# How to

## Resolve

## America's

## Gun Problem

**A 5 Step Plan with the potential to save thousands of lives each year**

# 109 a day
# 3,314 a month
# 39,773 a year
# 397,730 a decade
# 3,977,300 a century

The figures above represent the number of firearm-related deaths in the United States based on 2017 figures.

This book aims to show a realistic way in which these numbers can be dramatically reduced and thereby save thousands if not millions of lives.

# TABLE OF CONTENTS

# Preface

In February 2014 my family & I who are British citizens relocated to the United States due to my job being transferred from the United Kingdom to Dallas, Texas. We spent 4 enjoyable years in Dallas where we found the Texans to be welcoming and very friendly, before returning to the United Kingdom following my retirement in 2018.

If someone had told me in 2013 that one day, I would be writing a book about guns, I would never have believed them, partly because I had never considered writing a book on any subject and partly because the concepts of owning a gun, gun-rights and gun-control had never crossed my mind. It was a subject I had no interest in, probably because guns are not a significant political or social issue in the United Kingdom and rarely discussed.

My attention to the gun issue in the United States first occurred when around one month after starting work in my new office, a work colleague asked me if I had got a gun yet? Coming from a country where handguns are banned this came as quite a shock to me. My instant response was "No, why would I want a gun?" "For protection" stated my colleague. This surprised me as I had never felt concerned about my safety, or the safety of my family, and I was extremely dubious that a gun would make us safer. Whilst this was the 1st incident that made me aware of guns, it was the following two incidents that convinced me something was seriously wrong with the gun culture in the United States.

The first incident occurred on November 22, 2014, when a 12-year-old boy Tamir Rice took a toy gun to the Cudell Recreation Center in Cleveland Ohio, and started pointing it at various people. A concerned bystander called the police asking them to investigate this matter but did explain that they thought the gun was probably a toy. According to a police spokesman when the police arrived, they saw Tamir put the gun in his waistband and asked Tamir to put his hands up. Unfortunately, Tamir appeared instead to reach for his waistband and was quickly shot dead by the police[i]. What shocked me about this specific incident was how a child with a toy could be perceived as a life-threatening danger and that amongst developed countries, it was probably only in the United States that there would be an assumption that the gun was likely to be real.

The second incident occurred on June 12, 2016, when Omar Mateen, a 29-year-old security guard, killed 49 people and wounded 53 others in a terrorist attack inside Pulse, a gay nightclub in Orlando, Florida[ii]. At the time of the shooting, it was thought that Omar who had previously been a suspected terrorist was on a no-fly list, although subsequently this was found not to be the case. A debate then followed as to whether a person who is on a no-fly list should be legally allowed to buy a gun and a motion to ban suspected terrorists from acquiring guns was put to Congress. Amazingly this failed to move forward and at the time of writing this book, suspected terrorists are still allowed to purchase guns. A poll taken in June 2016 found that 86% of voters would favor a no-fly ban[iii]. How could Congress be so out of touch with public opinion? As will be examined later this can largely be explained by the influence the NRA and the gun lobby hold over elected Representatives.

The main argument against banning suspected terrorists on a no-fly list from buying a gun was that someone with the same name as a suspected terrorist may inadvertently be on the list and therefore denied their right to buy a gun. Since one is deemed innocent until proven guilty, Congress and gun enthusiasts argued that this right should not be denied. In reality, this is stating that a person having to wait a few weeks to clear his or her name from a list to obtain a gun is more important than preventing a terrorist from legally purchasing a gun which could be used to kill many innocent people.

Additionally, if someone without their knowledge, was incorrectly on a no-fly list it would surely be less of an inconvenience for them to wait to clear their name before getting a gun, as opposed to being prevented to board a plane at the airport. The reality is that the people most likely to be anxious to get guns immediately are those who are already planning to use a gun to harm themselves or others.

Following these incidents, I began to research the gun issue in detail and was shocked by the volume of gun-related deaths in the United States and the total lack of action to try and resolve the issue. There seems to be an acceptance of the status quo and a lack of desire to enact new measures to save lives. This can be summed up by the level of support for the NRA statement "The only way to stop a bad guy with a gun is with a good guy with a gun" The rest of the developed world would try to stop the bad guy getting a gun rather than supply a good guy with a gun.

The more I researched the gun issue, the more I became convinced that the concept, guns are good and help save lives, is fundamentally wrong, and that the exact opposite is true i.e. guns are bad and result in far more lives being lost than saved. Most of the arguments in favor of guns make no sense and when scrutinized seem to be either false or irrelevant.

What surprised me the most when researching the gun issue is how many people refuse to admit there is a gun problem in the United States, when all the evidence points to the fact that thousands of lives are needlessly lost each year as a direct consequence of gunfire. In reality, America has a huge gun problem, and the first and most important step to resolve this is to accept that there is a gun problem.

I am convinced there is a way to resolve the American gun problem and I have enjoyed writing this book and sincerely hope that the message that the book tries to portray will enable, or encourage, action to be taken, either by politicians enacting sensible gun policies or by individuals deciding not to possess guns, both of which, would save lives.

# Introduction

This book is split into 5 sections, with each section relating to a vital step that is required to both understand and hopefully resolve the problem of guns in the United States.

The 1st Section, or Step as we shall refer to each section in this book, is to accept that America does have a gun problem. In Chapter 1 we will look at a variety of statistics, which demonstrate the fact that America has a huge gun problem, which results in numerous unnecessary deaths and injuries every year. These statistics provide clear evidence that amongst developed nations the United States is unique in having a major gun problem and that the overall homicide rate is significantly higher than in other highly developed nations due entirely to the increased incidence of firearm homicides. Additionally, the statistics will demonstrate that in recent years the problem is getting worse.

In 2017 there were 39,773 firearm deaths in the United States[iv] which represents around 109 deaths per day. Gun-rights advocates frequently argue that this figure is misleading since over half these deaths are suicides and since the victim chose to end their lives these figures should be excluded. Whilst it is true that over half of firearm fatalities are suicides (in 2017 there were 23,854 firearm suicides[v] representing 60% of firearm fatalities) suicides should not be discounted. Any suicide is tragic and can have a devastating impact on relatives and close friends of the victim and as we shall see in Chapter 2 an easily accessible gun is by far the most efficient method to end one's own life.

Subsequent chapters in Step 1 will focus on firearm accidents, legal intervention shootings, and homicides. It should be pointed out that of the 39,773 firearm deaths in 2017 just 553[vi] (1.4%) were determined to be a result of legal intervention and as we shall see in

Chapter 4 the justification for many of these is dubious. In comparison there were 14,542 firearm homicides in 2017 i.e. for every legal intervention death there were over 26 firearm homicides. Particularly worrisome is the rapid increase in firearm homicides as the 14,542 homicides in 2017 represent a 32% increase since 2014[vii]. The final chapter in Step 1 focusses on mass shootings which seem to be getting ever more deadly. The sad fact that is despite frequent mass shootings the United States does nothing to try and prevent future mass shootings. This is in sharp contrast to other nations such as the United Kingdom, Australia, and New Zealand, who all took decisive action following a major mass shooting, to reduce the risk of future mass shootings.

The 2nd Step of this book aims to understand the reasons why guns are so popular in the United States. There are indeed many reasons which include culture, hunting, target shooting, protection, gun advocacy groups and to thwart a potential future tyrannical government. What is virtually unique in the United States is the extremely popular 2nd Amendment which states that to secure a free state the right to keep and bear arms shall not be infringed.

The strong gun culture in America along with a huge supply of well-marketed firearms and few restrictions on gun ownership explains the popularity of guns. It is vital for those who would like to see greater gun-control, to appreciate the popularity of guns and the reasons behind their popularity, as this sets boundaries on what is achievable. For example, a ban on handguns that has proved popular and effective in other countries is not a feasible option in the United States as it would be both unpopular and unconstitutional.

The 3rd Step of the book looks at arguments that are frequently made by Gun-rights Advocates, most of which on examination appear to be either false, irrelevant, or misleading. This includes statements such as "Guns don't kill people, people kill people". Although technically correct the phrase as we shall examine in Chapter 13 is meaningless and completely ignores the fact that guns make it easy for people to kill people.

Some of the arguments made by gun-rights advocates are valid to a limited extent such as the fact that Chicago despite strict gun-control does have a high homicide rate. The Chicago example is however an example of cherry-picking in that there are bound to be some cities with high homicide rates and strict gun-control. In reality, as we shall see in Chapter 14, Chicago has a high homicide rate despite having strict gun-control as opposed to having a high homicide rate because of strict gun-control. Moreover, whilst all gun-control measures should be encouraged, they can only have a limited impact when made at a city level, given the ease of transporting guns from nearby areas where there are fewer restrictions on guns.

Further chapters in Step 3 will disprove the dubious claims made by gun-rights advocates that guns help to protect individuals and also reduce crime, in particular, violent crime rates. Other arguments made by gun-rights advocates fail to recognize the dangers of guns for example the statement that if there were no guns then knives would be used may be partially true, but this fails to recognize that guns are much more deadly than knives. Also, the claim that mental health and not guns are the problem will be reviewed in Chapter 18. This claim fails to address the issue that mental health is a problem in all developed countries, but it is only in the United States that it is easy for those with mental health issues to obtain a gun. The final chapter in Step 3 looks at the extremely disrespectful conspiracy theory concerning the Sandy Hook Elementary school mass shooting.

The 4th Step of the book looks at various obstacles that are present making it more difficult to enact sensible gun safety regulations. Any other highly developed country experiencing the annual firearm death toll found in America would take decisive action to remedy the situation, but in the United States, little or nothing is done. Some of the obstacles are legal such as the 2008 Supreme Court judgment in the District of Columbia v Heller which makes restricting the rights of people to have free access to arms more difficult, as this right is no longer connected to the necessity of having a well-regulated militia. Other obstacles relate to the influence gun-rights advocates have on the gun debate. This includes NRA leaders who seem to be more concerned with supporting the firearm industry than in promoting gun safety. Additional obstacles include a lack of transparency in the firearm industry in the form of a register and research ban and obstacles relating to terminology, in particular the word "Control", used by those wishing to see more restrictions on guns. Gun-control is seen by many to be a tool used by authoritarian governments to restrict individuals' rights. This in turn leads to the obstacle of fearmongering, in which the most modest of gun-control proposals will be voted down because the doomsayers argue it is just the 1st step in the process of banning all guns and doing away with the 2nd Amendment.

The final obstacle which will be examined is money. The American firearm industry is huge and generates over $50 billion a year[viii]. Some of this money is then used to support gun-rights advocates such as the NRA and large sums of money are filtered into the hands of politicians in the form of political lobbying. This then ensures that these politicians support the firearm industry by blocking any proposals which may harm the profitability of the firearm industry.

The final section of this book – Step 5 looks at various ways in which the gun problem can be resolved. This includes addressing one of the arguments raised by gun-rights advocates that laws aimed at controlling gun ownership do not work because criminals do not obey laws, as this Step looks at ways in which illegal possession can be prevented. In Chapter 28 we will look at the lessons which can be learned from both the car and tobacco industries and how they can be incorporated into strategies to reduce gun-related fatalities. Both, car accident death rates and deaths caused by tobacco have fallen in recent years although as we shall see for very different reasons.

A barrier that needs to be overcome before it will be possible to enact any significant new gun safety policies is to ensure that public opinion is on the side of greater gun safety. As we shall see in Chapter 29 public opinion is in general in favor of greater gun safety; however, in this chapter, we will look ways in which this opinion can be built upon to reach a critical mass beyond which it will become more difficult to block sensible gun safety proposals.

Other chapters in this final Step will show how effective setting of goals and targets can be utilized to set up a comprehensive strategy to resolve America's gun problem, how technological advances can be used to make guns safer and how following a mass shooting the "Never Again" movement set up by students at Marjory Stoneman Douglas High School in Parkland, Florida can help to maintain a momentum in improving gun safety. The final chapter provides a comprehensive 20-point strategy, which if largely implemented, would significantly reduce the number of firearm fatalities in the United States.

# STEP 1

Acknowledging that America has a gun problem

# 1. Homicide & Firearm-related Statistics

Does the United States of America have an intentional homicide rate higher than most other countries? At first glance, as illustrated in the following table the answer would be no since it would appear that the 2017 intentional homicide rate of 5.3 individuals per 100,000 inhabitants[ix] in the United States is much in line with the rest of the world and is indeed below the world average rate of 6.1 homicides per 100,000 residents.[x]

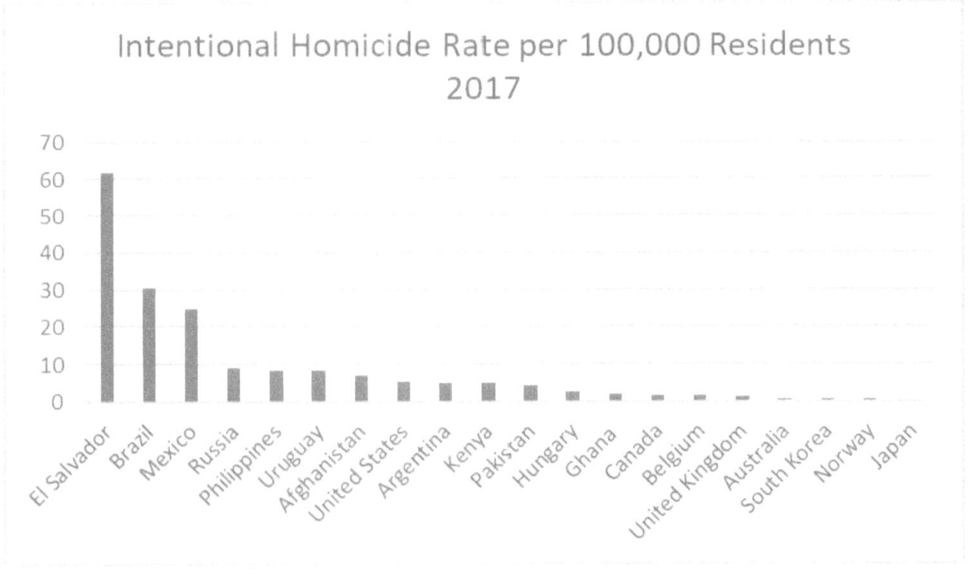


xi

A much different conclusion would however be reached if the intentional homicide rate in the United States was compared with other highly developed countries. A good measurement of a country's development is the Human Development Index 'HDI' as defined by the United Nations. In addition to taking into account GDP per capita, the HDI also factors in how income is turned into education and health opportunities that lead to higher levels of human development. Countries with the highest HDI ratings are referred to as having 'Very high human development' Based on 2017 data the United States had an HDI rating of 0.92 which placed it 15[th] in the world HDI ranking[xii]. Countries with high HDI ratings tend to have homicide rates significantly lower than average as can be seen from the following graph which shows the intentional homicide rate for the countries with the 20 highest HDI rating.

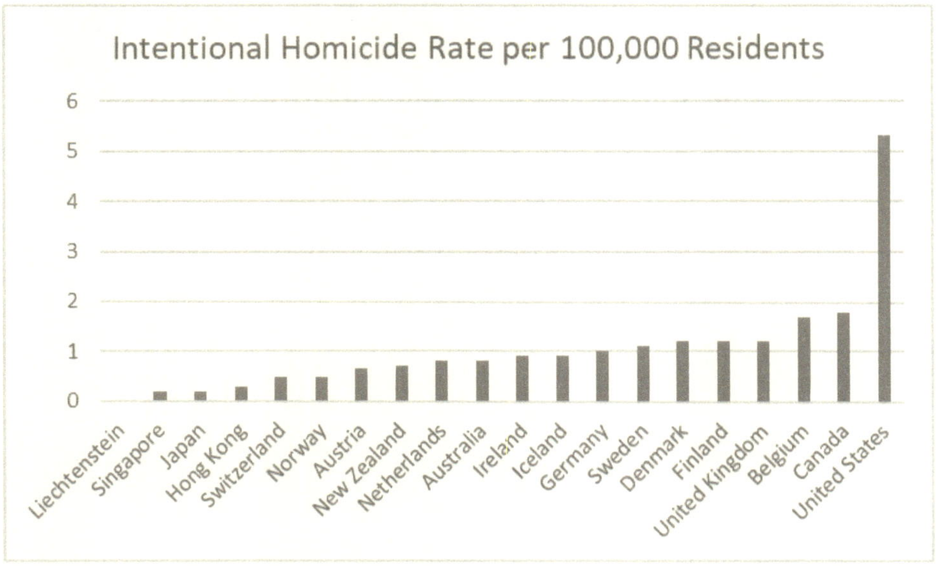


All 20 of these countries have an intentional homicide rate lower than the world average of 6.1 however, the intentional homicide rate for the United States is significantly higher than any other of the very high human development index countries. The United States rate of 5.3 is over 6 times greater than the average of the other 19 countries listed above and nearly 3 times the rate of the 2[nd] highest country Canada which has an intentional homicide rate of 1.8.[xiii]

The main reason why the United States has higher murder rates than the other top 20 very high human development countries becomes obvious when just analyzing firearm intentional homicide rates, as illustrated on the following chart [xiv]

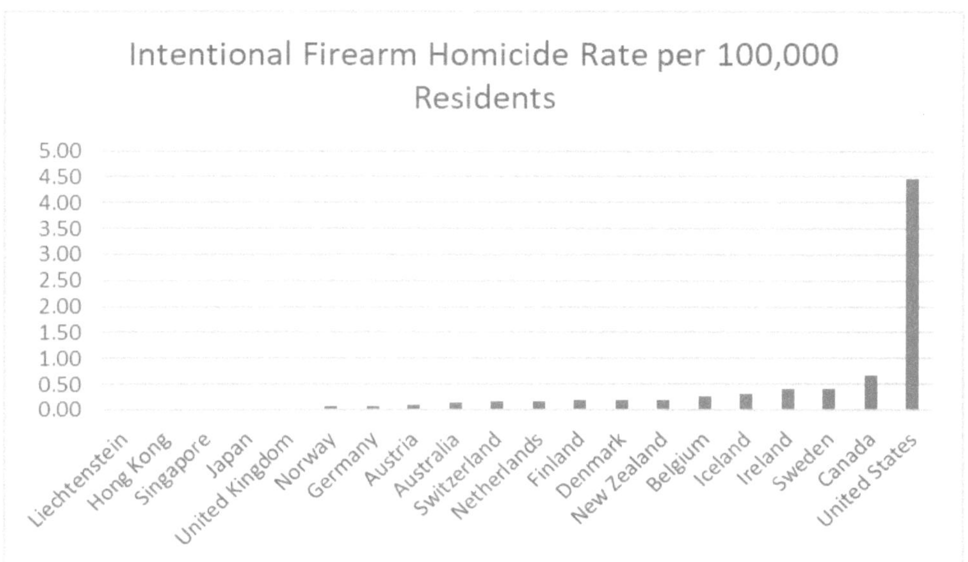


The United States intentional firearm homicide rate of 4.46 per 100,000 residents[xv] is over 25 times greater than the average of the other 19 countries listed above and over 6 times the rate of the 2nd highest country Canada which has an intentional firearm homicide rate of 0.67 per 100,000 residents.

Clearly, it is the incidence of firearm-related homicides which results in the United States having overall homicide rates much greater than the other highly developed countries. The reason for the higher firearm-related homicides becomes obvious when discovering that America with 4.4 percent of the world's population has 42% of the civilian-owned guns around the world[xvi]

More guns = more firearm homicides = more overall homicides. It is true that some homicides committed with firearms would be performed by other methods, such as knives or blunt objects if firearms were not readily available, but only to a limited extent for the simple reason that it is much easier to kill someone with a gun than with any other potential accessible weapon.

Unfortunately, the huge volume of available guns in America not only leads to a rise in homicides, but it also results in more suicides and accidental deaths as is evidenced when comparing total firearm deaths amongst highly developed countries.

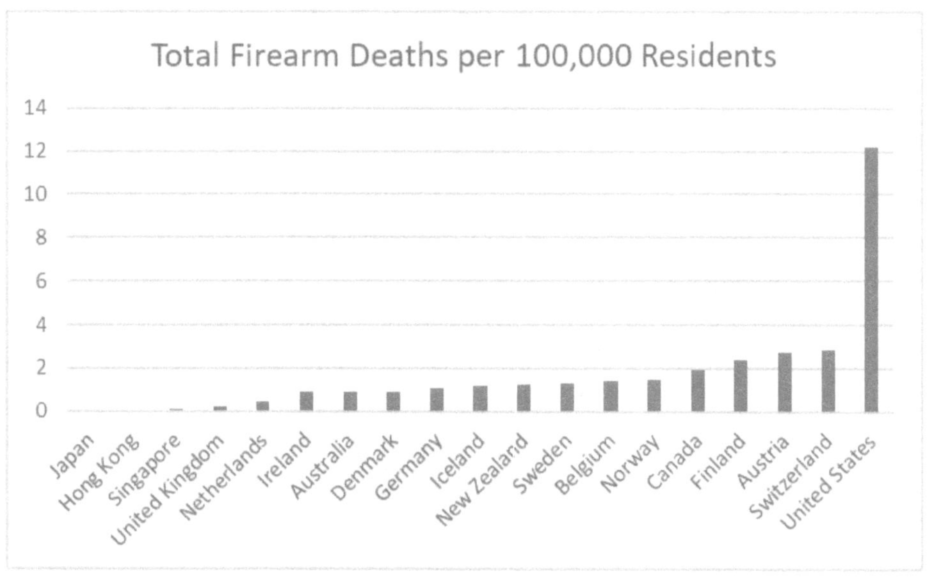


xvii

Note – figures for Liechtenstein were not available

The United States total firearm death rate (homicide + suicide + accidental + justified + unknown) of 12.21 per 100,000 residents is over 10 times greater than the average of the other 18 countries listed above and over 4 times the rate of the 2nd highest country Switzerland whose total firearm death rate is 2.84 per 100,000 residents.

The above table should convince any doubter that the United States does have a deadly gun problem. The tragic truth is that gun deaths impact so many lives in the United States, as can be seen from the following table which provides a breakdown of the number of firearm-related deaths in America for the period 2010 - 2017. Particularly worrisome is the fact that total firearm deaths have risen significantly in recent years.

# Firearm deaths in the USA 2010 - 2017

| Year | Suicides | Homicides | Unintentional | Legal Intervention | Undetermined | Total |
|---|---|---|---|---|---|---|
| 2010 | 19,392 | 11,078 | 606 | 344 | 252 | 31,672 |
| 2011 | 19,990 | 11,068 | 591 | 454 | 248 | 32.351 |
| 2012 | 20,666 | 11,622 | 548 | 471 | 256 | 33,563 |
| 2013 | 21,175 | 11,208 | 505 | 467 | 281 | 33,636 |
| 2014 | 21,386 | 11,008 | 461 | 464 | 275 | 33,594 |
| 2015 | 22,018 | 12,979 | 489 | 484 | 282 | 36,252 |
| 2016 | 22,938 | 14,415 | 495 | 510 | 300 | 38,658 |
| 2017 | 23,854 | 14,542 | 486 | 553 | 338 | 39,773 |

xviii

In addition to the 39,773 gun-related deaths in 2017, there were over twice this number of gun-related injuries and when you consider the impact on family and friends of the deceased coming to terms with the loss of life, or serious injury of a wife, husband, daughter, son, mother, father, sister, brother, girlfriend, boyfriend or other close friends, it is not unreasonable to assume that around half a million lives are significantly impaired by firearms each year.

It should be noted that the majority of firearm deaths are suicides and one could assume that the ready availability of firearms does not have a significant impact on suicides as there are many other methods of ending one's own life e.g. drug overdose, however as we shall see in the next chapter when we examine suicides in more detail, more guns do equate to more suicides for the same reason as it leads to more homicides i.e. guns not only make it easy to kill others, but they also make it easy to kill yourself.

Of particular concern is the fact that so many firearm-related deaths involve young people and as the following chart shows, for young men aged 15 -19, guns are the leading cause of death in the United States[xix].

# Gun violence is the most common cause of death for young men

*Causes of death for young men ages 15 to 19, 2016*

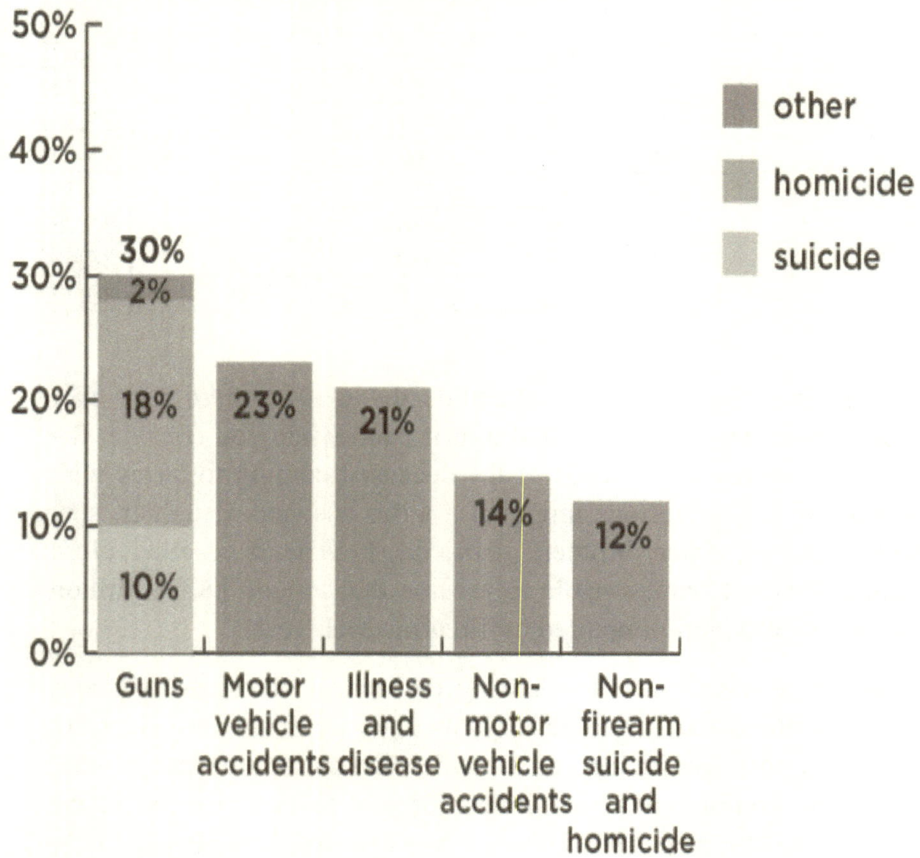


Source: Centers for Disease Control and Prevention, National Center for Health Statistics. Underlying Cause of Death 1999-2016 on CDC WONDER Online Database, released December, 2017. Data are from the Multiple Cause of Death Files, 1999-2016, as compiled from data provided by the 57 vital statistics jurisdictions through the Vital Statistics Cooperative Program

So how effective is gun-control and gun law regulation in the USA? At an overall level based on comparisons with other developed countries, it is not effective. This is because compared to other highly developed counties there are very few restrictions placed on gun purchases and ownership in the United States and this is almost certainly the reason why the United States has far more gun-related deaths and intentional homicides than any other highly developed country. In a later chapter, we will see that the states which place the most restrictions on gun ownership have significantly lower gun-related death rates than states with fewer restrictions.

Although all evidence points to the fact that more gun-control will reduce the number of homicides, suicides, and accidents, US citizens are passionately proud of their gun-rights and believe guns are essential for protection and to provide the opportunity to overthrow a possible future tyrannical government if the needs arise. The following chart plots public opinion on gun-rights v gun-control[xx]:

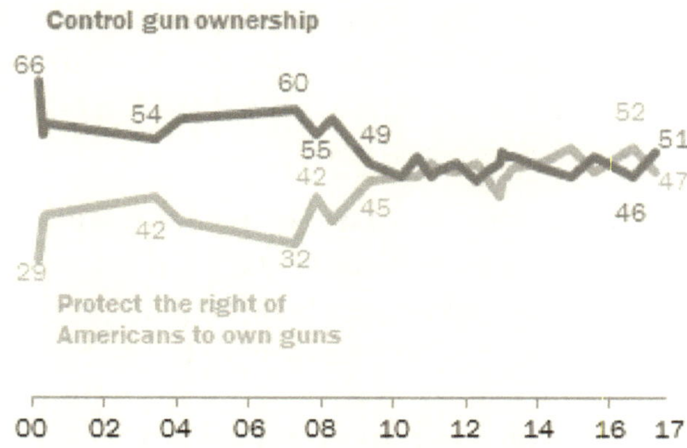



Since around 2010 public opinion in America has been split down the middle on whether it is more important to put more control on gun ownership or protect the right of Americans to own guns. In reality, those advocating for protecting gun-rights are more organized than those wanting strict control and hence organizations such as the NRA & gun manufacturers have been able to successfully halt many initiatives designed to help prevent greater gun-control policies from being initiated.

Changing the status quo is difficult but not impossible and hopefully, this book will give some insight into how firearm-related deaths could be significantly reduced. The most important 1[st] step in reducing firearm deaths is to come to terms with the fact that the

United States does have a gun problem, which results in the needless loss of thousands of lives each year. Without this acknowledgment, nothing will be done and excuses will continue to be made e.g. blaming a mass shooting on mental health issues and not guns. Wake up America, mental health is an issue in all countries but amongst highly developed countries it is only in the United States where it is easy for someone with mental issues to get hold of a semi-automatic firearm and go on a shooting spree.

One final statistic which should convince doubters that there is a gun problem in America is the fact that a study has found that guns kill 1,300 and wound around 5,800 American children under the age of 17 every year[xxi]. This is something that no other highly developed country would tolerate.

# 2. The Impact of Guns on Suicide

Given that the majority of firearm-related deaths are suicides, it is fitting to commence by examining the impact the ready availability of guns may have on the level of suicides in the United States. The key questions to be answered are firstly, does having easy access to guns increase the level of suicides, and secondly does the suicide rate matter given that those individuals are choosing to end their own lives.

In 2017 there were 47,107 recorded suicides in the United States, of which as evidenced in the previous chapter 23,854 were carried out by firearms. Guns, therefore, accounted for just over 50% of suicides in 2017. The following chart compares the suicide rate in the United States with other HDI countries [xxii]

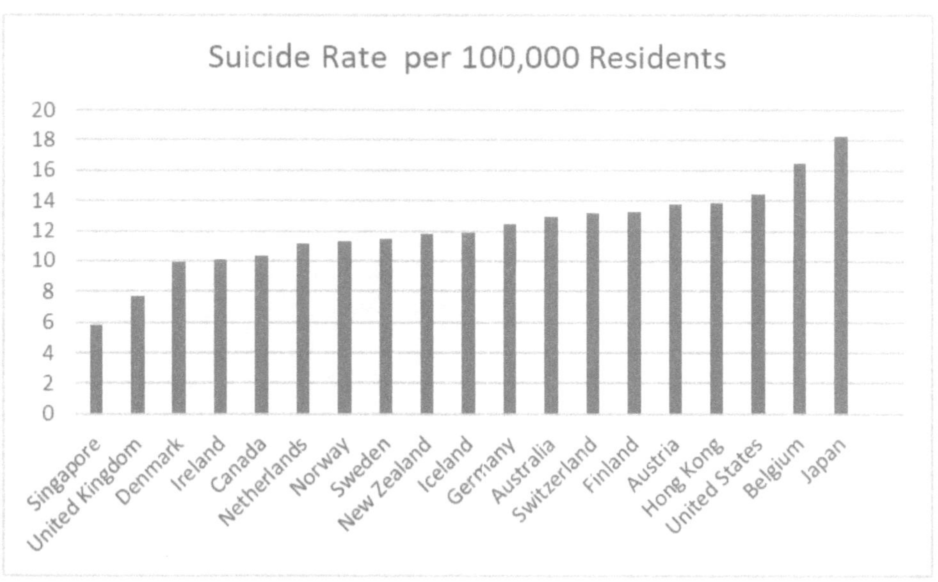

The United States suicide rate in 2017 of 14.46 individuals per 100,000 residents is higher than the average rate of 11.98 in the 20 most developed countries. Gun-rights enthusiasts will point to this figure not being materially greater than other countries, however, the causes of suicides are complex and gun ownership is only one cause for a country to have a higher suicide rate. That said as we shall see there is sufficient evidence pointing to the fact that the United States suicide rate would be significantly reduced if guns were not readily available to almost all US residents.

Of particular interest is the percentage of suicides performed by firearms in various countries. In the United States as we have seen over 50% of suicides are performed with firearms, whilst in other high-income countries where the prevalence of firearms in the household is lower, firearms account for only 4.5%[xxiii] of all suicides.

The following chart demonstrates that although guns are only the chosen method for around 6% of suicide attempts in America, they make up over 50% of fatal suicides. This discrepancy is because around 85% of gun suicides are fatal, compared to drug or poison overdosing which accounts for 71 percent of attempts but only 12 percent of fatalities.

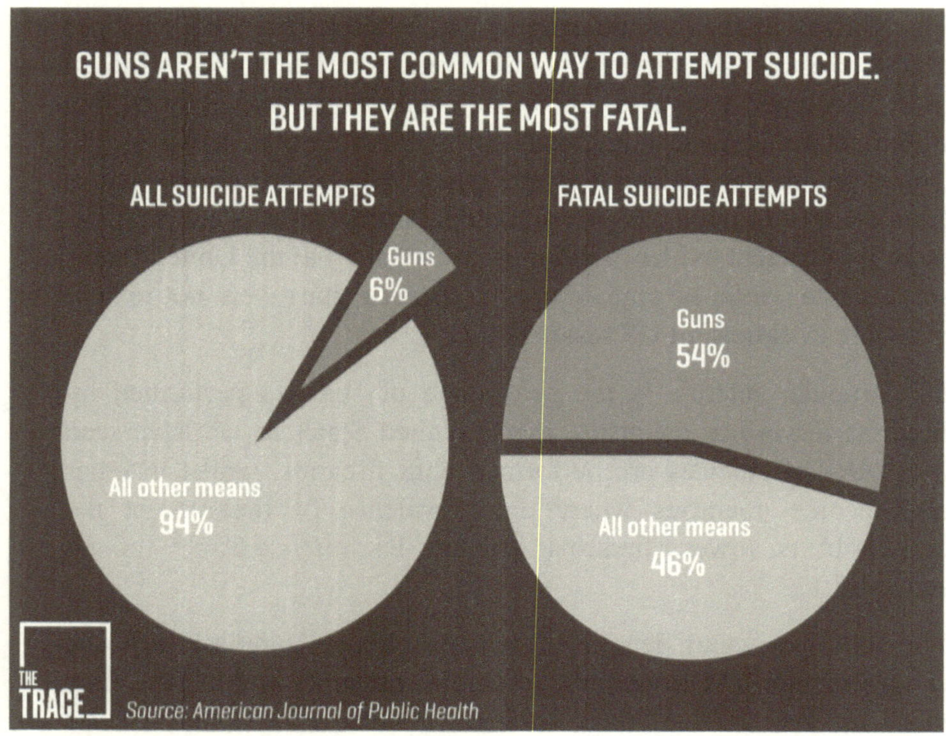



xxiv

The following chart based on data taken from 1989 – 1997 compares the fatality rates of the most common suicide methods and again demonstrates the effectiveness of firearms as a means of suicide.

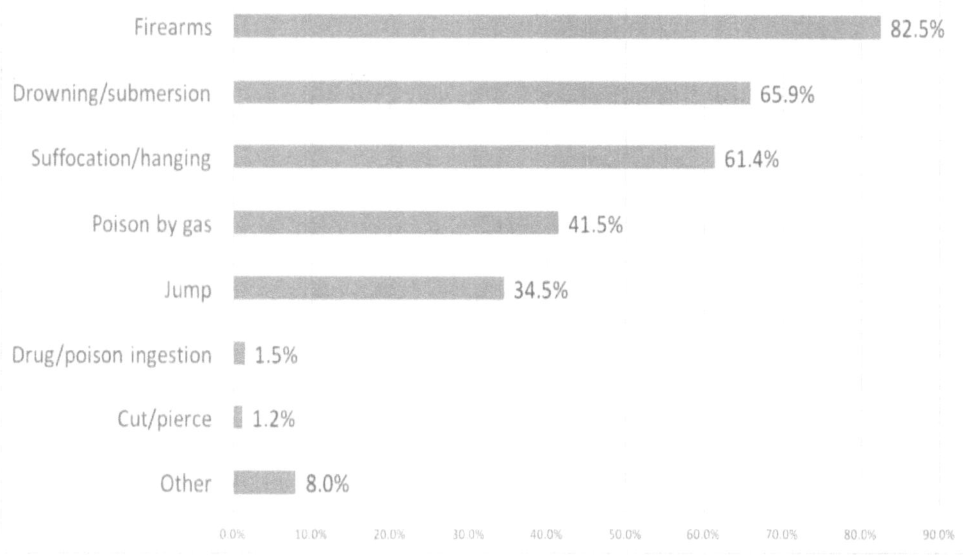



xxv

Unfortunately, as indicated in the previous chapter guns make it easy to kill yourself. Picking up a gun stored in your house and pulling the trigger is a quick and relatively painless method to kill yourself compared to many other suicide methods and of particular importance, there is little time to change your mind or to think about the consequences your death may have on your loved ones.

Following this logic, we would expect to see those states with the highest gun ownership having the highest suicide levels and indeed this is the case. Centers for Disease Control (CDC) surveys taken from 2001- 2004 found that the three states with the highest percentage of household gun ownership - Wyoming, Montana, and Alaska had suicide rates of around 20 people per 100,000, nearly double the national average of about 11 per 100,000. Conversely, the nine states with the lowest per-household gun ownership from 2001 to 2004 also had the nine lowest suicide rates. They were Hawaii, New Jersey, Massachusetts, Rhode Island, Connecticut, New York, California, Illinois, and Maryland.[xxvi]

Further support indicating that higher levels of gun ownership results in higher suicide rates is evidenced by an American Journal of Public Health (AJPH) study published in 2016 based on suicide rates between 1981 and 2013 [xxvii]. This concluded that increased gun ownership resulted in increased firearm suicide rates among both genders, and increased overall suicide rates amongst males.

A 2011 study by researchers at Harvard found that 82% of teens who killed themselves with a gun, used a gun belonging to someone in their home [xxviii], usually a parent. It is hard to imagine the grief and guilt felt by a parent if they were to discover that their son or daughter had killed themselves with a gun stored, clearly not safely, at home.

A common misconception surrounding failed suicides is that the individual who tried to kill themselves will keep trying to end their life until successful. Thus, the fact that firearm suicides are generally successful is irrelevant because eventually, they would have killed themselves even without access to firearms. Extensive research on this subject however shows that this is not the case. Only between 5-11% of people who unsuccessfully tried to kill themselves will eventually succeed in killing themselves, [xxix] which means the vast majority do not end up committing suicide. The reason for this is that suicide is usually an impulsive decision and a moment's reflection or heart to heart chat with a close friend or relative can encourage alternatives such as seeking counseling to prevent the urge to kill oneself from resurfacing.

In 2016 The Brady Campaign to Prevent Gun Violence produced a report titled "The Truth About Suicide and Guns"[xxx] This report demonstrates the link between suicide and guns in America. Within this report, there is a reference to 5 US case studies which found conclusive evidence that firearms in the home are associated with significantly higher rates of suicides and references to analysis combining the result of 14 national and international studies, which concluded that access to firearms increased the risk of suicide more than 3 times.[xxxi]

The answer to the first question posed at the beginning of the chapter is therefore a clear yes. Easy access to guns does increase the number of suicides. There is just no alternative suicide method which is both easy, quick, and generally lethal. Overdosing on pills which is the most common attempted suicide method fits the easy measure but is rarely lethal. Hanging which is the most common suicide method in many countries is quite effective but not easy to set up and a painfully slow method which is less likely to be done on impulse compared to pulling a trigger.

Individuals and organizations that support gun-rights and easy access to guns in the United States are generally dismissive about suicides. For example, if informed that there were 39,773 firearm deaths in 2017 as indicated in the previous chapter they would swiftly respond along these lines. Most of these are suicides and so should not be counted since the individual shooting themselves chose to end their lives. This logic not only fails to consider the impact that the suicide may have on close relatives and friends, but it also fails to consider that a depressed individual on the verge of wanting to kill themselves is probably not of sufficiently sound mind, to make the most important decision in their life, as to whether to commit suicide or not. As we have seen following a failed suicide attempt, the majority of individuals do not go on to kill themselves at a later date.

So, to answer the second question; does suicide matter. The answer is obviously yes. It is a tragedy to the individual their family and friends and anyone who may feel remorse for not having taken action or seen the warning signs to prevent the suicide. Of particular concern with firearm suicides are that these are frequently sudden impulsive decisions and if the gun had not been available it is likely that no suicide attempt would have been made. Even if the individual did then attempt an alternative suicide method such as drug overdose the method would probably fail and additionally, the individual would have time to reflect and seek help from others to prevent the suicide.

Within the Brady 2016 report "The Truth About Suicide and Guns" there is a quote from a father of a 13-year-old child who killed himself with a gun which is repeated below:

*"Cayman was a really, really happy kid. He wasn't being bullied at school. He had no real girl problems. He had a happy family. There were absolutely no warning signs. He got an e-mail about a homework assignment and probably 20 to 30 minutes later, my 13-year-old son took his life with a gun I hadn't thought about in years."*

This sums up the dangers of keeping a gun at home and the tragic nature of so many suicides particularly those of children. It seems fitting to end this chapter with a poem that describes how lives are intertwined and that any life lost whether, by homicide, suicide or natural causes diminishes us all.

The following poem "No Man is an Island" was written by the English Metaphysical poet John Donne in 1624.

No man is an island,
Entire of itself,
Every man is a piece of the continent,
A part of the main.
If a clod be washed away by the sea,
Europe is the less.
As well as if a promontory were.
As well as if a manor of thy friend's
Or of thine own were:
Any man's death diminishes me,
Because I am involved in mankind,
And therefore never send to know for whom the bell tolls;
It tolls for thee.

# 3. Unintentional Firearm Deaths

Although unintentional or in other words accidental firearm deaths represented only 1.2% of American firearm deaths in 2017, this still amounted to 486 accidental deaths for the year, which means on average there is more than 1 accidental firearm death every day. As a comparison in most full years, there are zero accidental firearm deaths in the United Kingdom.

Firearm accidental deaths are particularly tragic as they often involve children, either as the perpetrator or the victim and virtually all these deaths would be avoided if America had sensible gun policies in line with other highly developed nations.

For the period 2000-2017, 11,090 [xxxii] people died as a result of accidental shootings which equates to 616 unintentional firearm deaths per year, of which over 4,000 of the victims were aged under 25.[xxxiii]

In 2001 a report was written[xxxiv] demonstrating that individuals of all age groups are significantly more likely to die from unintentional firearm injuries when they live in states with more guns, relative to states with fewer guns. On average, states with the highest gun levels had nine times the rate of unintentional firearms deaths compared to states with the lowest gun levels. A federal government study[xxxv] of unintentional shootings found that 8% of such shooting deaths resulted from shots fired by children under the age of six.

The U.S. General Accounting Office has estimated that 31% of unintentional deaths caused by firearms might be prevented by the addition of two devices: a child-proof safety lock (8%) and a loading indicator (23%) which is a safety device that indicates at a glance whether a firearm is loaded and whether a round remains in the chamber. Despite these startling statistics many states do little or nothing to try and prevent unintentional deaths.

A key factor that would significantly reduce the number of firearm unintentional homicides, particularly for children, relates to gun storage. A 2018 study found that 4.6 million minors in the US live in homes with at least one loaded, unlocked firearm[xxxvi]. Another study of firearm storage patterns in the US found that of the homes with children and firearms, 55% were reported to have one or more firearms in an unlocked place, and 43% reported keeping guns without a trigger lock in an unlocked place.[xxxvii]

In another report, it was found that 73% of children under age 10 living in homes with guns reported knowing the location of their parents' firearms.[xxxviii] Parents and homeowners need to be made more aware of the dangers of not keeping firearms safely stored, and state or preferably federal laws relating to firearm storage would be beneficial in reducing unintentional firearm deaths.

Many gun-right advocates passionately believe that firearms should be stored loaded and ready to use in case of immediate threat, which is probably a reason why guns are so frequently left unlocked and loaded. The merits of this are at best questionable but downright irresponsible when children are resident.

Despite the evidence that securing guns safely would reduce the danger of accidental shootings, at the time of writing only 11 states have any laws relating to this matter and only Massachusetts has a law stating that all firearms must be kept locked. A summary of state gun storage and locking devise laws is shown below: [xxxix]

| Summary of State Laws Regarding the Safe Storage of Firearms | | | | |
|---|---|---|---|---|
| | | | | |
| State | Firearms Must Be Kept Locked | Locks Must Accompany Dealer Sales | Locks Must Accompany Private Sales | Locks Must Meet Standards or Be Approved |
| | | | | |
| California | Sometimes | Yes | Yes | Yes |

| Connecticut | Sometimes | Handguns Only | Handguns Only | Yes |
|---|---|---|---|---|
| Illinois | | Handguns Only | | |
| Maryland | | Handguns Only | | Yes |
| Massachuse tts | Yes | Handguns and Assault Weapons Only | Handguns and Assault Weapons Only | Yes |
| Michigan | | Yes | | |
| New Jersey | | Handguns Only | Handguns Only | |
| New York | Sometimes | Yes | | Yes |
| Ohio | | Offer Only | | |
| Pennsylvani a | | Handguns Only | | |
| Rhode Island | | Handguns Only | | |

It is interesting to note that based on the Giffords Law Center 2019 Annual Gun Law Scorecard, the state of Massachusetts, being the only state to require all firearms to be kept locked, has the 2nd lowest firearm overall death rate of 3.46 individuals per 100,000 residents, with only Rhode Island having a lower rate. The 3 states which sometimes require firearms to be kept locked also have low overall firearm fatalities, with New York being the 4th lowest, Connecticut the 6th lowest, and California the 7th lowest.[xl]

Everytown for Gun Safety[xli] has produced a website named #NotAnAccident Index which details all incidents since 2015 where a person aged 17 or under unintentionally kills or injures themselves, or someone else with a gun. In 2017 alone there were at least 286 unintentional shootings by children in America.

The following examples represent just a small sample of these unintentional shootings and demonstrate the tragic nature of some of these incidents; which could so easily be avoided if parents stored guns securely and ideally avoided storing any guns in homes where children are resident, or in cars when children are passengers.

November 13, 2017 – In Hermiston Oregon, a 7-year-old shot his 2-year-old brother in the head with a handgun found in his mother's car. The victim was taken to intensive care and fortunately, in this instance, the toddler survived. [xlii]

Tragically on the same date November 13, 2017, a 1-year old baby girl died after being shot by her 3-year-old brother in Memphis Tennessee. In this incident, a loaded gun had been inadvertently left beside the child's bed at night. [xliii]

October 23, 2017 - Cullman Alabama a 16-year-old boy accidentally fatally shot himself whilst Facetiming a friend. The boy was an experienced hunter and it is thought the accident occurred because he was unaware the gun was loaded. If the gun had a loading indicator this tragedy would probably never have happened. [xliv]

June 20, 2017 – Danville Arkansas a 2-year-old boy fatally shot himself. Family members told police they were not sure how the child reached the gun because it was normally stored on top of a cabinet in the bedroom. They told police they had seen him playing in the hallway and then heard the weapon discharge, after which they called 911. [xlv]

May 29, 2017 – St Petersburg Florida a 10-year-old boy was shot twice by an 11-year-old. Fortunately, the shots were in the arm and shoulder and not critical. Apparently, a 17-year-old boy brought a gun into the home while he was supervising several children. An 11-year-old was playing with the firearm and it went off accidentally. The teen was charged with aggravated child abuse. [xlvi]

March 11, 2017 – Fort Worth Texas a 3-year-old accidentally shot himself and another 3-year-old child outside a Chuck E. Cheese restaurant. The children had left the restaurant ahead of their parents and went to the family vehicle, where they found a .380-caliber pistol. As one of the children was playing with the weapon, it discharged, injuring the child in the hand and striking the other child in the back. Luckily, in this instance the injuries were not too serious. [xlvii]

January 31, 2017 – Rankin Mississippi a 4-year-old boy accidentally shot his 1-year-old brother at home, whilst the father was watching television and the mother was working on a project. The father thought the gun was securely stored in a gun vault, however, although the gun was in the vault and the door was shut and latched, it was not locked. Luckily the bullet missed the baby's chest by inches and the child recovered. [xlviii]

January 13, 2017 – Carthage Missouri a 10-year-old girl was fatally shot by either a 12 or 13-year old child who was in the home at the same time. One of the other children found a loaded gun in the residence, mishandled it, and caused the 10-year-olds death. [xlix]

It is hard to imagine how dreadful the family members of those impacted must feel when incidents such as those described above occur. Imagine this example situation to which sadly something similar must have happened so many times over the years. A father buys a gun but does not store it securely. A child in the house finds the gun and accidentally shoots and kills his younger sister. Result at least 4 lives ruined. The daughter is dead, the brother has to live with a lifetime of guilt growing up wondering how and why this terrible event happened and why did he need to fulfill his curiosity as to what may happen if he pulled the trigger. The father will be racked with guilt and depending on the circumstances may be charged with negligent homicide, in addition to feeling the grief on the loss of his daughter. The mother is likely to be furious with the father and also has to come to terms with the loss of her daughter. She may also feel guilty in not ensuring the gun was safely secured. All this because someone in the family thought a gun would make them safer. In a later chapter, we will see how the concept of guns making individuals safer is almost certainly a fallacy.

# 4. Firearm Legal Intervention Shootings

Legal intervention firearm deaths which may also be described as justifiable firearm homicides describe situations where an individual uses a gun to kill someone in self-defense or similar circumstances. This is not a legal charge, but rather a classification that police can use in an event where an individual died but no crime was committed, or as a defense in a homicide prosecution. Because the killing was justifiable, the person who committed the killing will not be held criminally liable for the death, though civil penalties may still apply under certain circumstances.

Legal intervention firearm deaths totaled 553 in 2017[l] and averaged 468 over the period 2010 to 2017. This represented around 1.3% of all firearm-related deaths. Obtaining information on these deaths is difficult but they can be broken down between those involving civilian firearms and those involving firearms shot by law enforcement officers.

In 2014 there were 229 justifiable homicides involving a private citizen using a firearm, reported to the Federal Bureau of Investigation's Uniform Crime Reporting (UCR) Program as detailed in its Expanded Homicide Data Table.[li]

While it is clear that guns are rarely used to justifiably kill criminals, there is a lot of conflicting data on how frequently guns are used in self-defense, where no criminal or suspected criminal is killed. Pro-gun advocates – from individual gun owners to organizations like the National Rifle Association – frequently claim that guns are used up to 2.5 million times each year in self-defense in the United States. There is little data to back up this claim and a more realistic figure can probably be found using National Crime Victimization Survey data to examine incidents where victims employed guns against offenders. Based on these figures between 1987 and 1990 there were an estimated 258,460 incidents of defensive firearm use giving an annual average of 64,615[lii]

In a 2004 book "Private Guns, Public Health" by Dr. David Hemenway, Professor of Health Policy at the Harvard T. H. Chan School of Public Health and director of the Harvard Injury Control Research Center, Dr. Hemenway states the claim that 2.5 million Americans use guns in self-defense against criminal attackers each year, is not plausible and nominates it as the most outrageous number mentioned in a policy discussion by an elected official[liii]. There probably have been more outrageous claims made by elected officials, but there does appear to be little empirical evidence to support this 2.5m figure.

The main reason why a homicide may be deemed to be justified is that it was necessary for self-defense. This would cover the case where an individual, feels threatened and that their safety, or safety of their loved ones is in jeopardy. In such situations, the presence of a firearm provides an opportunity for a quick and effective way to remove the threat. Ideally, just the sight of a firearm will be sufficient to cause an intruder to retreat but, in some cases, it may be necessary to shoot the aggressor.

The laws allowing individuals to protect themselves from criminal attackers are very strong in America and are summarized below:

<u>Stand your ground laws</u>

Stand your ground laws generally state that, under certain circumstances, individuals can use force to defend themselves without first attempting to retreat from the danger. The purpose behind these laws is to remove any confusion about when individuals can defend themselves and to eliminate prosecutions of people who legitimately used self-defense even though they had not attempted to retreat from the threat. States with Stand your ground laws differ on whether the law applies to instances involving lethal force, with some states retaining the duty to retreat when lethal force is involved and others removing the duty to retreat under all circumstances.

## The Castle Doctrine

The Castle Doctrine is a legal doctrine that designates a person's abode or any legally occupied place (for example, a vehicle or home) as a place in which that person has protections and immunities permitting one, in certain circumstances, to use force (up to and including deadly force) to defend oneself against an intruder, free from legal prosecution for the consequences of the force used. Where the Castle Doctrine applies there is less of a requirement to retreat as defined below.

## Duty to Retreat

Some U.S. jurisdictions require that a person retreat from an attack and allow the use of deadly in self-defense only when retreat is not possible or when retreat poses a danger to the person under attack.

It does seem understandable for the law to protect victims of crime and allow reasonable self-defense and even deadly force in certain situations. There is however a problem with a shoot-first mentality and a belief by homeowners that they can shoot intruders on sight without fearing any legal implications as illustrated by the following incidents.

On Oct 17, 1992, a Japanese 16-year-old exchange student Yoshihiro Hattori was on his way to a Halloween party when he was mistakenly dropped off at the wrong house. The panicked householder yelled "Freeze!" but Hattori, clearly misunderstanding the command, kept approaching. The householder fired a .44 caliber magnum bullet into Hattori's chest at nearly point-blank range, and the boy died before he could be taken to a hospital. The homeowner who was charged with manslaughter invoked the Castle Doctrine defense and was found not guilty by the jury. [liv]

In November 2013, Ronald Westbrook, a 72-year-old who suffered from Alzheimer's disease, knocked on a stranger's door in the early hours of the morning after slipping away unnoticed from his North Georgia home with his two dogs. Police said a man inside that home, 34-year-old Joe Hendrix, got a .40-caliber handgun, went outside to investigate, and shot Westbrook in a horrible mistake. This unlikely collision between two strangers, one deeply confused, another perceiving a threat, illustrates both the difficulties that caregivers face in keeping loved ones with Alzheimer's safe and the consequences of miscalculation in a state that celebrates its gun culture.[lv]

The attorney of the homeowner described his client as distraught, which is not surprising under the circumstances. This incident was probably recorded as a justifiable homicide but serves to illustrate even when homicides are deemed to be justified, they can result in much hardship not only for the victim but also for the individual having to make a snap decision as to whether to shoot or not. It is only natural for most people to feel remorse if they are responsible for ending another person's life and this will be magnified when in the cold light of day, it turns out that the victim was not a threat at all. The problem with using a gun in self-defense is that it involves having to make a quick decision where the person with the gun is going to be under huge stress. It is not possible to always make the correct decision, but the consequences of a wrong decision would be far less severe if no firearms were present.

According to an analysis by the Bureau of Justice Statistics on both violent and property crimes for the period 2007-2011[lvi], there were 338,700 violent or property crimes in which the attacker was threatened with a firearm i.e. just under 68,000 incidents a year, as opposed to 2.5 million, referred to earlier in the chapter. The 68,000 figure is in line with most other estimates of the incidence of self-defense actions involving firearms. It is fair to acknowledge that 68,000 is still a significant number of incidents and that in the majority of these cases an attack can be prevented without the requirement to kill or injure anyone.

As noted earlier a significant proportion of legal intervention firearm incidents and justifiable homicides are performed by law enforcement officers and these are reviewed in detail in the next chapter, which will also cover incidents where law enforcement officers are the victims of firearm homicides.

# 5. Police Shootings

Based on figures prepared by the FBI there was an average of around 400 annual fatal shootings of suspected felons by police forces, however, these figures are likely to be understated as police forces are not obliged to provide this information and only some of them do.[lvii]

Many human rights organizations believe this number to be far higher citing a lack of transparency in how these figures are reported. According to the Washington Post, 963[lviii] people were shot and killed by police in 2016 based on news reports, public records, social media, and other sources, with this figure increasing to 987[lix] in 2017.

The lack of transparency in these figures is concerning, but even assuming the FBI figures are the most accurate it still reflects a significant number of police firearm fatal shootings, which dwarves the number of people killed by law enforcement officers in other highly developed countries, for example.

Iceland – 1 fatality in 71 years[lx]
England and Wales – An average of 2.67 fatalities each year in the period 2004-2019[lxi]
Australia – An average of 3.5 fatalities each year in the period 2008-2011[lxii]
Germany – An average of 10 fatalities per year [lxiii]

The two key questions which need to be answered are why does the USA have significantly more fatal shootings by police than other peer countries? and are these shootings justified?

The most obvious reason for the high levels of police shooting fatalities is that all police are armed with firearms, however, since only 19 out of 197 recognized countries in the world do not routinely arm their police,[lxiv] it does not in itself explain why the levels are so much higher in America. Whilst having unarmed police may be an ideal in countries where gun ownership or gun crime is low it is not a practical solution for most countries and certainly not something to be considered in the United States where such a high proportion of felons are armed.

So apart from the fact that police are armed, the following are all factors which may increase the volume of police shooting fatalities in America:

- Poor training on when to use firearms
- Unwillingness to use non-fatal alternatives e.g. handcuffs, batons, pepper spray, tasers
- Failure to recognize mental disabilities which may be the reason a suspect does not comply with verbal requests
- Aiming to kill as opposed to injure
- Police being aware they are unlikely to be prosecuted for shooting a felon or suspected felon
- Racial tensions
- Safety in numbers - One more police shooting will not be noticed when there are police shooting fatalities almost every day

Whilst all the above are factors, particularly the lack of training, they are all overshadowed by the most significant reason for the uniquely high level of police shootings and fatalities in America, which is that almost all police shooting incidents occur because of the constant fear the police have that the suspect or felon may be armed and ready to shoot in self-defense. Amongst highly developed countries this fear is unique in America, as it is the only highly developed country in which there would be an assumption that the suspect is likely to be armed.

Virtually all shooting fatalities by law enforcement officers will be recorded as justifiable homicides and it is fair to say that a large proportion of these are justifiable and understandable. If law enforcement officers are in fear for their lives or believe other innocent lives are in danger then of course they should be able to use whatever force is necessary to prevent further violence and to protect themselves or their colleagues, without fear of repercussion.

Any individual who comes into contact with law enforcement officers must understand that being armed is endangering their lives. It makes the police fearful of their own lives and if there are several law enforcement officers present it just needs one of them to make the fatal shot. Given the strong laws protecting law enforcement officers acting in self-defense in America, the shooting of an armed suspect will almost always be considered as a justifiable homicide, even when it turns out in hindsight that there was little or no threat to the law enforcement officer.

It must be reflected that the vast majority of police incidents even those where the suspected felon is armed do not result in a fatal shooting. In most cases, an armed felon will follow police instructions and drop any firearm before being restrained and handcuffed. The fact so many suspects are armed with guns is a double-edged sword in that it both increases the volume of incidents where police are called to confront an armed suspect and also increases the chance that the police will feel the need to fire a fatal shot, due to the fear and threat the law enforcement officers feel when believing they are dealing with an armed suspect.

Since 2015 the Washington Post has kept a database on police fatal shootings[lxv] and breaks these down into various categories including the weapon carried by the suspected felon, whether the suspect was fleeing and if the suspect had a mental illness. For this purpose, we will use the 2017 database in which there were 987 fatal police shootings recorded.

<u>Weapon Type</u>

This records the weapon that the person who was shot was carrying at the time of the incident.

| <u>Weapon carried by suspected felon</u> | <u>Number of fatal police shootings</u> |
|---|---|
| Gun | 579 |
| Knife | 156 |
| Vehicle | 85 |
| Toy weapon | 26 |
| Other weapon | 47 |
| Unarmed | 68 |
| Unknown | 26 |
| Total | 987 |

Without knowing further details, it is impossible to know how many of these shootings were justified or necessary under the circumstances, and even when knowing more details, it may be difficult to pass judgment. For example, if a police officer thinks there is a 10% chance that a suspect with a gun will fire at him or a colleague, it is reasonable for them to shoot-first, even though it was probably not necessary. For this reason, in almost all cases where the suspect had a gun, the shooting can be deemed to be justified.

What is particularly concerning are those incidents where the suspect was unarmed or had a toy weapon. In the preface, we referred to the fatal shooting by police officers of a 12-year old boy who was brandishing a toy gun in a park. It is difficult to see how this could really be considered a serious threat particularly as the police had been notified that it was probably a toy gun.

A particularly tragic incident occurred when a 6-year old child was accidentally shot dead by law enforcement officers on December 21, 2017[lxvi]. This occurred when sheriff's deputies opened fire on a woman they had been chasing and one of the bullets pierced the wall of a mobile home the child was living in and struck the child in the abdomen. The woman, a suspected car thief who had been trying to break into the home, was also killed in the shooting near San

Antonio in Texas. The female suspect had been threatening deputies with a weapon and so this would appear to have been a justifiable shooting, however it highlights the dangers of any shooting incident where innocent bystanders can get caught in the crossfire. That these accidents can happen when trained law enforcers are shooting highlights the even greater danger when ordinary citizens fire on impulse.

Although the majority of police shootings are justifiable, there are a significant number of police shootings which on the surface do not seem reasonable. A police shooting is less likely to be justified when the suspect is fleeing and the Washington Post database helpfully breaks down the shootings based on whether the suspect was fleeing or not as follows.

| Method of fleeing | Number of fatal police shootings |
| --- | --- |
| Fleeing in car | 182 |
| Fleeing by foot | 124 |
| Fleeing other | 33 |
| Not fleeing | 597 |
| Undetermined | 51 |
| Total | 987 |

It is concerning that there were 339 fatal police shootings in which their target was fleeing and hence less likely to be posing an immediate threat.

The Washington Post database also keeps track of the number of fatal police shootings in which the suspect had some form of mental illness. In 2017, 236 of the 987 fatal police shooting involved the shooting of suspects with mental illness. There is a tendency for police to shoot when the suspect does not follow orders and it can be impossible for people with certain disability's e.g. autism to follow instructions.

It is also concerning that 122 of these 236 suspects with mental illness were armed with guns. Simply put - individuals with mental illness should not have access to firearms. This is not discrimination against those with mental disabilities, but rather a way of protecting those with mental illness; in addition to protecting all citizens from coming into contact with an armed mentally disabled individual. Most of the 122 suspected armed suspects with mental disabilities who were killed by police would still be alive if they had not been provided with a potentially lethal firearm.

It must be recognized that law enforcement officers perform stressful and dangerous duties, most are highly professional and deserve the utmost respect. It is therefore tragic when police officers are killed. The National Law Enforcement Memorial Fund keeps a detailed record of law enforcement officers fallen heroes[lxvii]. In 2018, 158 law enforcement officers died in the line of duty.

There are many ways in which law enforcement officers may be killed with shootings and auto crashes being the most common. The 2018 figure of 158 fatalities can be broken down as follows:

| How law enforcement officers are killed | Number of fatalities |
| --- | --- |
| Shot | 53 |
| Auto crash | 31 |
| Job-related illness | 48 |
| Struck by vehicle | 14 |
| Other | 12 |
| Total | 158 |

By comparison, even though police are not armed in the UK, just two law enforcement officers were killed in 2017. One of these occurred when a police officer was stabbed trying to prevent a knife-wielding terrorist entering Westminster Palace [lxviii] and the other when an officer was struck by a vehicle [lxix]. At the time of writing the last time a law enforcement officer was fatally shot was in

September 2012 when 2 female police officers were shot in an ambush following the report of a burglary.[lxx]

There does seem to be a vicious circle in America in which the more frequently law enforcement officers are shot, the more likely it is that police officers fearful for their own lives will shoot suspects in questionable circumstances. This in turn gives police bad publicity and hence makes it more likely that they will then be targeted by felons.

The over-riding message here is that possession of a gun in a confrontational situation, dramatically increases the risk that you will be shot. The reason for this being that it makes you appear to be a threat and therefore a legitimate target for your adversary. The main reason police shoot suspects are that they believe the suspect to be armed and dangerous.

Unfortunately, the vast presence of guns in America not only endangers those carrying guns it also increases the risk to those who are not armed. For example, police may assume that someone who moves their hand to take a cell phone from their pocket is attempting to take a gun from their pocket. Following an incident in which police shoot an unarmed suspect the excuse will always be "I thought he was armed". This only occurs in countries where it is not unusual for suspects to be armed.

# 6. Intentional Homicide

There are three general categories of intentional homicide, these being murder, manslaughter, and justifiable homicide. Justifiable firearm homicide deaths were covered in the previous 2 chapters. In this chapter, we will review intentional firearm homicides, which covers both murder and manslaughter. Based on 2017 figures and as noted in Chapter 1, the combined total of firearm murder and manslaughter deaths totaled 14,542 a figure 26 times greater than the number of justifiable firearm homicides figure of 553 for the same period.

Murder can be subdivided into several sub-categories the most common of which are first-degree murder and second-degree murder.

First-degree murder is the most serious of all homicide charges and applies to situations in which someone is accused of killing another person after having planned to kill the victim. It requires malice (evil intent) and forethought (planning).

Second-degree murder usually applies to cases in which someone may have intended to kill another person but did not have time to plan it. Second-degree murder may also apply to situations in which someone's actions were so wanton and reckless that the death of another person was readily foreseeable, even if killing someone was not the intention. Second-degree murders frequently result from a sudden outburst of anger e.g. road rage or a domestic argument. The dangers of having a loaded gun to hand in these situations are all too obvious. An incident that may have resulted in a bloody nose from a fist without a gun can result in a death or serious injury when a gun is available. One moment of extreme anger in an individual can ruin the lives of 2 people and their families in an instant when a gun is easily accessible. The victim and their family due to loss of life or injury and the perpetrator and their family through the likely incarceration which will follow the incident.

Manslaughter applies to instances where the accused did not plan the crime nor did he or she intend for the victim to die because of his or her actions. Manslaughter charges usually arise out of accidental circumstances where a person died because of the event. For example, a parent that leaves a baby in a hot car, or a driver who causes a fatal car accident through dangerous driving. Firearm-related manslaughter charges are probably not that common, in that the shooter must realize there is a significant chance that their actions will cause the death of their target. An example of firearm manslaughter would probably cover a case where someone recklessly shoots a gun through an open car window and unintentionally kills someone.

In reality, the classification of the homicide between the above categories is only important to the perpetrator, since it will determine their charges and sentencing when caught. To the victim and their families, it makes no difference if the tragic loss of life was a result of a first-degree murder, second-degree murder, or manslaughter.

The 2017 figure of 14,542 firearm-related homicides in the United States equates to nearly 40 fatal criminal shootings each day. As a comparison for England & Wales, there were just 32 firearm homicides in the 12 months ending March 2017[lxxi]. Put simply there are significantly more firearm homicides in the United States in 1 day than for a whole year in England & Wales.

It is true that the perpetrators of some of the firearm homicides would be able to use a different method for their murder if a firearm was not easily accessible but only to a limited extent. The key point to remember is that overall homicide rates in America are significantly higher than any of the other top 20 highly developed countries, due almost entirely to the alarmingly high (for a developed country) rate of firearm-related homicides, resulting from the combination of the huge number of guns in circulation, the relative ease to purchase firearms legally and the inability to prevent individuals from obtaining firearms illegally. We will examine ways of trying to prevent illegal ownership in Chapter 27, but for now, the key question is why do more guns result in higher overall intentional homicide rates? There are several reasons including the following:

Firstly, firearms unlike most other potential murder weapons are designed to kill and consequently, a significant proportion of firearm murder attempts will be successful. Firing at a relatively close range to the victim's torso or head is likely to kill them, which makes firearms an effective way of ending another person's life.

Secondly, pulling a trigger is easy and can also be quickly repeated.

Thirdly, using a firearm as a murder weapon gives the perpetrator little time to change their minds. Once the firearm has been aimed and the trigger has been pulled there is no going back. This is not the case with many other murder weapons such as strangulation which takes time and might be stopped when the attacker has second thoughts or notices the victim losing consciousness. With a blunt object, the attacker may stop after the first blow which knocks the victim to the floor. Generally, blunt objects are more likely to kill with repeated blows as opposed to a single blow. With a knife, the assailant may resist the temptation to stab too deep or may simply have insufficient strength to make a fatal wound.

Fourthly, using a firearm reduces the risk of the attacker being hurt or killed in retaliation. The low risk resulting from the fact that the shot can be fired without having to come into proximity of the victim. Most other murder weapons involve close contact with the victim which gives them more chance to fight back.

Fifthly, because a firearm can be shot from distance it makes it more difficult for the victim to retreat to safety.

In summary, firearms are so deadly because when they are used in murder attempts, they are effective, easy to use, quick, difficult to retract, hard to retaliate against, and not easy to evade.

A frequent argument between gun-rights and gun-control advocates is whether most murders are committed by strangers, or by individuals who have close contact with the victim. If most murders are committed by strangers then having a gun at home or in your car may be an effective deterrent against an intruder i.e. an effective method of protection. On the other hand, if most murders are committed by family members then having a gun in the home significantly increases the dangers for all individuals residing in the home. For example, following a domestic argument, an attacker in a fit of temper can quickly pick up a gun stored in the house and shoot other household residents.

So, are most homicides committed by strangers or acquaintances? Figures published by the Bureau of Justice Statistics based on homicides reported to the FBI between 1993 and 2008 show that between 21% and 27% of homicides for which the victim-offender relationship was known were committed by strangers and between 73% and 79% were committed by offenders known to the victims[lxxii].

This would suggest that the presence of a gun in the home increases the risk that residents will be homicide victims rather than reducing the risk. This will be explored further in Step 3 of the book in which the ineffectiveness of using guns for protection will be demonstrated.

There is a specific type of murder which amongst developed countries is uniquely prevalent in America that requires further analysis and this relates to incidents where an individual kills one or more other persons and then kills themselves. This is referred to as murder-suicide.

The Violence Policy Center periodically publishes details of murder-suicides in publications titled American Roulette: Murder-Suicide in the United States. The 6th edition published in June 2018 provides the following information for the 1st half of 2017[lxxiii].

- There were 296 murder-suicide events resulting in 663 murder-suicide deaths, of which 296 were suicides and 367 were homicides.
- Of the 296 murder-suicide events, 270 were known to involve a firearm (91 percent).
- Sixty-five percent of all murder-suicides involved an intimate partner. Of these, 96 percent were females killed by their intimate partners and 94 percent involved a gun.
- Forty-two of the homicide victims were children and teens less than 18 years of age.
- Fifty-two children and teens less than 18 years of age were survivors who witnessed some aspect of the murder-suicide.

It is probably not too surprising that 91% of murder-suicides involved firearms since as previously noted guns make it quick and easy to kill others and quick and easy to kill yourself.

A particularly tragic consequence of murder-suicides is that they frequently leave children parentless and without a shadow of a doubt the reason why murder-suicides occur in the United States at such an alarming rate is due to the volume and easy access of firearms and the high proportion of households in which firearms are stored.

There is another category of firearm homicide which requires further review and that is mass shootings which we will examine in the next chapter.

# 7. Mass Shootings



According to data from the Gun Violence Archive, in the United States, there were 382 mass shooting incidents in 2016 and 346 in 2017, [lxxiv] or in other words an average of approximately 1 mass shooting incident a day. This contrasts with FBI data which recorded just 20 active shooting incidents in 2016 and 30 in 2017[lxxv].

The huge difference in the Gun Violence Archive and FBI figures arises from the fact that there is no single accepted definition of a mass shooting. The Gun Violence Archive defines a mass shooting as an incident in which four or more individuals are shot and includes firearm injuries as well as fatalities. The FBI definition of a public mass shooting is one in which four or more people selected indiscriminately, not including the perpetrator, are killed, echoing the FBI definition of the term mass murder.

Regardless of the actual definition of the term mass shooting one thing is clear. These incidents occur far more frequently in America than any other developed country in the world as can be seen from the following analysis of 119 mass shootings which occurred in 25 developed countries between 1983 and 2013[lxxvi].

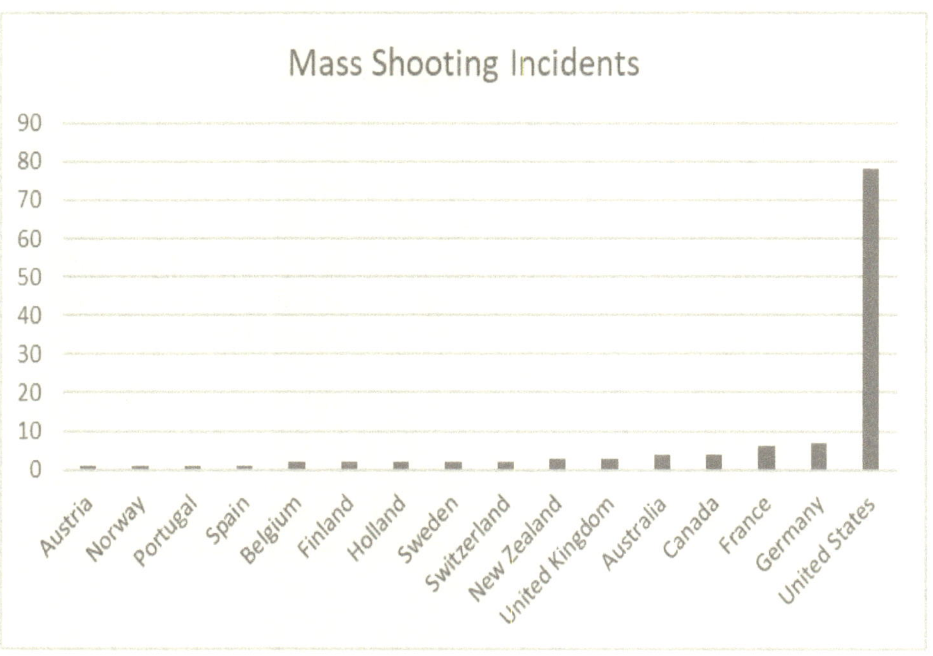



These figures would suggest that the FBI definition of mass murders or something similar has been used. There were 9 countries amongst the 25 included in this analysis with no mass shooting incidents in these 30 years, which do not appear on the above chart. Once again, the United States is an outlier when it comes to firearm-related incidents, with 78 of the 119 mass shootings. In other words, the United States had nearly double the number of mass shootings than all the other 24 countries combined in the same 30-year period.

In a separate CNN news report, it was noted that the United States has 31% of world-wide public mass shootings despite only having 5% of the world population.[lxxvii]

In addition to the frequency of the mass shootings in America, they have also become deadlier in recent years as is evident by the fact that 5 of the 10 deadliest mass shootings have occurred since 2016, with the deadliest occurring in 2017.

Below are brief details of the deadliest 10 mass shootings to have occurred in America since 1949 as published by CNN [lxxviii]

1. The Harvest Music Festival: 58 killed

October 1, 2017 - A gunman, identified as 64-year-old Stephen Paddock, fires from the 32nd floor of the Mandalay Bay Resort and Casino on a crowd of more than 20,000 gathered on the Las Vegas Strip for the Route 91 Harvest Music Festival. He kills 58 people and injures more than 500. Police believe the gunman then kills himself. It is the deadliest mass shooting in modern US history.

2. Pulse night club: 49 killed

June 12, 2016 - Omar Siddiqui Mateen, 29, opens fire inside Pulse, a gay nightclub, in Orlando. At least 49 people are killed and more than 50 are injured. Police shoot and kill Mateen during an operation to free hostages, officials say he was holding captive at the club.

3. Virginia Tech: 32 killed

April 16, 2007 - Student Seung-Hui Cho, 23, goes on a shooting spree, killing 32 people in two locations and wounding an undetermined number of others on the campus of Virginia Tech in Blacksburg. The shooter dies by suicide.

4. Sandy Hook: 27 killed

December 14, 2012 - Adam Lanza, 20, guns down 20 children, ages 6 and 7, and six adults at Sandy Hook Elementary School in Newtown, Connecticut, before turning the gun on himself. Investigators later find the shooter's mother, Nancy Lanza, dead from a gunshot wound.

5. First Baptist Church in Sutherland Springs: 25 and an unborn child killed

November 5, 2017 - A man walks into a small church in a rural Texas town and guns down 25 people. The shooter, identified by two law enforcement sources as Devin Patrick Kelley, is found dead after a brief chase, but it's unclear if he is killed or takes his own life. It is the deadliest mass shooting in Texas history.

6. Luby's Cafeteria: 23 killed

October 16, 1991 - In Killeen, Texas, 35-year-old George Hennard crashes his pickup truck through the wall of a Luby's Cafeteria. After exiting the truck, Hennard shoots and kills 23 people. He then takes his own life.

7. Walmart El Paso: 23 killed

August 3, 2019 – Patrick Crusius 21, walked into a Walmart carrying a WASR-10 rifle and opened fire killing 22 people and injuring 24. After leaving the Walmart Crusius drove to a nearby intersection, where he identified himself as the shooter and surrendered to the Texas Rangers.

8. McDonald's in San Ysidro: 21 killed

July 18, 1984 - In San Ysidro, California, 41-year-old James Huberty, armed with a long-barreled Uzi, a pump-action shotgun and a handgun, shoots and kills 21 adults and children at a McDonald's. A police sharpshooter kills Huberty one hour after the rampage begins.

9. University of Texas: 18 killed

August 1, 1966 - Charles Joseph Whitman, a former US Marine, kills 16 and wounds at least 30 while shooting from a tower at the University of Texas at Austin. Police officers Ramiro Martinez and Houston McCoy shoot and kill Whitman in the tower. Whitman had killed his mother and wife earlier in the day.

10. High school in Parkland, Florida: 17 killed

February 14, 2018 - A former student opened fire at Marjory Stoneman Douglas High School. The suspect, a former student, was expelled for disciplinary reasons, officials said. He was taken into custody shortly after the attack.

So, why are there so many more mass shootings in America than in other developed countries, and why are they becoming deadlier? All the following are factors; the sheer volume of firearms in circulation, the lack of control as to who can obtain firearms, the lack of restrictions on the type of firearms and ammunition available, and the lack of action following a mass shooting.

The volume of firearms in the United States has already been noted and the reasons behind this and the general lack of control on gun ownership and weapon availability will be reviewed later in the book. The remainder of this chapter will focus on how 3 countries, namely Australia the United Kingdom & New Zealand reacted following mass shootings in their countries, how effective their response was, and how this sharply contrasts with the continued lack of action following mass shootings in the United States.

<u>Port Arthur Massacre Australia</u>[lxxix]

On April 28 1996 Martin Bryant went on a mass shooting spree in Port Arthur Tasmania, killing 35 people and injuring at least 18. Martin Bryant had been able to legally obtain a Colt AR15 semi-automatic rifle although he was intellectually disabled since, at the time of purchase, no registration of guns outside of handguns was required in Tasmania.

Australians reacted to the event with widespread shock and horror, and the political effects were significant and long-lasting. The federal government led state governments, some of which (notably Tasmania itself and Queensland) had previously been opposed to new gun laws, to severely restrict the availability of firearms.

Under federal government co-ordination, all states and territories of Australia restricted the legal ownership and use of self-loading rifles, self-loading shotguns, and tightened controls on their legal use by recreational shooters. The government initiated a mandatory "buy-back" scheme with the owners paid according to a table of valuations. During the buyback, more than 700,000 firearms (both banned and legal) were surrendered to the police and destroyed. This represented a third of the guns that were estimated to be in the country at the time.

John Howard the Prime Minister of Australia at the time of the incident was able to introduce strict gun-controls as well as introducing firearms licensing with bipartisan support by the Commonwealth, states and territories of Australia.

Support for widespread gun reform following this tragic incident was overwhelming and the buy-back scheme was a great success with no further mass shootings in Australia for 22 years. This compares with 13 mass shootings in the 15 years prior to the 1996 buy-back[lxxx]. Sadly, there was a further mass shooting on May 11 2018 at a home in Osmington near Perth in Western Australia, which resulted in the death of 4 children and three adults. No amount of restrictions on firearms can eliminate firearm deaths or mass shootings but they can go a long way to significantly reduce the number of innocent people being killed or injured through firearms.

Whilst mass shootings are tragic, they only contribute to a relatively small proportion of overall firearm deaths and in some respects, the greatest achievement of the 1996 buy-back and increased gun regulations, is the reduction it helped to achieve, in overall firearm-related deaths in Australia post-1996. Between 1996 and 2016 the annual rate of gun deaths in Australia fell from 2.9 per 100,000 residents to 0.9 per 100,000[lxxxi]. Whilst it is true that Australian firearm deaths were already falling before 1996 the rate of decline accelerated post-1996. The extent to which the 1996 reforms reduced firearm deaths is difficult to quantify but it certainly did reduce overall firearm deaths and reduce the frequency of mass shootings.

The most important point to note from this is that following a large-scale mass shooting in Australia the government found bipartisan support to enact meaningful controls to try and prevent further mass shootings and that these actions have proved to be successful.

<u>Dunblane School Massacre Scotland</u>

On March 13 1996 Thomas Hamilton shot 16 children and one teacher dead before killing himself at the Dunblane primary school near Stirling in Scotland. It remains the deadliest mass shooting in British history.[lxxxii]. What was particularly tragic about this incident was the fact that most of the victims were aged just 5 years old.

The firearms used in this massacre included two pistols and two revolvers all of which had been legally obtained. The massacre in Dunblane prompted widespread outrage and a surge in public opinion to ban handguns. Consequently, after the massacre, public petitions were set up calling for a ban on the private ownership of handguns, and an official inquiry was set up which produced the Cullen Report[lxxxiii] recommending much tighter restrictions on gun ownership. Following further debate, two new Firearms Acts were passed, which outlawed private ownership of most handguns in Great Britain. These built upon a previous firearm act which had been set up following a mass shooting that killed 16 people in Hungerford in 1987 [lxxxiv]. This had banned the ownership of semi-automatic center-fire rifles and restricted the use of shotguns with a capacity of more than three cartridges.

Following the Dunblane mass shooting a government-led buy-back program was set up through which 162,198 handguns had been surrendered by January 2000. Since 1996 there have been no further school shootings in the United Kingdom and just one mass shooting incident in Cumbria in 2010 [lxxxv]

Total firearm homicides have also been substantially reduced following the new legislation, with the following firearm homicide comparison in the years before Dunblane and more recent available figures[lxxxvi]:

| Year | Number of firearm homicides |
|---|---|
| 1993 | 75 |
| 1994 | 75 |
| 1995 | 81 |
| 2014/15 | 20 |
| 2016/16 | 24 |
| 2016/17 | 27 |

In common with Australia, following a mass shooting the UK passed meaningful restrictions on gun ownership and initiated a successful buy-back scheme which has prevented further mass shootings and reduced the number of firearm homicides.

Christchurch Mosque Shootings New Zealand

On March 15 2019 there was a mass shooting at the Al Noor Mosque in the Christchurch suburb of Riccarton, followed by a mass shooting at the Linwood Islamic Centre. These attacks killed 50 people and injured 50 others. The attacks were carried out by a lone shooter, and police recovered five guns at the scene: two semi-automatic weapons, two shotguns, and a lever-action firearm. New Zealand's relatively unrestricted gun laws came under scrutiny after the shooting and their Prime Minister Jacinda Ardern immediately announced: "Our gun laws will change, now is the time. People will be seeking change, and I am committed to that"[lxxxvii]

Prime Minister Ardern was true to her word banning the sale of all military-style semi-automatics (MSSA) and assault rifles just six days after the March 15 shooting. Plans to tighten gun laws were announced and less than 1 month after the shooting Parliament passed the gun reform bill, the first substantial changes to New Zealand's gun laws in decades, by 119 to 1.[lxxxviii] The bill granted an amnesty of around 6 months for people to hand in the newly prohibited weapons through a government buy-back scheme.

An extremely impressive response by New Zealand who unanimously have prioritized the safety of their citizens ahead of special interest groups and those advocating gun-rights. The whole country came together to take decisive action to help prevent future mass shootings.

Having seen how effectively Australia the United Kingdom & New Zealand reacted to their mass shootings we shall now review how the United States has reacted to some of their recent mass shootings.

<u>Sandy Hook School shooting 2012</u>

As outlined earlier in the chapter this was a tragic incident in which 20 primary school children and 6 adults were shot dead at Sandy Hook Elementary School in Newtown, Connecticut. This was such a terrible event that it shook the nation. On the day of the shootings, a visibly shaken President Obama gave a televised address and had to pause twice to compose himself and wipe away tears. He stated: "We're going to have to come together and take meaningful action to prevent more tragedies like this, regardless of the politics"

Sadly, President Obama's words have fallen on death ears. On the 5th anniversary of the Sandy Hook Elementary School shooting it was noted that there had been more than one hundred attempts to enact various federal gun-control legislation and not a single one of these had passed[lxxxix].

What seemed at the time like the horrifying turning point in the American gun debate, a gunman in Newtown, Connecticut, slaughtering 20 children and six adult employees during the school day after killing his mother, now instead seems like the moment the United States decided no tragedy was too great to change federal gun laws. Almost all major attempts at federal legislation have failed, even as shootings with ever-higher body counts continue.

The Harvest Music Festival Las Vegas

On October 1, 2017, Stephen Paddock initiated the deadliest mass shooting in modern US history killing 58 people and injuring more than 500 before killing himself. The reason the attack was so deadly was that Paddock had access to bump stocks, which essentially convert semi-automatic weapons to fully automatic ones. The use of bump stock and a semi-automatic weapon allowed Paddock to fire more than 1,100 rounds before he turned the gun on himself. Following this massacre, a bill to ban bump stocks was introduced which unusually gained bipartisan support. And despite opposition from the NRA, the use of bump stocks was banned with the final date to destroy or turn in the devices being 21 March 2019.[xc] This is a rare success for those supporting gun-control although pro-gun advocates have said they are prepared to fight the rule in court.

The contrast between the lack of action in America and the effective action in Australia the United Kingdom and New Zealand could not be starker. The typical course of action following a major mass shooting in the United States is as follows:

1.  Offer thoughts and prayers to the victims
2.  Say that now is a time for grieving and not discussing the merits of further gun-control
3.  Do nothing – If an attempt is made to tighten federal gun regulation it will fail
4.  Await the next mass shooting and repeat these 4 steps.

To understand the reason for this lack of action it is necessary to understand, the constitutional legal restraints imposed on gun-control by the Second Amendment and the passion with which American citizens love their guns. Both of these will be explored in Step 2 of the book. Additionally, the stranglehold organizations such as the

NRA and gun manufacturers have in restricting action to curb gun violence, will be examined in Step 4 of this book.

# STEP 2

Understanding why guns are so popular in America

# 8. The Second Amendment

*A well regulated militia, being necessary to the security of a free state, the right of the people to keep and bear arms, shall not be infringed.*

These 27 words enshrined in the Bill of Rights as the Second Amendment are considered sacrosanct by the majority of Americans.

But what do these words mean and do they have any relevance in the 21st century? To help answer these questions we need initially to define the meaning of some of the keywords.

- Militia – At the time the Bill of Rights was drafted "Militia" were military forces drawn from the citizenry. Men from sixteen to sixty were required to join a company and train intermittently. They were also required to bring their own musket.

- Well Regulated – Today this would probably refer to some amount of governmental rules and control in addition to being well trained; however, this meaning was different in the 18th century. According to Alexander Hamilton, this meant a select militia of only the most ardent men. Based on the Articles of Confederation it would appear to refer to a militia with sufficient weaponry. Additionally, Well Regulated may simply mean well disciplined.

- Free State – Some have asserted that this is a generic term referring to a republican government, however, it is generally considered to refer to individual states.

- The Right of The People – This is generally considered to be an individual right for personal protection or militia service.

- Keep and Bear Arms – This is probably the most debated phrase within the Second Amendment. Many people believe this refers to the right to carry guns in an individual capacity for self-defense. Scholars however believe it was originally intended just to cover the rights in a military context.

The precise legal interpretation of the Second Amendment has changed over the years. In 1939 the U.S. Supreme Court considered the matter in United States v. Miller. The Court adopted a collective rights approach, in this case, determining that Congress could regulate a sawed-off shotgun that had moved in interstate commerce under the National Firearms Act of 1934 because the evidence did not suggest that the shotgun "has some reasonable relationship to the preservation or efficiency of a well-regulated militia" The Court then explained that the Framers included the Second Amendment to ensure the effectiveness of the militia [xci].

The 1939 precedent stood for nearly 70 years until the U.S. Supreme Court revisited the issue in the case of District of Columbia v. Heller in 2008. The plaintiff in *Heller* challenged the constitutionality of the Washington D.C. handgun ban, a statute that had stood for 32 years. In a 5-4 decision, the Court, meticulously detailing the history and tradition of the Second Amendment at the time of the Constitutional Convention, proclaimed that the Second Amendment established an individual right for U.S. citizens to possess firearms and struck down the D.C. handgun ban as violative of that right[xcii].

This ruling in effect dissected the second part of the Amendment *"the right of the people to keep and bear arms, shall not be infringed."* From the first part of the Amendment *"A well regulated militia, being necessary to the security of a free state"*. In other words, the right for people to have free access to arms is no longer connected to the necessity of having a well regulated militia. Consequently, the general understanding of the meaning of the Second Amendment to most American citizens covers either one or both of the following:

1.  We need a well-armed militia i.e. citizens with guns to secure our freedom. This is generally translated as citizens needing to be armed in order to overthrow a potentially dangerous or tyrannical government.

2. All citizens have an individual right to bear arms i.e. to be freely able to purchase guns with little or no restriction.

Understanding these 2 separate concepts helps explain why the Second Amendment is so popular in the United States.

Firstly, the concept of a well-armed militia i.e. armed citizens has tremendous support since this is what enabled the Americans to defeat the British, in the American War of Independence. Additionally, even today with a well-established Constitution and democratic electoral system there is a general lack of trust in the Government and a fear that it may one day be necessary to use the force of the militia to overthrow the Government.

Secondly, many Americans believe that possessing a gun helps to protect them and their families, and hence they feel the right to freely own guns for self-defense purposes is important. The Second Amendment, following the 2008 Supreme Court decision, helps to cement this basic right to freely obtain guns. In Step 4 of this book, we will examine how this ruling is both an obstacle and a potential opportunity for those wishing to introduce more restrictions on gun ownership.

Returning to the first half of the Second Amendment we need to consider if a well regulated militia has any relevance today and if it could be used to overthrow a government. When the Second Amendment was drafted the military as we know it today did not exist. The country, therefore, depended on a well-armed militia to defend itself. This not only enabled the country to defend itself against foreign invaders but also provided the opportunity to overthrow the government if it was perceived that the government was no longer acting in the interest of the citizens.

The militia does still exist in the United States and is defined by the Militia Act of 1903. Militia is primarily used to describe two groups within the United States:

- Organized militia – consisting of State militia forces; notably, the National Guard and Naval Militia.

- Unorganized militia – composing the Reserve Militia: every able-bodied man of at least 17 and under 45 years of age, not a member of the National Guard or Naval Militia.

The National Guard represents a reserve component of the United States Armed Forces. Composed of National Guard military members and units from each state. The National Guard can be deployed or mobilized for both federal and domestic missions. There are approximately 350,000 guardsmen currently serving[xciii].

The Naval militia is made up of retirees or reserve members of the Navy, Marine Corps, and the Coast Guard. When the militia's services are needed, they are allowed to receive supplies from the federal government and use available facilities designated for reserves[xciv].

With regards to Unorganized Militia, it is unlikely that they would ever be called up for duty, which is just as well since many men between the ages of 17 and 45 are probably not even aware they belong to the Unorganized Militia and the chances they are well regulated is slim. It is possible, although unlikely, that Unorganized Militia could be called upon based on the example of the law in Georgia, which states the following:

*When the militia of the state is called into federal service under the Constitution and laws of the United States, the Governor shall order out for service the organized militia or such part thereof as may be necessary; and, if the number available is insufficient, the Governor may call for and accept from the unorganized militia as many volunteers as are required for service in the organized militia[xcv].*

The Georgia law implies that volunteers would be sought rather than there being a demand to utilize all members of the Unorganized Militia. In reality, the most likely event in which the services of Unorganized Militia would be required would be in the event of a natural disaster event such as flooding, hurricane, or earthquake, although this could be extended to cover instances of civil unrest.

With the acceptance that the Militia does still exist in both an organized and unorganized sense, the next question to be answered is if the Militia could realistically use force to overthrow a government? The answer to this question is a resounding no.

Even on the assumption that the militia was well regulated and consisted of millions of citizens, there is no way it could compete with the US Military. The US military belongs to The Department of Defense which is an executive branch department of the federal government of the United States charged with coordinating and supervising all agencies and functions of the government concerned directly with national security and the United States Armed Forces[xcvi]. In other words, the military acts on behalf of the government and so the militia would have to overpower the military to overthrow the government.

The US military includes the Army, Marine Corps, Navy, Air Force, and Coast Guard and as of 2017 spends around $610 billion annually to fund its military forces. All branches are armed with modern military-grade weapons and the concept of armed civilians even with legally or illegally purchased semi-automatic weapons and other firearms available to civilians confronting the US military armed with tanks, bombers, missiles, etc. is just ridiculous.

Just as difficult to imagine is how the well-armed militia would co-ordinate their efforts to overthrow the government. Would they target government buildings across the nation or alternatively target Congress, The Senate, or The White House?

Even more problematic would be how do you unite the armed militia? There is currently a great political divide and intense partisanship in the United States, which in reality means that some members of the militia would only want to overthrow an extreme right-wing government, whilst others would only want to overthrow an extreme left-wing government. In practice, there would likely be conflict within the militia, whose members will have different political views. For every member of the militia wanting to overthrow the government, there may be another one just as determined to support the government. This could give rise to tension within the militia which in turn could escalate into a civil war. It should not be forgotten that the deadliest war in American history was the Civil War (1861 - 1865) with 618,222 casualties. The only other war which comes close to this death toll was World War 2 in which there were 405,399 American casualties[xcvii].

The concept of a well-armed militia overthrowing a government, which may have been a realistic proposition when the Bill of Rights was ratified in 1791, is no longer realistic in the 21st century. Today, governments in highly developed countries are replaced through the ballot box i.e. the democratic electoral system and not overthrown through the use of force. That said it is still possible, although extremely unlikely, that a government could lose the plot completely and become so dangerous, as to require immediate replacement. If this did happen one would hope that the military would realize it could no longer act for the government and immediately step in to ensure as smooth as possible transition of government. In effect, the military would switch sides as opposed to being overpowered by a civilian-led militia. It would also be hoped that Congress and the Senate would step in to impeach and remove a rogue President, long before the military felt the need for action.

In reality, if American citizens were to have any influence in overthrowing a government it would be done through peaceful demonstrations. This would enable all US citizens to participate as opposed to the outdated sexist and ageist definitions of the Unorganized Militia. In the 21st century freedom of speech is a much more powerful tool than any weapon. It is also worth noting that when the media reports on conflicts between demonstrators and law enforcement, it is generally the side that uses unreasonable force that loses public support, with public support being the most vital component in determining if a government is overthrown or supported.

Whilst the phrase *"A well regulated militia, being necessary to the security of a free state"* was relevant in the 18th century, a more modern equivalent would be something along the lines of *"A strong military being necessary to the security of a free state."* And when it comes to the strength of the military the United States has no close rival, spending more on defense than the next seven countries combined[xcviii].

Despite the impracticality of a well-armed militia overthrowing the government today, the Second Amendment is seen as a vital part of the Constitution and most Americans not only support the Second Amendment but are also proud of it. A poll taken in 2018 by the Economist & YouGov demonstrated that the Second Amendment is supported by the overwhelming majority of American citizens, with only 21% of American citizens stating that they would like to see the Second Amendment repealed[xcix], compared to 60% who are opposed to a repeal. This popularity largely stems from the fact that the Second Amendment means that all Americans have a right to bear arms or in other words freely obtain firearms with few restrictions and as we shall see in the next chapter Americans love their guns.

Given the popularity of the Second Amendment, it is often used as an argument to prevent new gun restrictions from being set up, frequently through the use of fearmongering tactics. For example, if a politician believes it should be made more difficult for criminals to obtain firearms which in itself would be a popular viewpoint, gun-rights activists will falsely claim that this politician will repeal the Second Amendment and confiscate all guns.

Anyone who would like to see new and sensible gun restrictions set up must be aware of the sanctity of the Second Amendment, which has been around for over 200 years and like it or not, is here to stay for the foreseeable future.

# 9. Reasons for owning a gun

The current interpretation of the Second Amendment clearly gives Americans a constitutional right to own firearms with only limited restrictions. This in itself, however, does not explain the desire amongst so many Americans to possess firearms.

To understand why citizens of the United States owns around 42% of all civilian-owned guns in the world[c], we need to examine the reasons behind the desire American citizens have, to own guns. As can be seen from the chart below the 3 main reasons for owning guns are for protection, hunting, and sport shooting[ci].

---

## Most gun owners cite protection as a major reason for owning a gun

*% of gun owners saying each is a major reason why they own a gun*

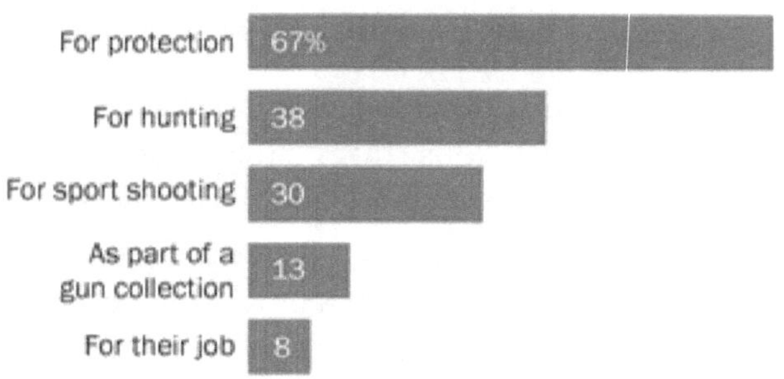


Source: Survey of U.S. adults conducted March 13-27 and April 4-18, 2017.
"America's Complex Relationship With Guns"

**PEW RESEARCH CENTER**

---

Note these figures add up to more than 100% as some gun owners may provide more than one major reason why they own a gun.

As can be seen, two-thirds of American gun owners state that a major reason why they own a gun is for protection. This is not surprising since most Americans, both gun owners and non-gun owners, believe that gun ownership makes you safer. In an NBC/Wall Street Journal poll taken in March 2018, it was found that 58 percent of respondents agreed with the statement that gun ownership does more to increase safety by allowing law-abiding citizens to protect themselves. By contrast, 38 percent said that gun ownership reduces safety by giving too many people access to firearms and increasing the chances for accidental misuse[cii].

It seems only natural to assume that having possession or easy access to a gun will make you safer since this will provide the opportunity to scare off any intruder or person attacking you and if necessary, the ability to shoot the aggressor before they can harm you. The reality however is the total opposite.

Following a very detailed review of scientific literature conducted by researchers at UC San Francisco and published online by the Annals of Internal Medicine in January 2014, it was concluded that someone with access to firearms is three times more likely to commit suicide and nearly twice as likely to be the victim of a homicide as someone who does not have access[ciii]. The review included studies about deaths by suicide and homicide but not accidental deaths.

Interestingly, there was a striking gender difference in the data. When firearms were accessible, men were nearly four times more likely to commit suicide than when firearms were not accessible, while women were almost three times more likely to be victims of homicide. This is consistent with men making more impulsive decisions to kill themselves with a gun and women being victims of male partners with access to firearms.

The link between firearm access and increased suicide risk was covered in Chapter 2 and the reason why easy access to firearms doubles the chance of being a victim of homicide will be covered in more detail in Chapter 16 which demonstrates that the presence of a gun poses more danger than protection.

One would hope that those who own guns for protection receive adequate training in how to safely use and store firearms, however, an article published in 2017 by the journal Injury Prevention [civ] found that for those gun owners who said they own a handgun for the sole purpose of protection, 57 percent said they had received formal training. In other words, 43% have not been trained on how to use their potentially deadly weapon. Even more concerning is that only 15 percent of gun owners said they had received any training or materials that addressed suicide, which is extremely alarming when around two-thirds of all gun deaths in the United States are self-inflicted.

The second most cited reason for owning a gun is hunting with 38% of gun owners stating this is a major reason why they own a gun. Whilst this seems quite a high figure it should be noted that the number of active hunters is continuing to decline. According to the US Fish & Wildlife Service, the number of people who stated they hunted at least once in the year has declined steadily from 14 million in 1996 to 12.5 million in 2006[cv]. This decline is probably associated with the general population shift from rural to urban areas.

The third most cited reason for owning a gun is sport or target shooting with 30% of gun owners stating this is a major reason why they own a gun. According to Statista, there were 30.46 million participants in target shooting in 2017[cvi], which is significantly higher than the number of hunters. This would appear to suggest that many participants in target shooting do not use their own guns and instead use the guns supplied at the target range, whilst hunters tend to use their own firearms.

One difference between those who own guns for protection and those who own them for hunting or target shooting is how the guns are likely to be stored. Those who own their guns for protection are more likely to have them loaded and easily accessible whilst those who own them for hunting or target shooting are more likely to have their guns unloaded and or safely stored in gun safes. Hunters and target shooters are therefore more likely to be responsible gun owners than those who own guns for protection.

According to the Pew Research Center, 38% of gun owners state they have a gun that is both loaded and easily accessible to them all of the time when they are at home, and 26% say they carry a gun outside their home all or most of the time[cvii]. It is safe to assume that the 26% who have a gun with them almost all the time cited self-protection as a major reason for owning a gun. The sad reality is that those owning a loaded and accessible gun for protection, are endangering themselves and their family members.

Although not cited as a being a specific major reason for owning guns the following, which will be examined further in the following chapters, are probably all factors that help explain the huge volume of firearms held in the United States.

- Children growing up in homes with guns, particularly if they are trained to use them are more likely to want to own a gun when they are adults, or they may inherit their parents' guns.
- The ease of purchase. A simple process with limited background checks will encourage people to purchase guns
- Gun Shows, which promote large volumes of customers and are an excellent way to market guns
- The NRA and gun manufacturers who actively lobby and promote gun ownership
- The irrational fear that soon there may be a ban on gun sales, and the better get a gun now whilst we can mentality.

Overall, there is no denying the popularity of guns in the United States, whether it be for protection, hunting, sport shooting, or any other reason; but exactly how many guns are there in the country? As we have previously noted according to the UNODC – small arms survey[cviii] around 42% of civilian held guns can be found in the United States. This figure must be an estimate however since there is no definitive measure on the number of civilian-owned guns, due to legal restrictions on keeping a database on gun registration.

A June 2018 report from the Small Arms Survey estimates that American civilians own 393 million guns, both legally and

otherwise, out of a worldwide (civilian) total of 857 million firearms[cix].
If this is correct it would mean that the Americans' world share of all civilian-owned guns has increased from 42% to 46% and that there are more guns than people in the country. No wonder there is such a high toll of firearm-related fatalities and injuries.

# 10. Gun Culture

In the previous chapter we examined the reasons why Americans own guns, but why are guns so much more popular in the United States than in any other country in the world? The need for protection and the opportunities for hunting and sport shooting exist in most other countries. The reasons for the unrivaled American passion for guns are complex and varied, but the initial starting point for the popularity of guns is associated with the history of guns and the strong gun culture this has created.

 Historically there has been a strong militia spirit in America which derived from the dependence of arms for protection from foreign armies and Native Americans. Survival depended upon everyone being armed and capable of using a weapon. This was enshrined further with the effective use of firearms in the American War of Independence and the creation of the Second Amendment.

Closely related to the militia tradition was the frontier tradition in which guns were required for self-defense during the 19th century westward expansion of the American frontier. Although the gun has not been a necessary part of daily survival for over a century, generations of Americans continue to embrace and glorify guns. In modern times gun culture is now promoted by western cowboy and gangster films & television programs.

With regard to films and Hollywood, the Michigan Youth Violence Prevention Center in 2013 wrote a BLOG titled Hollywood's Unapologetic Portrayal of Gun Violence[cx]. The writer was commenting on the fact that he witnessed a young boy accompanied by his parents watching the Quentin Tarantino film "Django Unchained". The title character in this film is a bounty hunter who receives monetary rewards for each individual he kills. This and similar films perpetuate the notion that it is both cool and acceptable to carry automatic weapons to take down the bad guys.

Heroes and heroines in films are often portrayed as violent individuals who are rewarded for their behavior. Frequently films or TV shows will show violent scenes with repetitive gunshots being fired in public places in which there is absolutely no concern for any collateral damage this may cause. Another misconception portrayed in movies is the fact that the gun yielding heroes never or rarely get killed, whilst the bad guys always do end up dead. In real life, the extreme risk-taking hero would be dead within 30 seconds. According to the American Academy of Child and Adolescent Psychiatry (AACAP), a typical American child will view more than 200,000 acts of violence on television and in film before reaching the age of eighteen. [cxi]

A more modern media platform in which gun violence is portrayed can be found in first-person shooter video games such as Call of Duty, in which players go around killing characters appearing on the screen. These games are extremely popular and as of December 2015, the Call of Duty series had sold over 250 million copies[cxii].

Violence in films and video games are frequently cited by gun enthusiasts as a reason for the high incidence of gun homicides and mass shootings in America, as opposed to the ease of purchase and the sheer volume of firearms. Whilst this is partially true it fails to acknowledge the fact that these violent films and games are prevalent in other countries that do not experience the same volume and severity of gun violence as the United States. The reality is that the portrayal of violence and particularly gun violence adds fuel to the dangerous situation created in which anyone can easily access powerful firearms.

The gun culture which leads so many Americans to idolize their weapons tends to be self-perpetuating in several ways. The popularity of guns has enabled gun manufacturers and the NRA to become powerful and effective in marketing, promoting guns, and political lobbying. It also gives rise to something which is almost exclusively an American phenomenon and that is the Gun Show.

A Gun Show is an event where promoters generally rent large public venues and then rent tables for display areas for dealers of guns and related items, and charge admission for buyers. The Bureau of Alcohol, Tobacco, Firearms and Explosives (ATF) estimates that there are 2,000 gun shows held in the United States each year, whilst the National Association of Arms Shows estimate that there are as many as 5,200 gun shows held each year which generate billions of dollars in sales.[cxiii]

In addition to promoting gun sales, gun shows also provide the perfect venue for promoting gun-rights and Second Amendment issues. Gun-rights groups frequently set up booths at gun shows to distribute literature and recruit members and no new potential member is too young to influence. Children are allowed to attend gun shows and will inevitably be influenced by the glorification of guns which will be occurring in abundance. The influence parents may have on their children is best summed up by a comment on a website in which someone asked if children are allowed to attend gun shows. One of the responses was as follows – *"I take my kids all the time. They like it. The children are the future and we need to instill our values in them regardless of what the anti-gunners think."*

Parents glorifying guns to their children are a significant reason for the self-perpetuating gun culture in the United States and this is amplified by the sheer volume of firearms, which means so many children have grown up in the presence of guns.

Telephone polls, from Gallup and the Pew Research Center in 2017 estimated that around 42% of people in the United States live in a household where guns are present. The Pew Research Center poll also indicated that 48% of adults grew up in a home where a gun was present and that 72% of adults have shot a gun at some point in their lives[cxiv]. Although the majority of American children live in homes where no guns are present, the vast majority of children will have visited friends or relatives in homes where guns are present and are therefore likely to have come into contact with firearms.

In 1995, political scientist Robert Spitzer said that the modern American gun culture is founded on three factors: the proliferation of firearms since the earliest days of the nation, the connection between personal ownership of weapons and the country's revolutionary and frontier history, and the cultural mythology regarding the gun in the frontier and modern life[cxv].

One thing is certain there is no other country in the world where the gun is held in such high esteem as in the United States.

# 11. Gun Availability

The previous 3 chapters focused on reasons why there is such a high demand for firearms in the United States with, the Second Amendment, belief that guns provide protection, and gun culture all having a major impact. To ensure this demand is met the gun industry, gun lobbyists, and organizations such as the NRA work tirelessly to ensure this demand is met with an adequate supply of firearms.

To meet the demand for both purchasing and owning guns it is necessary for there to be a high volume and variety of well-marketed firearms readily available for purchase. Additionally, there needs to be relatively few restrictions in allowing potential new customers from acquiring and owning firearms.

For a typical American wanting to purchase a firearm, there is a wide choice of weapon type and manufacturer to choose from. The weapon types include the following:

- Handgun - a short-barreled firearm designed to be fired with only one hand. The two most common handgun sub-types in use today are revolvers and semi-automatic pistols.
    - Revolver - a repeating handgun that has a revolving cylinder containing  multiple chambers and at least one barrel for firing.
    - Semi-automatic pistol - a type of pistol that uses the energy of the fired cartridge to cycle the action of the firearm and advance the next available cartridge into position for firing. One cartridge is fired each time the trigger of a semi-automatic pistol is pulled.
- Long gun - a category of firearms with longer barrels than most other types. In small arms, a long gun is generally designed to be held by both hands and braced against the shoulder.

- Rifle  -  a portable long-barreled firearm designed  for precision shooting, to be held with both hands and braced against the shoulder for stability during firing, and with a barrel that has a helical pattern of grooves ("rifling") cut into the bore walls.
- Shotgun - a firearm that is usually designed to be fired from the shoulder, which uses the energy of a fixed shell to fire several small spherical pellets called shot, or a solid projectile called a slug.
- Semi-automatic firearm - a firearm that not only fires a bullet each time the trigger is pulled but also performs all steps necessary to prepare it to discharge again assuming cartridges remain in the firearm's feed device. Typically, this includes extracting and ejecting the spent cartridge case from the firing chamber, re-cocking the firing mechanism, and loading a new cartridge into the firing chamber. To fire again, the trigger is released and re-pressed.
- Automatic firearm – a firearm that continuously fires rounds as long as the trigger is pressed or held and there is ammunition in the magazine/chamber.

All the above categories of weapons except automatic firearms are freely available in most states. Under federal law, fully automatic weapons are technically legal only if made before 1986, when Congress passed the Firearm Owners Protection Act. There are additional state laws placing restrictions on certain categories in particular semi-automatic weapons.

The Bureau of Alcohol, Tobacco, Firearms and Explosives produce an annual report which shows the volume of manufactured firearms on an annual basis. This provides an insight into both the huge volume of manufactured guns and the most popular categories of firearms. The 2016 annual firearms manufacturing and export report are summarized as follows[cxvi]:

| Type of weapon | Total manufactured in 2016 |
| --- | --- |
| Pistols | 4,720,075 |
| Revolvers | 856,291 |
| Rifles | 4,239,335 |
| Shotguns | 848,617 |
| Misc. firearms | 833,123 |
| Total manufactured | 11,497,441 |

From the figures above it is clear that the two most popular categories of firearms are pistols and rifles. Of the 11.5 million firearms manufactured in 2016 only 376,818 i.e., just over 3% were exported. That such a small proportion of firearms were exported is no surprise given the huge demand for firearms in the United States. Approximately one-third of American firearms are imported[cxvii].

The actual volume of gun sales would appear to be significantly higher than the number manufactured, based on FBI background check the number of firearm sales for the period 2015 - 2018 were as follows: [cxviii]

| | |
| --- | --- |
| 2015 | 23,141,970 |
| 2016 | 27,538,673 |
| 2017 | 25,235,215 |
| 2018 | 26,181,936 |

FBI background checks are considered to provide a very good estimate of actual firearm sales and it is worth noting that the 2016 figure was a record level, due in part to the Pulse Nightclub mass shooting and the fear that there may have been more restrictions placed on guns if Hilary Clinton had won the 2016 presidential election.

Marketing is an important aspect for gun manufacturers and based on 2017 sales the most popular handgun is the Sturm Ruger Lightweight Compact Pistol (LCP). This is a semi-automatic pistol and comes in a wide variety of colors and is marketed as follows on the Ruger website[cxix]:

- Compact and lightweight, the LCP® is designed to fit a variety of holsters.
- Textured grip frame provides a secure and comfortable grip.
- Fixed front and rear sights are integral to the slide, while the hammer is recessed within the slide.
- Rugged construction with through-hardened steel slide and one-piece, high-performance, glass-filled nylon grip frame.
- Includes finger grip extension floorplate that can be added to the magazine for comfort and improved grip.
- Black Oxide, alloy steel barrel.
- Also includes one 6-round magazine.

One of the most popular rifles is the semi-automatic AR-15. The AR-15 is an assault-style rifle that is easy to obtain and capable of causing a high volume of casualties. The AR-15 is a particularly controversial firearm as it has frequently been used to perpetrate mass shootings. Regardless of the carnage, an AR-15 can cause, manufacturers boast that an experienced shooter could fire as many as 45 rounds in one minute with an AR-15, and magazines containing fresh ammunition can be swapped out in a matter of seconds. [cxx]

It would, therefore, appear that the high demand for firearms is being met by a well-established and professional supply of firearms. There is just one final ingredient required to enable the gun industry in the United States to become so dominant and that is the legality and ease of purchase of firearms for American citizens.

Current federal laws place few restrictions on both the type of firearms that can be sold and on who is allowed to purchase firearms. Below is a summary of the most relevant recent Federal laws concerning firearms:

- Firearm Owners Protection Act (FOPA) 1986 - Prohibited the sale to civilians of automatic firearms manufactured after the date of the law's passage. Required Alcohol, Tobacco, Firearms and Explosives (ATF) approval of transfers of automatic firearms [cxxi].
- Gun-Free School Zones Act (1990): Prohibits unauthorized individuals from knowingly possessing a firearm at a place that the individual knows, or has reasonable cause to believe, is a school zone [cxxii].
- Brady Handgun Violence Prevention Act (1993): Requires background checks on most firearm purchasers, depending on seller and venue [cxxiii].
- Federal Assault Weapons Ban (1994–2004): Banned semiautomatics that looked like assault weapons and large-capacity ammunition feeding devices. This law expired in 2004 and has not been replaced [cxxiv].
- Protection of Lawful Commerce in Arms Act (2005): Prevents firearm manufacturers and licensed dealers from being held liable for negligence when crimes have been committed with their products [cxxv].

As can be seen the failure to re-enact the Federal Assault Weapon Ban and the Protection of Lawful Commerce in Arms Act have reduced federal restrictions in recent years. There are also few restrictions on who can purchase firearms with restrictions only applying to those convicted of a felony or misdemeanor with a sentence exceeding 2 years, and those who were involuntarily admitted to a mental facility.

Federal law also prohibits the possession of a handgun or handgun ammunition by any person under the age of 18; however, there is no minimum age for the possession of long guns or long gun ammunition. In most states, there are few additional restrictions on firearms with forty-four states having a provision in their state constitutions similar to the Second Amendment to the United States Constitution, which protects the right to keep and bear arms.

In February 2018, just a few days after Nikolas Cruz shot 17 people dead at the Douglas High School mass shooting in Parkland Florida, the Business Insider published an article showing just how easy it is to buy a semi-automatic weapon in the United States[cxxvi]. Cruz, a 19-year-old former student of the school, was legally able to buy the AR-15 rifle he used to perpetrate the shooting. At this time Florida did not require fingerprints, a special permit, or even a waiting period to buy a gun. This is common in some parts of the US, where you can walk into a store and walk out with a semi-automatic gun in your hand in minutes.

In Virginia, you can buy a semi-automatic gun "in 15 minutes," Roanoke Firearms owner John Markell told the New York Time's Michael Barbaro. Roanoke Firearms is where Seung-Hui Cho, who killed 32 in a shooting spree on Virginia Tech's campus bought a Glock after passing two background checks.

It took a reporter from the Philly Inquirer seven minutes to buy an AR-15, the semi-automatic gun used in many of the US' deadliest mass shootings. In Orlando, buying the AR-15 took just 38 minutes two days after the shooting spree that killed 49 people at the city's Pulse nightclub, the Huffington Post reported.

Although some states have stricter regulation for certain types of firearms, such as assault rifles, in many states semi-automatic guns are typically treated similarly to any other firearm purchase. In most states, the store will run two background checks, a state check, and a federal check. The background checks provide nearly instantaneous results but in a majority of states, private sellers are allowed to sell guns without performing any kind of background state or federal checks.

In the case of the deadliest mass shooting in modern times at the Las Vegas Harvest Music Festival in October 2017, gunman Stephen Paddock bought 33 firearms in the year before the crime. Twelve of these were semiautomatic rifles that were rigged with legal devices that allowed the guns to fire like an automatic weapon. All of Paddock's purchases were completely legal. With no criminal record, Paddock would pass any background check. Nevada, where Paddock lived, does not impose any waiting period on gun purchases. The state allows anyone who is at least 18 years old to own a firearm and does not limit the number of guns a person can purchase in a single sale. [cxxvii]

It would appear that background checks are not particularly effective if the likes of Paddock can pass them. This is reflected by the fact that according to FBI figures only around 1 percent of federal background checks are rejected. Despite the low rejection rate, background checks are still an important tool in helping to prevent gun violence as the FBI data revealed that more than 1 million people failed background checks in the 14 years before 2013. The majority of these failures (578,000) were due to a felony or serious misdemeanor conviction, with other reasons for rejection including drug use or mental health issues. [cxxviii]

With a huge demand for firearms, a huge well-marketed supply of firearms, and very little restriction on who can purchase firearms, it is no wonder the firearm industry in the United States dwarves the figures in any other country.

The National Shooting Sports Foundation (NSSF) have published figures showing that the total economic impact of the firearms and ammunition industry in the United States increased from $19.1 billion in 2008 to $51.4 billion in 2017, a 169 percent increase, while the total number of full-time equivalent jobs rose from approximately 166,000 to almost 310,000, an 87 percent increase in that period[cxxix].

# 12. Gun-rights Advocacy Groups

Gun-rights Advocacy Groups are groups that actively work to protect individual citizen's rights to keep and bear firearms. They are strongly opposed to virtually all attempts to impose any form of gun-control, assist in the marketing of guns, and actively encourage gun ownership, which they believe is good for the nation. Gun-rights advocacy groups also engage in political lobbying and provide financial support to politicians who support greater gun-rights and to those who oppose gun-control.

Gun-rights advocacy groups including the following:

Gun Owners of America (GOA) [cxxx] – is an organization with over 2 million members. The declared purpose of GOA is to preserve, protect, and defend the second amendment rights of gun owners, including promoting and developing a greater understanding and awareness regarding the importance and benefits of firearms ownership and conducting education and policy related to such rights. An objective of the GOA is to generate public awareness of the dangers of not having a gun ready for protection and to encourage gun owners not to lock up their best means of self-defense.

Second Amendment Foundation (SAF) [cxxxi] - is a United States nonprofit organization that supports gun-rights, publishes gun-rights magazines and public education materials, funds conferences, provides media contacts, and has assumed a central role in sponsoring lawsuits in the support of gun-rights. The Citizens Committee for the Right to Keep and Bear Arms (CCRKBA) is the lobbying affiliate of the SAF. As of January 2015, both groups reported having over 650,000 members.

National Association of Gun-rights (NAGR)[cxxxii] – is a gun-rights advocacy group which considers itself the "conservative alternative" to the NRA. The group spends most of its energy attacking lawmakers deemed too soft on Second Amendment issues via direct mail, robocalls, and low-cost television ads. The group has gained notoriety for its aggressive lobbying tactics and attack ads. The NAGR claims to have around 4.5 million members.

National Shooting Sports Foundation (NSSF)[cxxxiii] - is an American national trade association for the firearms industry. The organization has more than 8,000 members. The members are not individuals but rather firearms manufacturers, distributors, retailers, shooting ranges, sportsmen's clubs, and media. The NSSF mission is "To promote, protect and preserve hunting and the shooting sports". In addition to promoting gun ownership[cxxxiv].

There are many other smaller gun advocacy groups including the following:

Jews for the Preservation of Firearms Ownership – mainly Jewish members
Pink Pistols – a gay gun-rights organization
Redneck Revolt – A far-left group


Additionally, there are many gun advocacy groups operating at a state-level.

Last and certainly not least is the most powerful and influential gun advocacy group in the world:

National Rifle Association (NRA) [cxxxv] – is an American nonprofit organization that advocates for gun-rights. Founded in 1871, the group has informed its members about firearm-related legislation since 1934. Founded to advance rifle marksmanship, the modern NRA continues to teach firearm safety and competency. The organization also publishes several magazines and sponsors competitive marksmanship events. The NRA has approximately 5 million members.


A 2017 Pew Research Center study found that around 14 million Americans consider themselves NRA members, which is well above the real membership number of 5 million. This may be attributed to the fact that the NRA has millions more of Americans who support them and will tell pollsters they are members, even when they are not members. [cxxxvi]

The NRA has been hugely successful over the years in encouraging gun ownership, supporting pro-gun-rights politicians, and in preventing proposed new gun-control measures from being implemented.

The NRA continues to increase its influence on American citizens and in July 2017 launched an online streaming service called NRATV. This is a part lifestyle and part gun-lobby channel with the aim of making you want to buy firearms. NRATV is a free, very well-designed, and smoothly navigable video-streaming website sponsored mainly by gun and ammunition manufacturers— Mossberg, Smith & Wesson, Sig Sauer. It offers a spectrum of programming that runs from harmless gun-nuttery at one end to face-melting propaganda at the other[cxxxvii].


The NRA are huge political lobbyists and donate staggering amounts of money to support politicians, who support gun-rights. In the 2016 presidential election, the NRA spent $30.3 million in support of Donald Trump and an additional $20 million supporting pro-gun-rights Republicans in competitive Senate races [cxxxviii]. In October 2016 alone, according to the Center for Public Integrity, roughly one out of every 20 television ads in Pennsylvania was sponsored by the NRA. That same month, the group paid for one in nine ads in North Carolina, and one of every eight in Ohio. The ads implied that Hilary Clinton and the Democrats would leave law-and-order abiding citizens defenseless.

It is not just the money however which helps the NRA promote gun-rights. In February 2018 just 5 days after the Parkland school mass shooting, Politico Magazine published an article titled "Why the NRA Always Wins" in which they argue it is more to do with culture than money[cxxxix]. This article states that it is because the NRA has built a movement that has convinced its followers that gun ownership is a way of life, central to one's freedom and safety, that must be defended on a daily basis. The gun-control majority on the other hand only gets worked up in the days after public mass shootings, even though such events accounted for only a small proportion of gun fatalities. Then the news coverage shifts, political prospects for action diminish, and the majority gravitates to other political matters while guns continue to take lives in suicides, domestic violence incidents, other crimes, and accidents every day.

Although the NRA remains powerful and popular there are signs that the tide is beginning to turn, based on polls taken in 2018 in the aftermath of the NRA's response to the high-school shooting in Parkland, Florida. The NRA response in question was to attack media coverage on the shooting and to call for more armed security at schools.

In March 2018 a NBC News/Wall Street Journal poll found that 40% of people surveyed had a negative view of the NRA, while 37% had a positive view. That represented a significant drop from April 2017, when the same poll found a 45% positive to 33% negative divide. It was the first time since 2000 that the poll registered a negative net favorability rating for the gun-owners group. An Economist/YouGov poll released in February 2018 found that for the first time in the poll's tracking, "significantly more Americans express a negative opinion of the National Rifle Association than a positive one. Overall, 45% of people surveyed held an unfavorable view of the NRA, while 36% had a favorable view. That was a decline from October 2017 when the NRA held a 40% favorable to a 36% unfavorable edge. A Quinnipiac poll released on February 20 2018 found that 38% of respondents thought the NRA supports policies that are good for the US, while 51% said the group supports policies that are bad for the US[cxl].

One reason for the recent decline in NRA popularity is likely to be suspected links between the NRA and Russia. FBI investigations resulted in the indictments of Russian agents on charges of developing and exploiting ties with the NRA to influence US politics, including the illegal funneling of money through the NRA to influence the 2016 presidential campaign[cxli]. These suspicions have gained traction following the conviction of Maria Butina a Russian gun-rights activist who established a close relationship with the NRA and who in April 2019 was sentenced to 18 months in prison after pleading guilty to conspiracy to act as an illegal foreign agent[cxlii].

Despite the fall in public support and the damage caused by Russian links, the NRA remains a powerful gun advocacy group.

# STEP 3

# Countering the Gun-rights Arguments

# 13. Bumper Sticker Mentality

Many of the phrases gun-rights advocates frequently repeat are nothing more than bumper sticker slogans, which are overly simplistic, but catchy. Some of the popular phrases are repeated so often that the message they attempt to portray become embedded in people's minds to such an extent that they are widely held to be both true and relevant.

In this chapter, we will analyze the following three popular slogans which are used as arguments to either support gun-rights or denounce gun-control.

- "Guns don't kill people, people kill people"
- "When guns are outlawed, only outlaws will have guns"
- "The only way to stop a bad guy with a gun is with a good guy with a gun"

Although these phrases have little substance, they have become powerful tools that gun-rights activists use to deflect against any attempts to criticize guns or impose restrictions on guns. Additionally, they empower politicians to suggest that the United States does not have a gun problem. No matter how damming the statistics on gun crime and no matter how many mass shootings there are, many politicians will blame firearm deaths on just about anything other than the gun.

It is now time to dissect the 3 slogans in question.

- "Guns don't kill people, people kill people"

This bumper style slogan was made popular by the NRA and to analyze the phrase "Guns don't kill people, people kill people" we need to separate the two clauses in the statement.

Guns don't kill people – This is incorrect because as we saw in Chapter 1 there were 39,773 gun-related deaths in 2017 alone. All these fatalities were a direct result of a shot being fired from a gun. If a water pistol had been used instead of a gun then the target would be wet but uninjured. With a gun the target if hit, will either be dead or injured. Guns are specifically designed to kill which is why they are used in the military.

People kill people – this clause is correct; people do kill people. People may kill others on purpose or by accident and they may kill themselves either on purpose or by accident. People kill people using many types of methods including guns, pills, knives, blunt objects, or by using their own bodies.

What gun-rights advocates are trying to say is that it is not the gun that kills, but rather the person firing the gun who kills. This is nonsense and could be applied to absolutely anything, dangerous, or non-dangerous alike e.g. butterflies don't kill people, people kill people, or nuclear bombs don't kill people, people kill people, when clearly a nuclear bomb is more dangerous than a butterfly. The 1st clause is superfluous since it could apply to any noun and the second clause is stating the obvious since all homicides and suicides are perpetrated by people.

A more logical interpretation of the statement "Guns don't kill people, people kill people", would be "People with guns kill people" however this only tells half the story. In reality, the true statement should be "Guns make it easy for people to kill people". This applies to homicide, suicide, and accidents. Guns are not only designed to kill they are also designed to make it easy for people to kill. The prevalence of guns in the United States is the sole reason why their murder rate is much higher than in any other highly developed country.

If you are being pedantic you can argue that guns don't kill by themselves, but in combination with people they do kill and they are a dangerous combination.

- "When guns are outlawed, only outlaws will have guns"

This is a slogan used to warn of the dangers of confiscating guns from law-abiding citizens. The logic follows the 3 arguments below:

1. If guns are outlawed only criminals will have guns.

2. A state of affairs in which only criminals have guns is dangerous.

3. Therefore, guns should not be outlawed

There are 2 ways in which these statements can be analyzed depending on whether it is a complete ban on guns which is being considered, or if it is just greater restrictions on gun purchases or ownership which is being considered.

In the situation where there is a complete ban on guns then statement 1 will be true i.e. only outlaws will have guns because anyone owning a gun would automatically become a criminal. In this scenario, however, statement 2 will not apply since the criminals will include the following categories, good citizens, police officers, military, etc. who are not generally dangerous. They will only have become criminals due to the outlawing of guns. In reality, a total ban on guns is never likely to be proposed and even less likely to be actioned, so this interpretation is somewhat irrelevant.

In the more likely scenario where just greater restrictions on firearms are being proposed then the 1st argument will be false. It will not just be criminals who have guns. The police and most law-abiding citizens who desire a gun will still have access to guns. Since the 1st argument is false the other 2 arguments are not relevant since they will not apply.

In reality, sensible restrictions on gun ownership and gun purchases reduce the danger imposed by outlaws or criminals in two ways. Firstly, restrictions based on weapon type e.g. banning semi-automatic weapons may limit the amount of damage an outlaw can initiate. Secondly, restrictions based on who can own or acquire firearms e.g. banning people on no-fly lists from acquiring guns will result in fewer outlaws having firearms.

It is worth noting the difference between the prevalence of firearms used in crimes between the United States and the United Kingdom. In the United States, data collected by the FBI for 2011 show that firearms were used in 68 percent of murders, 41 percent of robbery offenses, and 21 percent of aggravated assaults nationwide[cxliii]. By comparison for the year ending March 2019 in England & Wales firearms were used in 4.9% of murders and approximately 2.1% of robberies.[cxliv]

The strict gun regulations in the UK would, therefore, suggest that in general, outlaws in countries where there are few firearms do not have guns. This suggests that a more accurate translation of the phrase "When guns are outlawed, only outlaws will have guns" would be "When guns are outlawed, most outlaws won't have guns".

- "The only way to stop a bad guy with a gun is with a good guy with a gun"

The above slogan was coined by the NRA Executive Vice President, Wayne LaPierre at a news conference on December 21, 2012, just 1 week after the tragic mass shooting at Sandy Hook elementary school had left twenty young children and six adults dead. Wayne LaPierre then asked Congress to put armed security into every school in the United States. The theory is that when the bad guy with a gun comes along there will need to be a good guy to shoot him down before the bad guy does any, or at least not too much, damage.

This slogan is wrong on many levels. Firstly, the use of the word "only" is not correct, since there are many ways in which a bad guy with a gun can potentially be stopped, although no single method, including the good guy with a gun method, will always succeed. Possible methods would include the following with the effectiveness of each method depending on the situation.

- o Putting your hands up to show you are not a threat and telling the bad man you will co-operate – this is effective in burglaries or robberies in which the bad man is more interested in taking your possessions rather than your life. Is it worth risking your life to save your TV from being taken?

- o Retreating to a safe place – this is effective if you see the bad man with a gun before they see you

- o Persuasion – this may be effective in situations where the bad guy is familiar with the intended victim e.g. a wife explaining to her ex-husband to think about their children and the effect of having their mother dead and their father incarcerated for life.

o Playing dead – this may be effective in mass shooting situations where retreat is not possible

o Someone, either the intended victim or bystander calling 911 – Effective when the caller will not be noticed by the bad guy

It is true that except for persuasion, or a prompt response to a 911 call, none of the above stop the bad man with a gun. They do however buy time and time is not on the side of the bad guy as in most cases the bad guy will eventually be arrested.

It also has to be acknowledged that a good guy with a gun, especially when the good guy is a trained police officer is an effective way to stop a bad guy with a gun and indeed probably the most effective way. In most situations however it puts the good guy at enormous risk. A good guy with a gun will immediately become a threat and hence a target for a bad guy with a gun. If the good guy is a trained police officer than the good guy is most likely to prevail but if the good guy is an ordinary citizen then it is 50-50 whether the good guy or the bad guy will prevail.

Another problem with the word "only" is that it could be a bad guy with a gun who stops a bad guy with a gun. This no doubt happens quite frequently in gang or drug-related warfare.

Given that there are alternatives to good guys with guns stopping bad guys with guns, the slogan would be more reasonable if the words "the only" were simply replaced by the word "a" i.e. "A way to stop a bad guy with a gun is with a good guy with a gun"

The next problem with the slogan is the definition of good guy and bad guy. In movies, the distinction is usually quite clear, but in real life, the definition of good and bad may be more blurred. A good guy may purchase a gun to protect his family and property. Years later the good guy may have a row with his wife become drunk and violent and become a bad guy. Similarly, a teenager may become addicted to drugs and commit crimes to fund his habit, a clear example of a bad guy. Twenty years later, following rehab, this guy has served his time and learned his lesson. He now has a responsible job and is a loving husband and father. This bad guy has turned into a good guy. The majority of people are good most of the time but many have the capability of turning bad under certain circumstances e.g. divorce, job loss, financial difficulties, alcohol, or drug problems.

Whilst accepting that the statement "A way to stop a bad guy with a gun is with a good guy with a gun" is technically correct and that in most instances it will be obvious who is the good guy and who is the bad guy, the slogan still fails to reach the heart of the matter. This being why does the bad man have a gun in the first place.

All other highly developed countries have more restrictive firearm laws than the United States which are designed primarily to prevent bad guys from getting guns. Additionally, when there are fewer guns in circulation it is more difficult for bad guys to get guns illegally. Instead of trying to find a good guy to remove the threat of a bad guy, it would make much more sense to make it as difficult as possible to stop the bad guys from getting guns.

This underlines a basic problem in the United States which is the general acceptance that it is impossible to stop bad guys from getting hold of guns. This simply is not the case and in other highly developed countries bad guys by and large are successfully prevented from obtaining firearms. In Step 5 of this book, we will examine ways in which the bad guys can be prevented from having guns, but for now, we need to translate the "The only way to stop a bad guy with a gun is with a good guy with a gun" into a more sensible slogan and suggest the following – "The best way to stop a bad guy with a gun is to stop the bad guy getting a gun"

In summary, the phrases below should be replaced as follows:

"Guns don't kill people, people kill people" = "Guns make it easy for people to kill people"

"When guns are outlawed, only outlaws will have guns" = "When guns are outlawed, most outlaws won't have guns".

"The only way to stop a bad guy with a gun is with a good guy with a gun," = "The best way to stop a bad guy with a gun is to stop the bad guy getting a gun"

# 14. What About Chicago or Switzerland

A common statement that proponents of gun-rights will use to argue that gun-control is ineffective is "What about Chicago" or alternatively "What about Switzerland".

Chicago has a high firearm homicide and crime rate whilst having relatively strict gun-control laws compared to most other cities in the United States. On the surface, this would suggest that the stricter gun-control laws in Chicago are at best ineffective and at worst a cause of the high levels of gun crime. So, when new gun-control measures are proposed anywhere in the country, either at a city, state, or federal level they are ridiculed by inferring it doesn't work for Chicago.

Switzerland has a high level of gun ownership and low levels of firearm homicide and crime. Gun-rights enthusiasts use this as an argument suggesting that the high levels of gun ownership in the United States are not a problem. Look at Switzerland they have lots of guns and no crime, therefore there is no reason to make new laws that will decrease gun ownership.

In this chapter, we will examine the situation in Chicago and Switzerland to determine if there is any merit in either of these statements. Let's start with Chicago.

Firstly, does Chicago which is America's 3rd largest city deserve the reputation it has of being the murder capital of America? In one sense yes, in that there are more murders in Chicago than in any other American city. In 2018 there were 561 homicides in Chicago which was considerably more than the larger cities of New York with 278 homicides and Los Angeles 243 homicides.[cxlv]

A more accurate interpretation of the risk of being murdered in any particular city is the murder rate per 100,000 residents. In 2018 based on police data and news reports for large cities, St Louis was the most dangerous city with a homicide rate of 60.9 per 100,000 residents which was nearly treble the Chicago rate of 20.7 per 100,000. Based on the table below showing the murder rate for the most dangerous large cities Chicago had the 12[th] highest homicide rate[cxlvi].

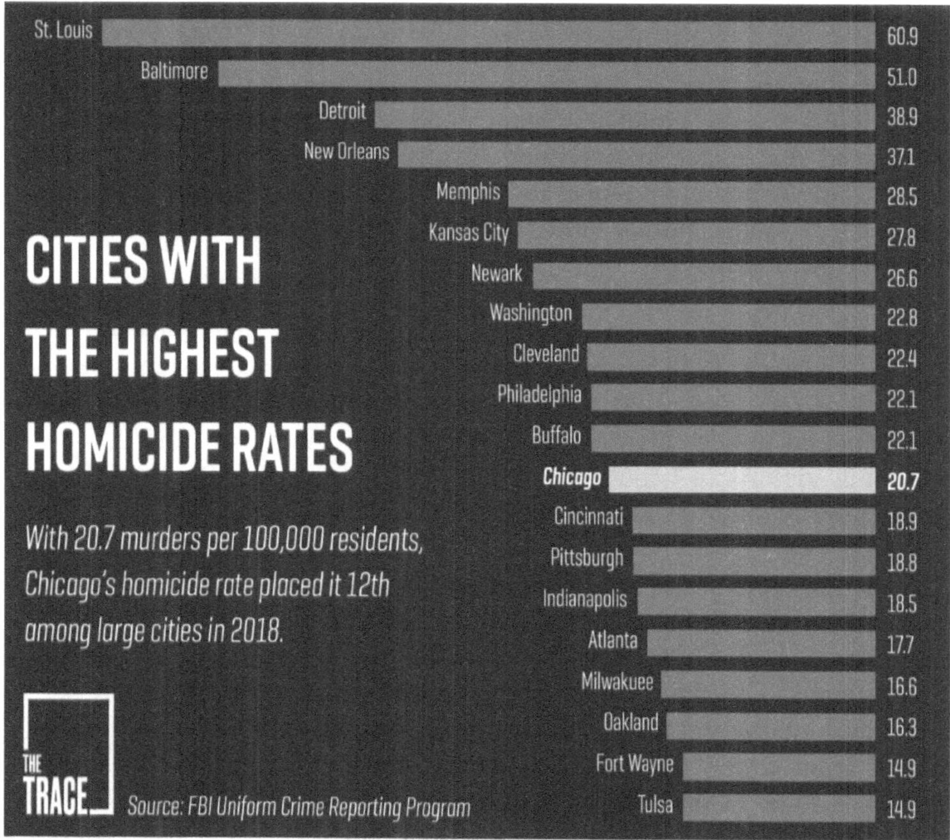


Although Chicago does not have the highest murder rate in the country, it does have to be recognized that Chicago does have a serious homicide problem.

The next thing to consider are the reasons behind the high levels of violence and homicide in Chicago. In reality, these are complex and varied. Chicago has a long history of organized crime and back in the days of prohibition was the home of the American mafia figure Al Capone. Today the problems are more centered around poverty and gang culture. Racial and economic segregation within Chicago has resulted in extreme poverty within clustered districts which tends to lead to more violence and homicide.

In addition to poverty, gangs have long been a problem in Chicago and an article published in the Chicago Sun-Times on June 11 2018 argues that the rise in social media is altering the Chicago gun culture and fueling violence. Gangs put a premium on retaliation for perceived disrespect. In the past, insults rarely spread beyond the block. Now, they're broadcast via social media to thousands in an instant[cxlvii]. Gang culture and the ready availability of guns is a dangerous combination.

 Regardless of the reason, it has to be recognized that guns are a major problem in Chicago, with the vast majority of the 561 homicides recorded in 2018, being firearm homicides. According to the Chicago police, there were 2,391 shooting incidents and 2,948 shooting victims in Chicago in 2018[cxlviii]. This represents around 8 people being killed or injured by a gun every day.

Given the reputation of Chicago's strict gun-control and the acceptance that firearms are a major problem in the city we now need to consider just how strict their gun-control policies are? According to Chicago Police, the claim that Chicago has the strictest gun laws in the country is a common misconception that ignores major legal decisions passed in recent years. Historically Chicago did have some of the country's strictest gun laws, however, in 2010, the Supreme Court struck down Chicago's handgun ban and in 2013, the city ended its gun registry. Police also point to the fact that most guns used in Chicago crimes are bought outside the city or even the state. Comparing gun restrictions to other major cities like New York and Los Angeles, The University of Chicago crime lab says the cities are pretty comparable, and when it comes to who can buy so-called assault weapons, New York and LA have tougher laws.[cxlix]

It would, therefore, appear that the claims gun-rights advocates make about Chicago are exaggerated in that Chicago does not have the highest homicide rate or the strictest gun-control measures. That said the argument does hold some water in that it must be recognized that the homicide rate is high, guns are a big problem and Chicago does have relatively strong gun-control measures.

The reality is that the effectiveness of any gun-control measures which cover only a small area such as a city is limited because it is so easy to bring in firearms from neighboring areas. The effectiveness of gun-control measures is dependent both on the size of the area being controlled and the difficulty in crossing the border. Thus, control at a country or federal level is the most effective since it involves the most distance to smuggle firearms plus border checks. State-level controls may or may not involve large distances but do not involve any border checks. City controls are the least effective as distances are short and there are no checks when driving into a city. This is not to say that cities should not bother to introduce gun-control measures and Chicago and other cities with even stronger gun-control measures such as New York and Los Angeles should be applauded for their efforts. Some gun-rights activists argue that Chicago has a homicide problem due to its firearm restrictions, but a more accurate statement would be that Chicago has a homicide problem despite its firearm restrictions.

Whilst on the subject of gun-control effectiveness it will be helpful to review the impact that state-level gun-control measures have on homicide rates. To assist in this matter, The Giffords Law Center to Prevent Gun Violence has produced an excellent website which provides an Annual Gun Law Scorecard for each state[cl].

This grades states based on the following six key policies designed to save lives from gun violence:

1. Background Checks – Federal law allows guns to be bought at gun shows, online, and in private sales without undergoing a background check. This deadly loophole allows felons,

domestic abusers, and others legally prohibited from owning firearms to get guns. Twelve states have addressed this issue by requiring background checks for all gun transfers, while six states have partially closed the loophole by covering just handguns or sales at gun shows. After Connecticut enacted its private sale background check sales, gun homicides dropped by 40%

2.  Child Access Prevention – Fourteen states have comprehensive laws to protect children from accessing guns by imposing liability on people who negligently store firearms. Massachusetts alone requires that all firearms be stored locked and unloaded. Incidentally in 2017 Massachusetts had the lowest gun death rate per 100,000 people in the entire country. Thirteen states have partial child access prevention laws imposing liability only against people who intentionally, knowingly, or recklessly store firearms so minors could, or do, gain access.

3.  Concealed Carry Permitting – The presence of guns in public makes it all too likely for everyday conflict to turn deadly. While all states allow some form of carrying concealed weapons (CCW), the degree to which states regulate these varies widely. Nine states have strong permitting systems that grant law enforcement discretion to deny CCW permits based on factors such as dangerous behavior. Twenty-nine states have laws that require CCW permits but set few qualifications to obtain them. Twelve states do not require a permit at all to carry concealed.

4.  Domestic Violence – Recognizing the fact that abused women are five times more likely to be killed if their abuser owns a firearm this is one of the few areas in which there is a federal law, which prohibits domestic abusers from purchasing guns. Federal law does not however have a system to ensure abusers surrender firearms they already own. Twenty-three states require abusers to transfer their firearm to law enforcement or a licensed dealer and provide proof to a court that they have done so. Fourteen states

partially address this problem by requiring abusers to surrender their guns but not mandating that they require proof. This leaves thirteen states that place no additional restrictions on domestic violence abusers.

5. Extreme Risk Protection Order (ERPO) – Also known as gun violence protective order or gun violence restraining order provides a mechanism for family, household members, or law enforcement to petition a court to temporarily remove guns from people at proven risk of harming themselves or others. Just three states being California, Oregon and Washington have strong ERPO laws that allow families and law enforcement to petition to remove guns from at-risk individuals. Connecticut and Indiana have partial ERPO laws that allow only law enforcement to make the petition to remove guns.

6. Military-Style Weaponry – Military-style firearms and accessories include assault weapons, large-capacity ammunition magazines, and silencers. These products are not intended for hunting or self-defense and are specifically designed to make it easier to kill high numbers of people in a short amount of time. Six states have comprehensive laws in place to prohibit this type of weaponry and four states have partial laws regulating these weapons and accessories but not prohibiting them entirely.

The grading is based on a system that assigns positive point values to gun safety policies such as private sale background checks and negative points to dangerous laws such as permitless concealed carry. Each state is then awarded either an A B C D or F grade, with an A grade reflecting the best gun safety laws and an F grade reflecting the least additional safety laws. Those states awarded an A or B grade in 2017 deserve mention and are ranked in order as follows:

Grade A – California, New Jersey, Connecticut, Massachusetts, New York, Maryland, Hawaii

Grade B – Illinois, Rhode Island, Washington, Delaware

There were seven states awarded a C grade and seven awarded a D grade, which sadly leaves 25 states being awarded an F grade.

The relationship between a state's gun law strength and the firearm death rate in the state is highly significant with those states having strong gun laws suffering lower firearm death rates per capita than those states with weaker gun laws. This can be readily seen from the table below which shows the average firearm death rate per capita in 2017 for each grade.

| Grade | Average gun death rate per 100,000 |
| --- | --- |
| A | 6.0 |
| B | 8.9 |
| C | 11.2 |
| D | 13.8 |
| F | 15.9 |

If the F grade states enforced similar laws to those in the Grade A states, they would probably reduce their firearm death rates by over 50% within a few years. Sadly, public opinion and the elected politicians in many of the F grade states are opposed to introducing sensible gun safety policies which would save so many lives and injuries.

Of the 10 states with the lowest gun death rates, eight are graded A or B, and all the 10 states with the highest gun death rates are graded F. The evidence that strong state gun laws reduce firearm death rates is overwhelming.

As noted earlier, gun safety measures at a federal level would be even more effective than at a state-level, which leads us to the other claim made by gun-rights enthusiasts – "What About Switzerland"? They have a lot of guns and a low homicide rate.

It must be recognized that Switzerland does have a relatively high gun ownership rate with the small arms survey estimating there are around 2.33 million civilian-held firearms in the country, representing around 27.6 guns per 100 residents [cli]. Additionally, Switzerland does have a relatively low homicide rate with 0.59 homicides per 100,000 residents in 2018.[clii]

The reason the Swiss have high gun ownership levels is because Switzerland only has a small standing army and relies much more heavily on its militia system for national defense. This means that most able-bodied civilian men of military age are required to keep weapons at home in case of a national emergency. By law, these weapons must be kept locked and their issue of 72 rounds of ammunition must be sealed, and strictly accounted for. With regard to civilian weapons, most cantons (the Switzerland equivalent of a state) require handgun registration. Any ammunition bought on the private market is also registered[cliii].

Whilst it is recognized that the Swiss homicide rate is below the average of the twenty most highly developed countries, total firearm deaths per capita in Switzerland are the second-highest amongst these countries, although significantly lower than the country with the highest firearm death rate, that country being the United States. In 2016 Switzerland had the 3rd highest firearm death rate per 100,000 population in Europe. The European country with the highest firearm death rate was Serbia, which probably not coincidentally, also had the most civilian held guns at 39.1 guns per 100 residents in 2017, significantly more than any other European country[cliv].

Like Chicago, there is some if only a little substance to the Switzerland argument, however, the Chicago and Switzerland examples are both cherry-picked. There is bound to be some city in the United States with strict gun-control and high homicide rates and similarly, there is bound to be a country somewhere in the world with high gun ownership and low homicide rates.

To turn the tables, a much more convincing statement could be made for those arguing for greater gun safety and regulation in any country, other than the United States. If in this country there were proposals to encourage gun ownership or reduce firearm restrictions, the obvious counter-argument would be "What about the United States of America". The United States is a highly developed country with high levels of gun ownership, high levels of firearm-related deaths, and high levels of intentional homicides (when compared with other highly developed countries).

# 15. Guns Reduce Crime

A common argument used by gun-rights advocates is that the more guns there are, the less crime, and in particular, violent crime there will be. The theory being that violent crime declines in places where there are more legal gun owners carrying weapons. The reason for the suggested decline being that potential criminals would be worried that their intended victim or a passer-by may be armed and hence decide not to act on any criminal activity they were considering.

The guns reducing crime argument is based on the research of an economist named John Lott who has written a popular book titled "More Guns Less Crime"[clv] and other published studies on this topic. In particular, John Lott argues that right-to-carry laws are correlated with decreases in violent crime. This conclusion was based on complex and some argue manipulated statistical data, however, these views are often cited by academics, politicians, and pro-gun private citizens and have frequently been effective in firearm policy debates.

The argument that more guns means less crime comes from Lott's research in the 1990s, which suggested that states that passed more lenient concealed-carry laws saw a drop in crime rates. However, a comprehensive study on the effects of right-to-carry laws performed in 2017 by the National Bureau of Economic Research (NBER) [clvi] looked at the relationship between gun laws and crime rates over a longer period and found that Lott's initial theory does not hold up. Indeed, their analysis found the exact opposite effect in that violent crime rates increased with each additional year such a right-to-carry statute was in place, presumably as more people were carrying guns. By 10 years after the adoption of a right-to-carry law, violent crime rates were 13 to 15 percent higher than predicted had such laws not been in place.

An earlier report was conducted by a sixteen-member panel of the United States National Research Council (NRC). In 2004 who a report titled

"Firearms and Violence: A Critical Review". This examined Lott's statistical methods in detail, including the computation of the statistical uncertainties involved. The committee found no credible evidence that the passage of right-to-carry laws decreases or increases violent crime.[clvii]

In the book "More Guns Less Crime" there is a table showing the results of analysis on the relationship between gun ownership and crime rates based on 1995 data[clviii]. This portrays a strong negative relationship between gun ownership and crime rates. The conclusion from this analysis however is so far-fetched it beggars belief. This conclusion is that a 1% increase in gun ownership reduces violent crime by 4.1%. This is not possible since it implies that if there was universal gun ownership there would be virtually zero violent crime and if there was zero-gun ownership there would be astronomically high levels of violent crime. One thing is for sure is that if a 1% increase in gun ownership did reduce violent crime by 4.1% then the United States would have the lowest violent crime rates in the world by a huge margin.

In reality arguing whether more guns increase or reduce crime or violent crime rates based on evidence on gun ownership in the United States is difficult to evaluate and there is unlikely to be a significant correlation between violent crime rates (excluding homicides) and the volume of guns in circulation, or right to carry laws, hence the different conclusions:

John Lott        more guns = less crime
NBER             more guns = more crime
NRC              more guns has no impact on crime

The different conclusions and unclear link between gun prevalence and crime rates may arise from two factors which act in opposite directions. On the one hand, some potential criminals may decide not to perform a criminal act for fear of being shot in the act of perpetrating the crime. On the other hand, a criminal with easy access to a gun may feel empowered by having a loaded gun at the ready and pluck up the courage to perform a crime they would not have committed without the gun.

Whilst the relationship between gun volume and crime rates is unclear, the relationships below regarding the concept of more guns are undeniably true:

More guns = more intentional homicides

More guns = more suicides

More guns = more accidental firearm deaths

More guns = more undetermined firearm deaths

More guns = more justifiable firearm deaths

The argument that more guns reduces crime falters even more when comparing crime rates in the United States to those of other developed countries. To assist in this matter the Institute for the Study of Civil Society a UK company known as CIVITAS prepared a paper titled Comparisons of Crime in OECD Countries[clix]. The figures are based on a United Nations survey of crime trends and although somewhat dated, in that the figures are based on police recorded crime in 2006, it does provide some interesting information. A total of 36 countries are included in the analysis and the United States has higher than average crime rates in all 6 crime categories covered. In summary, the figures for the United States are as follows:

| Crime | Rate per 100,000 | Position out of 36 * |
| --- | --- | --- |
| Intentional homicide | 5.0 | 3rd highest |
| Rape | 28.6 | 4th highest |
| Robbery | 133 | 8th highest |
| Assault | 262 | 16th highest |
| Burglary | 715 | 13th highest |
| Vehicle theft | 258 | 10th highest |

* Note higher positions = worse crime rates

If guns do reduce violent crime one would expect the United States to have the lowest or at least close to the lowest crime rates in all these categories due to the sheer volume of guns in circulation and the fact that there is a right to carry in all states. This is not the case with the figures above showing that the United States crime rates are above average in all 6 of the categories listed above demonstrating that more guns do not result in less crime.

There is another claim that gun-rights advocates frequently make which is that the rate of violent crime in the United Kingdom is much higher than the rate of violent crime in the United States and that the reason for this is the very strict gun-control laws in the United Kingdom which includes a ban on handguns. The exact opposite viewpoint was made by the British CNN host Piers Morgan following the Sandy Hook school mass shooting in December 2012 where he stated that the United Kingdom is a safer country than the US because Britain has strict gun-control laws vis-a-vis the United States. Following the airing of this program a barrage of claims was advanced by pro-gun advocates quoting statistics showing that the United Kingdom has between 4 to 10 times more violent crime per capita than the United States. Is this true?

With regards to reported figures on violent crime, the gun-rights advocates are correct in that the United Kingdom does report much higher violent crime rates than the United States. The problem is that this is comparing apples with oranges. There are huge differences in the definition of violent crime between the two countries.

In England & Wales violent crime is defined as follows:

Violent crime contains a wide range of offenses, from minor assaults such as pushing and shoving that result in no physical harm through to serious incidents of wounding and murder. Around a half of violent incidents identified by both BCS and police statistics involve no injury to the victim[clx].

In the United States violent crime is defined as follows:

In the FBI's Uniform Crime Reporting (UCR) Program, violent crime is composed of four offenses: murder and nonnegligent manslaughter, forcible rape, robbery, and aggravated assault. Violent crimes are defined in the UCR Program as those offenses which involve force or threat of force[clxi].

The UK definition of violent crime is far more wide-ranging than the American counterpart and consequently, there will inevitably be a higher level of recorded violent crime there. There is probably insufficient data to determine which country has a higher rate of violent crime and to some extent, the answer would depend on the definition used, but one thing is for certain and that is the United States has a higher level of intentional homicides than the United Kingdom, due almost entirely to the volume and general lack of restrictions on firearms.

# 16. Guns Required for Protection

In Chapter 9 it was noted that the majority of American citizens believe that owning a gun makes you safer and is the most effective method of protection. Indeed, the belief that guns provide protection is the main reason why so many Americans own guns, but as revealed in Chapter 9 the truth is the exact opposite in that owning guns dramatically increases the risk of death or injury to both gun owners and their families.

Part of this apparent contradiction stems from the fact that protection and self-defense frequently get conflated, with the incorrect assumption that guns being effective for protection and effective for self-defense are the same thing - They are not. A gun in certain circumstances may provide an effective method of self-defense but at the same time greatly jeopardize the safety (protection) of the person using a gun in self-defense.  The legal definition of self-defense is "the use of force to defend oneself" On this basis i.e. the requirement to use force then nothing which can legally be owned by a civilian would be more efficient than a gun. Access to a gun provides a quick, simple, effective, and powerful method to repulse an attack. The problem is that thwarting an attack is not the same as keeping oneself safe and owning a firearm greatly increases the risk of death or injury to oneself or family members.

It is worth repeating the research at UC San Francisco[clxii] which concluded that someone with access to firearms is three times more likely to commit suicide and nearly twice as likely to be a homicide victim as someone who does not have access. When firearms were accessible, men were nearly four times more likely to commit suicide than when firearms were not accessible, while women were almost three times more likely to be victims of homicide. This study did not consider accidental deaths which would also increase the risk of death or injury to gun owners and their families, especially when children are present.

The link between firearm access, suicide, and firearm accidents has been covered in earlier chapters, but why does access to firearms double the chance of being a victim of homicide? There are several reasons which include the following:

- Increased chance of being killed by a partner or other close relation living in the home. Many homicide victims are killed either by their own firearm or a firearm belonging to someone else living in the home. This is particularly true for women. Indeed, over half of American female homicide victims are related to intimate partner violence, with the vast majority of the victims dying at the hands of a current or former romantic partner[clxiii].
- Increased chance of being involved in a murder-suicide incident, either as the victim or the perpetrator. This also highlights the fact that as well as making it more likely that having access to a firearm will make you a homicide victim it also significantly increases the chance that in a sudden fit of anger you become the murderer, particularly if you have a loaded gun at hand.
- Being armed may make individuals take more chances, such as confronting intruders. This is not without risk when the intruder may also be armed.
- Being armed makes you a target. When you are armed you present a danger to others and as such, they are more likely to shoot you to remove the threat you pose.
- Any confrontation in which law enforcement officers are present pose a significant risk to anyone brandishing a firearm, regardless of whether the gun is being used to perpetrate a crime or to prevent a crime. Police have to react quickly and may not always come to the correct conclusion as to the motives of different gun wielders.

The notion that having a gun helps protect yourself is frequently demonstrated by using fearmongering tactics to highlight the dangers of not having access to a gun. A good example of this occurred before the 2016 presidential election when the NRA aired a commercial titled "Don't let Hillary Clinton leave you defenseless".

In this commercial, a woman, home alone and asleep in her second-floor bedroom, wakes with a gasp to the sound of breaking glass. As an intruder lurks in the shadows of the ground floor of the home, our protagonist bounds out of bed to grab her phone while simultaneously entering the combination on a nearby gun safe. An announcer explains what we're seeing: "She'll call 911. Average response time: 11 minutes. Too late. She keeps a firearm in this safe for protection. But Hillary Clinton could take away her right to self-defense." Like magic, the gun safe suddenly disappears. "And with Supreme Court justices," the announcer continues, "Hillary can". Don't let Hillary leave you protected with nothing but a phone." The woman, gripped by fear, drops her phone (in slow motion, of course). We don't see what happens next, but a closing scene that shows police tape around her home offers a rough idea[clxiv].

Setting apart the highly dubious claim that Hilary Clinton would take away her right to own a gun, the commercial is fundamentally wrong in that it implies the woman in the commercial would be safer if she had access to a gun, when the research conducted by UC San Francisco demonstrated that women are almost 3 times more likely to be victims of homicide when firearms are accessible.

There are other studies which highlight the dangers to women of having a firearm at home:

In a study in the *Journal of Trauma*, A.L. Kellermann, director of the RAND Institute of health, and his coauthor J.A. Mercy concluded: "More than twice as many women are killed with a gun used by their husbands or intimate acquaintances than are murdered by strangers using guns, knives, or any other means.[clxv]"

Another large case-control study compared women who were murdered by their intimate partner with a control group of battered women. Only 16 percent of the women who had been abused, but not murdered, had guns in their homes, whereas 51 percent of the murder victims did. In fact, not a single study to date has shown that the risk of any crime including burglary, robbery, home invasion, or spousal abuse against a female is decreased through gun ownership.

Though there are examples of women using a gun to defend themselves, they are few and far between, and not statistically significant.[clxvi]

Finally, what should be the most concerning statistic is that based on data from 25 high-income countries, women in the United States accounted for 84 percent of all female firearm victims and 70 percent of all female homicide victims, even though they only represented 32% of the sample population. The analysis concluded that more women are homicide victims when firearms are more available [clxvii]. This demonstrates the dangers of attackers having firearms whilst indicating little advantage if any in the women being armed to defend themselves. It must be remembered that most female homicides are not perpetrated by strangers as the NRA commercial gun-rights advocates would have us believe.

The next thing to consider is how frequently are guns used in self-defense and what are the most common forms of self-protective behavior. The figures below are from the Bureau of Justice Statistics, National Crime Victimization Survey, 2013-2015, Special Tabulation.[clxviii]

Violent Crimes

| Self-protective behavior | Number of violent crimes | Percentage of violent crimes |
|---|---|---|
| Took no action or kept still | 6,375,500 | 38.7% |
| Threatened or attacked - firearm | 175,700 | 1,1% |
| Threatened or attacked – other weapon | 304,800 | 1.8% |
| Threatened or attacked – no weapon | 4,005,500 | 24.3% |
| * Nonconfrontational tactics | 4,887,400 | 29.6% |
| Other reaction | 710,800 | 4.3% |
| Unknown reaction | 32,900 | 0.2% |
| Victim not present | n/a | n/a |

| Total | 14,492,600 | 100% |
| --- | --- | --- |

<u>Property Crimes</u>

| <u>Self-protective behavior</u> | <u>Number of property crimes</u> | Percentage of violent crimes |
| --- | --- | --- |
| Took no action or kept still | 5,777,400 | 12.4% |
| Threatened or attacked - firearm | 109,000 | 0.2% |
| Threatened or attacked – other weapon | 16,300 | <0.1% |
| Threatened or attacked – no weapon | 286,000 | 0.6% |
| * Nonconfrontational tactics | 928,700 | 2.0% |
| Other reaction | 132,700 | 0.3% |
| Unknown reaction | 13,200 | <0.1% |
| Victim not present | 39,410,300 | 84.4% |
| Total | 46,673,600 | 100% |

* Nonconfrontational tactics include yelling, running, arguing.

As can be seen, firearms were used in just 0.2% of property crime and 1.1% of violent crimes during the 3 years 2013-2015. Concerning property crime, the main thing to note is that 84.4% of property crimes take place when the victim is not present, usually during the day when the residents are at work. This is not surprising since one would expect criminals to check no-one was at home before entering a property to reduce the risk of being injured or arrested.

An important factor to consider in offsetting the potential benefit of having a gun available to repulse a violent or property crime against the risk involved in having access to a gun at all times is the timescale of the benefits and risks. The majority of the population will never be involved in a violent crime, or be at home during a property invasion, hence any potential benefit a gun may provide would be non-existent. Even those who are innocently involved in a violent or property crime situation will only experience the possible benefit of having access to a gun for perhaps 15 minutes of their life. On the other hand, the increased danger of suicide, accident, or homicide by a partner or family member when guns are quickly available is omnipresent. Except for law enforcement officers, the only people this may not apply to would be criminals who are much more likely to be frequently involved in situations where they require a gun.

Although guns do not provide an effective method of protection there are many other ways in which individuals can protect themselves or family members including the following:

<u>Protection against property crime</u>

- Fitting burglar alarms
- Setting up CCTV
- Fitting high-quality locks
- Living in a low crime area
- Ensuring adequate insurance on property and contents

<u>Protection against violent crime</u>

- Avoid confrontation
- Avoid walking alone at night
- Avoid flaunting high-value items
- Avoid entering high crime hotspots

In conclusion, guns may be considered to be an effective self-defense method however, they are used much less frequently than gun-rights advocates claim. Protection however is far more important than self-defense and it is clear that guns do not help protect people. All evidence suggests that the presence of firearms substantially increases suicide risk for men, homicide risk for women, and accidental risk for children.

# 17. If there were no Guns, Knives would be Used

A frequent argument that gun-rights advocates use when being challenged with the fact that there are so many firearm homicides in the United States is that if guns were restricted other methods would be used to perpetrate the killings, such as a knife or a blunt object. A similar argument is used for suicides, in that if a gun was not available the person wanting to commit suicide would use a knife, pills, or some other method. Whilst it is true that some of these suicides or homicides would still occur if a gun was not available the majority would not.

Over 50% of all successful suicides in 2016 were, as noted in Chapter 2, performed with a firearm[clxix]. For intentional homicide the dominance of firearm's being the weapon of choice is even greater with a gun being the murder weapon in 74.5% of all homicides carried out in 2016[clxx]. In summary, the reason for the prevalence of the use of guns in suicide and homicide is that guns unlike any other item readily available to civilians are specifically designed to kill. Guns are not only frequently lethal they are easy and quick to use, easy to conceal, difficult to retreat from, and minimize the risk of the attacker being overpowered. For suicides in particular the gun is quick, relatively painless, and generally lethal as there is no chance for going back once the trigger has been pulled.

The statement that if there were no guns, knives or other types of weapons would be used is misleading in 2 ways. Firstly, for the reasons noted above regarding the convenience of using a firearm, it is likely that many murders would never even be attempted if a firearm was not available. Secondly, even assuming that there would be no drop in the number of attempted homicides if all attempted firearm homicides were substituted to attempted knife homicides; there would be a huge reduction in the number of homicide victims. The reason for this being simply that guns are much more lethal than knives.

The Perelman School of Medicine at the University of Pennsylvania performed a study over 5 years, from January 2003 to December 2007 on penetrating trauma victims [clxxi] comparing the fatality rate of gunshot and stabbing victims and concluded as follows:

33% of patients with gunshot wounds died
7.7% of patients with stab wounds died

Put simply a gunshot is over 4 times deadlier than a stabbing. From this simple fact, we can estimate the number of lives which would be saved if there were no guns and all attempted firearm homicides and suicides plus accidental firearm incidents were performed with a knife instead of a gun.

For the basis of the calculation, we will assume that a gun is exactly 4 times deadlier than a knife and that this proportion is consistent for homicides, suicides, and accidents. As noted in Chapter 1 there were 39,773 firearm fatalities in 2017, in which case the number of fatalities would be a quarter of this number i.e. 9,943, or in other words, 29,830 lives would be saved each year. This would amount to just under 3 million lives a century. Whilst this calculation is an oversimplification, it does serve to illustrate how many lives are lost because ordinary citizens are armed with weapons specifically designed to kill as opposed to instruments intended to cut bread.

Another factor to be considered is that knives are not an efficient tool to use for mass murders. Guns unlike most other murder weapons readily available to civilians can kill or injure many people in a short amount of time and consequently, firearms are used in virtually all mass murders in the United States. Indeed, if you perform an internet search for mass murder in the United States the results just list "mass shootings" as opposed to the broader result of "mass murders". It is just taken for granted that any mass murder in the United States will involve a firearm.

Whilst mass murder attempts not involving firearms do occur in other countries (presumably because firearms are not easily accessible) they are usually much less lethal. To help illustrate this point on the same day that a gunman killed 27 and wounded 2 at

Newtown Connecticut, a knife-wielding maniac wounded 22 and killed zero people in China. Why was the Newtown incident much deadlier than the Chinese incident? Simple answer – The American mass murderer had easy access to guns whilst his Chinese counterpart did not[clxxii].

Another point to consider is that the countries with the highest rate of firearm homicides tend to have the highest rate of overall homicide rates. As evidenced in Chapter 1, of the twenty most highly developed countries, the two countries with the highest overall intentional homicide rate are the same 2 countries which have the highest firearm intentional homicide rate, namely Canada & the United States. The United States having the unfortunate distinction of having both the highest firearm and overall intentional homicide rate of these highly developed countries.

The connection between overall homicide rates and firearm homicide rates can be underlined even further by the following table which lists the 4 countries with the highest intentional homicide rate in the world. [clxxiii] [clxxiv]

| Country | Intentional Homicide Rate | Firearm Homicide Rate |
|---|---|---|
| El Salvador | Highest in the world | 3rd highest in the world |
| Jamaica | 2nd highest in the world | 4th highest in the world |
| Venezuela | 3rd highest in the world | 2nd highest in the world |
| Honduras | 4th highest in the world | Highest in the world |

The same 4 countries appear in the top 4 list for both the most firearm-related homicides and overall intentional homicides. This is surely no coincidence and shows a clear link between high levels of firearm homicide rates and high levels of overall intentional homicide rates.

# 18. The problem is Mental Health, not Guns

When gun-rights supporters react to the latest mass shooting or the concept that America does have a gun problem, a typical response will be something along the lines of "We don't have a gun problem it's a mental health problem".

To determine the relevance of this statement we need to ask the following 4 questions:

1. Does America have a mental health problem?
2. Is the mental health problem greater in the United States than in other developed countries?
3. Are people with mental health issues more prone to harm or kill themselves, or others, than the general population?
4. How difficult is it for people with mental health issues to obtain guns?

The answer to the first question is a resounding yes. The United States does have a serious mental health problem. Mental Health America (MHA) has produced a web page titled "The State of Mental Health in America 2018" [clxxv] which contains the following headline data:

- 18% of adults i.e. around 43 million Americans have a mental health condition
- Nearly half of those affected have a co-occurring substance abuse disorder
- 56% of American adults with a mental illness did not receive treatment

- Over 1.7 million youths with major depressive periods did not receive treatment
- 9.6 million Americans with mental health conditions have experienced suicidal thoughts

The answer to the 2nd question is also yes. Mental health does appear to be a greater problem in the United States than in other countries. According to the World Health Organization (WHO), the United States has the highest prevalence of mental health disorders in the world. Based on the WHO research over a 12-month period, 27 percent of adults in the U.S. will experience some sort of mental health disorder. Mental health disorders include mood disorders, anxiety disorders, attention-deficit/hyperactivity disorder, and substance abuse. Over one's entire lifetime, the average American has a 47.4 percent chance of having some kind of mental health disorder[clxxvi].

It should be noted that the WHO has recorded significantly greater levels of mental health problems than the MHA and this highlights the difficulty in obtaining consistent definitions and in the measuring of mental health problems.

The answer to the third question is where the arguments that mental health, not guns are the problem begins to falter. Although the majority of Americans believe that people with mental health problems are more likely to commit violent crimes, homicide, or a mass shooting the reality is the exact opposite.

The BBC has published a series of articles under the banner of "Criminal Myths" one of which is the myth of the link between mass shootings and mental health which lists many studies and facts on this matter, including the following: [clxxvii]

A 2004 analysis of more than 60 mass murders in North America, for example, found that just 6% were psychotic at the time of the killings. A 2016 study found that when it comes to mass shootings, those with mental illness account for "less than 1% of all yearly gun-related homicides". Other studies indicate that people with mental disorders account for just 3-5% of overall violence in the US, much lower than the prevalence of mental illness in the general population of up to 18%. This 18% figure is consistent with the MHA 2018 study.

The BBC article also notes that individuals suffering from mental illnesses are three times more likely than the average person to be victims of violence, as they are more vulnerable. In other words, those with mental health problems are much more likely to be a victim of a violent crime than the perpetrator of a violent crime. With regard to mass shootings, the article also notes that large attacks also require a level of planning and organization that often defies many with serious mental illness. Put simply many people with mental illness are just not mentally capable of planning a deadly mass murder.

So, to answer the third question posed at the beginning of the chapter the answer is that people with mental health issues are not more prone to harm or kill others than the general population. They are however significantly more prone to harm or kill themselves than the general population.

A study performed in the United Kingdom by King's College London found that individuals with psychotic disorders, such as schizophrenia or bipolar disorder, are 12 times more likely than the national average, to commit suicide in the first year following diagnosis. The risk remains four times greater than the general population up to ten years after diagnosis[clxxviii]. Whilst this study was performed in the United Kingdom it is not unreasonable to expect that similar results would be obtained in the United States.

In the United States, the National Institute of Mental Health (NIH) provides publications on mental health information which includes a page on suicide[clxxix]. This lists several bullet points highlighting the main risk factors for suicide. Included in this list is "depression and other mental health disorders" and also "having guns or other firearms in the home". The link between access to guns and suicide was reviewed in Chapter 2 and making it easy for those with mental health problems to obtain or have access to guns just compounds the problem and inevitably results in more suicides.

Now based on the analysis of this chapter, does the answer to the 4th and final question "How difficult is it for people with mental health issues to obtain guns" actually matter? Well, it should matter, for one good reason, and for one reason of consistency.

The good reason is that those with mental health problems, in particular, should be prevented from having easy access to a gun which makes committing suicide quick, painless, and efficient. As discussed, those with mental health problems are much more likely to feel suicidal than the general population, and to protect these vulnerable individuals their access to firearms should be restricted as much as practical. It must never be forgotten that suicide is tragic and affects not just the deceased, but all the family and friends of the individual taking their own life. Additionally, many individuals with mental health issues can be treated and go on to lead successful and happy lives, long after the momentary thought of ending their own life has passed.

The consistency reason on whether the ease of access to firearms for individuals with mental health matters, is based on the popular view that these individuals are more dangerous than the general population. If this is the case then it would make sense to endeavor to restrict their access to firearms. It is this exact point that highlights the inconsistency in those who argue that mental health and not guns are the problem and this inconsistency is found at the highest level i.e. the President of the United States.

In November 2017, just hours after 26 people were killed in a mass shooting at the First Baptist Church in Sutherland Springs in Texas, President Trump quoted the following, as reported in the New York Times. "I think that mental health is your problem here," Mr. Trump told reporters at a news conference in Japan, the first stop on his 12-day overseas trip. Based on preliminary reports, the gunman in Sutherland Springs, Tex., was a "very deranged individual," he said. "We have a lot of mental health problems in our country, as do other countries." "But this isn't a gun's situation," Mr. Trump added[clxxx].

One would, therefore, expect that people who believe that mass shootings are frequently a mental health problem would want to make it more difficult for those affected individuals to have access to firearms. This is where the inconsistency comes in as these are the same people who want to remove restrictions preventing those with mental health issues from acquiring guns.

Shortly after his inauguration, President Trump signed legislation repealing a regulation enacted by President Barack Obama intended to add the names of mentally ill Americans registered with the Social Security Administration to the database for gun purchase background checks. The regulation, a response by Mr. Obama in part to the 2012 school shooting in Newtown, Conn., would have affected those unable to work because of severe mental impairment and unable to manage their own Social Security financial benefits. In February 2017, both houses of Congress passed a resolution revoking the resolution. President Trump's aides said at the time that he signed it because he did not want to deprive law-abiding citizens of their constitutional rights.[clxxxi]

The issue of constitutional rights is frequently cited by gun-rights advocates, who believe that the right for most individuals to possess a gun is sacrosanct and should only be removed in certain extreme circumstances. This belief is an obstacle to sensible gun law reform which will be analyzed in Step 4 of this book. In this example the constitutional right for a depressed mentally ill person to acquire a gun is not in his or her best interest, since if the gun is ever used it is most likely to result in a suicide.

Finally, to answer the question of how easy is it for mentally ill people to obtain guns the answer is in most cases, very easy. The following summary of the relevant Federal Law below is taken from the Giffords Law Center web page on Extreme Risk Protection Orders.

Under federal law, a person suffering from mental illness is not prohibited from purchasing and possessing a gun unless he or she has been formally, and involuntarily, committed to a mental institution, found not guilty by reason of insanity, or undergone some other formalized court proceeding regarding his or her mental illness. Similarly, a person who has committed a violent act towards others is not prohibited from possessing guns under federal law unless he or she is the subject of a domestic violence restraining order, has been convicted of a felony, or has been convicted of a domestic violence misdemeanor.[clxxxii]

So, how accurate is the argument that mental health and not guns are the problem behind the high firearm death toll in the United States? Well, the fact that it highlights America's mental health issues is a good thing, but overall, it only scores 1 out of 3.

Yes – Mental health is a problem
No – Mental health is not the reason behind most mass shootings or high firearm homicide rates
No – Guns are a problem.

It is worth stressing the inconsistency in those who argue that the problem is mental health and not guns. If mental health is such a rampant problem in the United States causing mass shootings and increased homicide rates, then it strengthens the argument to make access to firearms more difficult. Why would you want easy access to guns if you believe there are so many individuals with mental health problems likely to go on a shooting spree?

# 19. Sandy Hook Conspiracy Theory

As summarized in the chapter on Mass Shootings, a tragic incident occurred on December 14, 2012, when twenty school children aged 6 & 7 along with six adults were shot and killed by a crazed gunman at the Sandy Hook Elementary school in Newtown, Connecticut. Following the shooting President Obama made a speech that was so poignant it is difficult to read without feeling tears welling up. A summary of the speech can be found on the President Obama White House Blog and is repeated below:

*"We've endured too many of these tragedies in the past few years. And each time I learn the news I react not as a President, but as anybody else would -- as a parent. And that was especially true today. I know there's not a parent in America who doesn't feel the same overwhelming grief that I do.*

*The majority of those who died today were children -- beautiful little kids between the ages of 5 and 10 years old. They had their entire lives ahead of them -- birthdays, graduations, weddings, kids of their own. Among the fallen were also teachers -- men and women who devoted their lives to helping our children fulfill their dreams.*

*So, our hearts are broken today -- for the parents and grandparents, sisters and brothers of these little children, and for the families of the adults who were lost. Our hearts are broken for the parents of the survivors as well, for as blessed as they are to have their children home tonight, they know that their children's innocence has been torn away from them too early, and there are no words that will ease their pain.*

*As a country, we have been through this too many times. Whether it's an elementary school in Newtown, or a shopping mall in Oregon, or a temple in Wisconsin, or a movie theater in Aurora, or a street corner in Chicago -- these neighborhoods are our neighborhoods, and these children are our children. And we're going to have to come together and take meaningful action to prevent more tragedies like this, regardless of the politics.*

*-This evening, Michelle and I will do what I know every parent in America will do, which is hug our children a little tighter and we'll tell them that we love them, and we'll remind each other how deeply we love one another. But there are families in Connecticut who cannot do that tonight. And they need all of us right now. In the hard days to come, that community needs us to be at our best as Americans. And I will do everything in my power as President to help.''*[clxxxiii]

Not too surprising considering the strength of the gun lobby, President Obama had little success in enacting any significant new laws which would reduce the chances of these types of mass shootings from re-occurring. The 2 main federal proposals being "An Assaults Weapon Ban" and "Universal Background Checks" both being defeated in Congress.

Whilst it is true that the above proposals would not prevent most shooting fatalities or most mass shootings, Universal Background Checks would reduce the number of firearm fatalities and an Assault Weapon Ban would help to lessen the number of casualties in a mass shooting. Frustrating as this lack of action is, even more disturbing is the fact that following the shooting several Sandy Hook conspiracy theories have arisen including the following:

- The United States Government was involved in the shooting, with the objective being to push through new gun-control legislation [clxxxiv]
- Iranian television promoted theories blaming Israeli death squads for the shooting [clxxxv]
- A professor at Florida Atlantic University stating that the shooting did not occur and claiming political motives for the coverup [clxxxvi]
- A claim made by Alex Jones who runs the web site Infowars that "no one died" at Sandy Hook Elementary School

because the Uniform Crime Reports showed no murders in Newtown for 2012, and that the victims were "child actors". [clxxxvii]

The Alex Jones claim is the one most frequently cited and is fundamentally flawed as the murders were included in Connecticut state records rather than the Newtown statistics. This fundamental flaw is however not the major concern. The real problem here is how can anyone be conned into believing the tragedy never occurred, and that the grieving parents and children seen on the news coverage were actors. The disrespect being shown to the innocent victims and families of the school children and their teachers is staggering.

Not only are the Sandy Hook Conspiracy theories disgusting in the message they portray, but they also encourage certain sick individuals to threaten and intimidate the families of those affected by the school shooting. This is particularly true with the Alex Jones Infowars claim as his Infowars website has a huge following and although it has now been banned from many platforms as of September 2018 it was still receiving 1.15 million visits per month[clxxxviii]. The parents of one of the children killed in the shooting have had to relocate seven times after receiving death threats and online harassment and now live in a high-security community hundreds of miles from where their 6-year-old is buried[clxxxix].

Many of the Sandy Hook families have filed defamation suits against Alex Jones. The complaints from all these families allege that Jones used his internet and radio platforms to push the conspiracy theory that the shooting, in which a gunman killed twenty first-graders and six adults at the school in Newtown, Connecticut, was a staged event. The lawsuits claim that Jones' false narratives have brought him attention and money, while the families have suffered deep personal pain as well as abuse from fans of Jones. In December 2019 Alex Jones was ordered to pay $100,000 in the Sandy Hook defamation case in legal fees and court costs.[cxc]

Following the lawsuits, Jones has acknowledged that he believes the massacre "really happened," but that the families were being used by the Democratic Party[cxci]. This changed narrative of Alex Jones highlights the fact that politics is being placed above the lives of innocent children and their families. Some gun-rights advocates are concerned that highly publicized mass shootings may encourage tighter restrictions on guns and hence wish to pretend the mass shooting never occurred, or that it was set up by those wanting to control gun ownership. On the other side of the political divide, it also has to be acknowledged that some proponents of gun-control like to make political capital out of high-profile mass shootings.

In November 2014 a documentary was published titled "We Need to Talk About Sandy Hook" [cxcii]which promotes the conspiracy theory alleging that the tragedy at Sandy Hook was a hoax designed to increase popular support for gun-control. At the time of writing on the Internet Movie Database (IMDb), there were 26 user reviews on this documentary. Interestingly every review either gave the documentary a 10 out of 10 or 1 out of 10 rating i.e. the highest or the lowest rating possible with nothing in-between. This highlights the polarizing nature of these conspiracy theories. Around 2/3 of the reviewers gave the documentary 10 out of 10, which may not be too surprising as it is likely to be people who want to believe in this type of conspiracy theory that purchase the documentary.

With regards to general public opinion on the Sandy Hook shooting a poll was taken by Fairleigh Dickinson University in April 2013[cxciii], which found that 25% of Americans think that facts about the Sandy Hook shootings are being hidden, with a further 11% unsure. Whilst it is only a minority who believe in some form of conspiracy theory it is still a significant minority and it is concerning that so many people can believe in the complete nonsense of the shooting either being carried out by the government or that it never happened and that the victims and their families were all actors.

In reality, it is unlikely that 25% of the American population truly believe that the shootings did not occur, or were performed by the government to promote gun-control. Some people will say yes, they do believe in conspiracy theories because it suits their political viewpoint. In this example, some gun-rights advocates may say they do believe in the conspiracy theory even though deep down they know that the tragedy did occur and was the result of a crazed individual who had easy access to a semi-automatic weapon.

Unfortunately encouraging the proponents of the Sandy Hook Conspiracy theory is dangerous as it encourages the aforementioned harassment of the innocent victims and their families.

There is also a certain irony in the viewpoint that the shooting was set up by the government to promote gun control. As with most mass shootings in the United States, no meaningful new gun-control regulations were enacted. The very fear however that there would be new gun-control resulted in increased gun sales of around 3 million in the 5-months following the shooting[cxciv].

It is sad that such a tragic event should both fail to result in any new meaningful legislation and also give rise to conspiracy theories. Hopefully one day it will be possible to make effective changes to gun culture and laws, which will significantly reduce the number of annual firearm fatalities. There are however many obstacles in the way, which will be explored in Step 4 of the book.

# STEP 4

# Understanding the obstacles to change

# 20. District of Columbia v Heller

On reading the Second Amendment *"A well regulated militia, being necessary to the security of a free state, the right of the people to keep and bear arms, shall not be infringed."* it would seem reasonable to interpret this as basically meaning that people must be allowed to keep and bear arms for the specific purpose of maintaining a well regulated militia. As discussed in Chapter 8 this interpretation was cemented by a 1939 Supreme Court ruling in United States v Miller. This ruling allowed for the regulation of certain weapons provided that it did not impact the efficiency of a well regulated militia. In the ruling, the Court explained that the Framers included the Second Amendment to ensure the effectiveness of the militia[cxcv].

This interpretation was however overturned in 2008 in the District of Columbia V Heller case where the plaintiff Heller challenged the constitutionality of a Washington D.C. handgun ban. In this case, the U.S. Supreme Court answered a long-standing constitutional question about whether the right to "keep and bear arms" is an individual right unconnected to service in the militia, or a collective right that applies only to state-regulated militias.

By a five to four margin, the Court held that the Second Amendment protects an individual right to possess firearms for lawful use, such as self-defense, in the home. Accordingly, it struck down as unconstitutional provisions of a D.C. law that effectively banned possession of handguns by non-law enforcement officials and required lawfully owned firearms to be kept unloaded, disassembled, or locked when not located at a business place, or being used for lawful recreational activities.

According to the Court, the ban on handgun possession in the home amounted to a prohibition on an entire class of 'arms' that Americans overwhelmingly choose for the lawful purpose of self-defense.

Similarly, the requirement that any firearm in a home be disassembled or locked made it impossible for citizens to use arms for the core lawful purpose of self-defense. These laws were unconstitutional under any of the standards of scrutiny the Court has applied to enumerated constitutional rights[cxcvi].

Whilst it is dubious that this meaning was as originally intended by the framers of the Second Amendment, there is no doubt that it is a popular interpretation. Shortly after the Supreme Court ruling, a Gallup poll asked the following question:

*Do you believe the Second Amendment to the U.S. Constitution guarantees the rights of Americans to own guns, or do you believe it only guarantees members of state militias such as National Guard units the right to own guns?*

A massive 73% of respondents responded that it does guarantee the rights of Americans to own guns, with only 20% believing it only guarantees the rights of state militia members[cxcvii]. This underlines the popular support for the Right to Bear Arms in the United States.

On the face of it, this Supreme Court ruling is a major blow to those who would like to see tighter firearm regulation in the United States. It certainly does place a huge obstacle to some of the more drastic solutions to America's gun problem. For example, the handgun ban introduced in the United Kingdom following the Dunblane school mass shooting would be unlawful following the Heller decision. In reality, however, the obstacle this ruling imposes is not as significant as it may appear for 2 reasons.

Firstly, most new laws it would prevent were never realistic possibilities in the United States, regardless of the Heller decision. As an example, a federal handgun ban although effective in reducing homicide rates in other countries is not a realistic proposition in the United States and would never be proposed as it would be political suicide due to the overwhelming public support for the right to bear arms. The District of Columbia v Heller ruling has set a clear boundary for which all proponents of gun-control must be aware. Blanket bans on guns at federal, state, or municipal levels are not a realistic proposition and are unlawful.

Secondly, in the Ruling, it was made clear that the Second Amendment right is not absolute and a wide range of gun-control laws remain presumptively lawful, according to the Court. These include laws that (1) prohibit carrying concealed weapons, (2) prohibit gun possession by felons or the mentally retarded, (3) prohibit carrying firearms in sensitive places such as schools and government buildings, (4) impose conditions and qualifications on the commercial sale of arms, (5) prohibit "dangerous and unusual weapons, and (6) regulate firearm storage to prevent accidents[cxcviii]. In other words, sensible laws on gun safety would not be prevented from the Ruling.

A good example in which to determine the extent the Heller ruling can be used to prevent new gun-control laws is whether this would prevent a ban on Assault Weapons? In February 2018, the Washington Post published an article on this matter noting that to date Courts have ruled that the Second Amendment does not protect the right to own Assault Weapons.

In 2017 a federal appeals court considered whether a Maryland law passed following the Sandy Hook massacre banning assault weapons was unconstitutional. This law had been passed in the aftermath of the Sandy Hook massacre, which left 20 first-graders and six adults dead after a man bearing an AR-15-style weapon stormed the school in Newtown, Conn. The court ruled that the ban on assault weapons like the one Adam Lanza used at Sandy Hook was constitutional. This was the fourth time in the past decade that a federal appeals court had ruled that a ban on assault weapons was permissible under the Second Amendment and at the time of writing no federal appeals court has ever held that assault weapons are protected.

The bans on semiautomatic guns or assault weapons have been upheld for 2 reasons. Firstly, banning them, the courts have said, does not curtail the right of self-defense protected by the Constitution, since there are plenty of other weapons such as handguns and regular long guns available for people to protect themselves. Secondly, the courts have said, states and municipalities have legitimate reasons to ban AR-15-style weapons because of the dangers they pose, to schools, innocent bystanders and police[cxcix].

So, in summary, the District of Columbia v Heller ruling does not present an insurmountable obstacle for those wishing to enact sensible and realistic restrictions on gun purchases and ownership. It can also be argued that this ruling is beneficial in that it sets a clear boundary.

For example, if a modest safety proposal is suggested such as closing the gun show loophole, or strengthening background checks, the NRA and other gun-rights advocates will argue that this is just the start of a slippery slope and before too long there will be a complete ban on guns. They install a fear that "We're coming to get your guns" and this mentality is frequently used as an attack against any senate, congress, or presidential candidate who is in favor of strengthening gun control. The response to these accusations should be along the lines, that we respect the District of Columbia v Heller decision and have no intention of taking your guns, as we recognize this would be illegal. This ruling should make the coming to get your guns claim obsolete.

# 21. NRA Leadership

In Chapter 12 we reviewed the impact that Gun-rights Advocacy Groups have had in promoting gun ownership and in blocking proposals to tighten regulations on firearms. Here it was noted that the National Rifle Association (NRA) was the largest, most successful, and influential of the many Gun-rights Advocacy Groups.

The NRA represents a huge obstacle in promoting and enacting sensible gun policies, which would significantly reduce the firearm-related death toll in the United States. The ability of the NRA to influence politicians and impact gun-related laws must not be underestimated and we will examine some of the successes the NRA has had later in the chapter. It is however not so much the NRA itself which is so problematic, but rather the NRA leadership and the direction the NRA has taken in recent years. To understand this further we need to delve into the history of the NRA.

The NRA was founded in 1871 by two Civil War veterans to improve the dismal shooting abilities of the typical Union soldier. The original mission focused on hunting, conservation, marksmanship, and firearm safety education, and there was no mention of protecting the Second Amendment right to bear arms. Indeed, for nearly a century, the NRA actively lobbied for gun-control.

The NRA backed the nation's first federal gun laws after the Prohibition Era when tommy gun–wielding gangsters warred in the streets of Chicago. The National Firearms Acts of 1934 and 1938 placed heavy taxes and regulations on machine guns, sawed-off shotguns, and silencers; prohibited felons from owning weapons; and required gun owners to register with the federal government. NRA leader Karl T. Frederick not only endorsed the legislation, but he also went so far as to state, "I have never believed in the general practice of carrying weapons. I think it should be sharply restricted and only under licenses."

NRA support for gun-control continued up to the 1960s when assassinations and street violence rocked the nation. When it emerged that Lee Harvey Oswald had used a rifle purchased via an NRA mail-order advertisement to assassinate President John F. Kennedy in 1963, NRA Executive Vice President Franklin Orth backed the banning of mail-order sales. And when members of the Black Panther Party marched on the California Capitol carrying shotguns and rifles, the NRA supported state legislation prohibiting "open carry" in public places[cc].

The attitude of the NRA began to change in the late 1960s following the passing of the Gun-control Act of 1968. This Act banned interstate shipments of firearms to private individuals and sales of guns to minors, drug addicts, mental incompetents, and convicted felons. The Act also strengthened the licensing and record-keeping requirements for gun dealers.[cci].

The NRA didn't like the 1968 law, viewing it as overly restrictive, but also didn't see it as a slide toward tyranny. The top NRA officer, Franklin Orth, wrote in the association's publication American Rifleman that "the measure as a whole appears to be one that the sportsmen of America can live with". By the second half of the 1970s, the NRA faced a crossroads. Would it remain an Establishment institution, partnering with mainstream entities, and focusing on shooting competitions? Or would it roll up its sleeves and fight hammer and tongs against the gun-control advocates? This question was answered in May 1977 at the annual meeting of the NRA in a confrontation now referred to as the "Revolt at Cincinnati". [ccii]

On May 21, 1977, and into the morning of May 22, a rump caucus of gun-rights radicals took over the annual meeting of the National Rifle Association. The rebels wore orange-blaze hunting caps and spoke on walkie-talkies. The Old Guard was caught by surprise whilst the NRA officers sat up front, on a dais, observing their demise. The organization, about a century old already, was thoroughly mainstream and bipartisan, focusing on hunting, conservation, and marksmanship. It taught Boy Scouts how to shoot safely. But the world had changed, and everything was more political now. The rebels saw the NRA leaders as elites who lacked the heart and conviction to fight against gun-control legislation.

What unfolded that hot night in Cincinnati forever reoriented the NRA from a sporting and marksmanship club into arguably the most powerful lobbying organization in the nation's capital and certainly one of the most feared. The NRA are the people who say no, they are absolutist in their interpretation of the Second Amendment. The NRA learned that controversy isn't a problem but rather, in many cases, a solution, a motivator, a recruitment tool, and an inspiration.

Following the Revolt at Cincinnati, the old guard was ousted and Harlon Carter (who had served time for shooting dead a Mexican teenager) became the new NRA Executive Vice President. He spelled out the new approach as "No compromise, No gun legislation". The NRA began grading politicians from A to F on gun-control legislation. Those with the best report cards were given campaign money; the rest earned the wrath of the NRA's ballooning membership. The leadership adopted a new motto "The Right of the People to Bear Arms Shall Not Be Infringed". Any proposed piece of gun legislation was framed as the first step toward total disarmament.

In more recent years led by Executive Vice President Wayne LaPierre, the NRA continues to exert huge political influence. In 2013, when support for universal background checks rose to 91 percent after the Sandy Hook Elementary School shooting, the organization blocked congressional efforts to pass background-check amendments. NRA members are unmoved by stories about their early leaders' support for gun-control. "Then was then," said one NRA supporter recently, on Guns & Ammo's online forum. "Now is now."

The NRA used to tout its independence from gun manufacturers — branding itself as the century-old voice of average-joe hunters and sport shooters. Today, though, the organization bolsters its funds with million-dollar donations from 22 different gun makers. The NRA received up to $52.6 million in industry donations between 2005 and 2013, according to one report, it makes $1 from every purchase. The gun manufacturers' influence is clear: Today, the NRA's answer to every mass shooting is more firearms — even in schools and churches. "Today's NRA is a virtual subsidiary of the gun industry," said Josh Sugarmann, executive director of the Violence Policy Center, a gun-control organization. "While the NRA portrays itself as protecting the freedom of individual gun owners, it's actually working to protect the freedom of the gun industry to manufacture and sell virtually any weapon or accessory."[cciii]

The current NRA leadership poses 2 obstacles for those who believe that reducing the number of firearm fatalities is important. Firstly, as highlighted above, the NRA leaders believe they should be acting as a surrogate to the gun industry, and secondly, they are very successful in their objective of opposing gun safety laws.

In June 2016 CBS published an article noting that over 100 gun-control proposals had been proposed to Congress and not a single one had passed into law. This was written just after the June 12, 2016, Orlando mass shooting at a time when it was thought that the shooter Omar Mateen was a suspected terrorist and, on the no-fly list. At the time the article was written the Senate was due to vote on four more gun-control proposals. The Democrats had proposed two: one that would ban suspected terrorists from being able to purchase a gun and another that would expand background checks. The article noted that those two proposals, plus two less restrictive measures offered by Republicans, are all expected to fail[cciv]. The article was correct the proposals all failed. The article continues to note the following-

After every mass shooting, Democrats on Capitol Hill have tried to revive the gun-control issue by introducing new legislation. Two weeks after a Tucson mass shooting in 2011 a trio of gun-control bills were proposed. One would have closed the so-called gun show loophole by requiring sellers at gun shows to perform the same background checks that licensed gun dealers must conduct. Another would have banned the manufacture and sale of magazines with a capacity of more than 10 rounds of ammunition. The third proposal would have stopped a person on the terrorist watch list from obtaining explosives or guns. None of them gained traction.

Rep. Carolyn McCarthy, D-New York, who retired from Congress in 2015, spent 18 years on Capitol Hill fighting to renew the assault weapons ban, close the gun show loophole and ban high-capacity magazines. Her husband was killed and her son was severely injured when a gunman shot passengers on a Long Island Rail Road commuter train in 1993. McCarthy repeatedly introduced these proposals in every Congress, but none of them passed muster. The National Rifle Association's (NRA) stranglehold over Congress is largely responsible for the inaction[ccv].

What is remarkable about the NRA success in blocking sensible gun safety regulation is that in most instances they do not have public support in their favor. For example, a poll taken by Quinnipiac in February 2018 found that 67% of Americans favored a nationwide assault weapon ban[ccvi]. There are even some gun-control policies that are supported by NRA members. A Monmouth University poll taken in March 2018 found that 69% of NRA members expressed support for comprehensive background checks i.e. background checks which would apply to all gun sales, rather than just purchases made at licensed retailers, according to the gun-control advocacy group Giffords Law Center [ccvii]. One would hope that the NRA Leadership would act on this disconnect with its own members, however, things are unlikely to change unless as identified in Chapter 12, public support for the NRA continues to fall.

Regardless of any internal problems the NRA currently has, it must be recognized that the NRA leaders have been very successful in their objective of preventing new gun-control laws to be passed. So, what is the secret of their success in influencing Congress to block these measures? The answer is that they have mastered the art of effective political lobbying, which leads us neatly into the next chapter.

# 22. Political Lobbying

As noted in the previous chapter, the NRA has been extremely effective in ensuring Congress block any efforts to pass new laws placing restrictions on gun ownership. This has largely been achieved through political lobbying, but what exactly is political lobbying?

Political Lobbying frequently referred to as Lobbying, is defined as trying to influence the thinking of legislators or other public officials for or against a specific cause[ccviii]. Political lobbying is a highly controversial phenomenon, often seen in a negative light by the American public and some critics describe it as a legal form of bribery or extortion. Although there are rules which must be followed, lobbying has been interpreted as constitutionally protected free speech and a way to petition the government for the redress of grievances, two of the freedoms protected by the First Amendment of the Constitution[ccix].

Much of the lobbying i.e. the influencing of politicians is done through monetary contributions which are important in the American electoral system, as tremendous amounts of money are spent in campaign financing. For the 2016 elections, $2.4 billion was spent on the presidential contest (includes primaries) and $4 billion on congressional races. This includes spending by campaigns, party committees, and outside sources. In comparison in the United Kingdom, there is a cap of approximately $29.5 million on political spending[ccx].

So how important a player are gun-rights advocacy groups in the political lobbying arena? On the face of it they are not big players at all. The following table lists the 5 largest political lobbying industry sectors and the amount they spent in 2018: [ccxi]

| Pharmaceuticals/Health products | $283,967,894 |
| Insurance | $157,424,794 |
| Electronics Manufacturing & Equipment | $147,851,718 |
| Business Associations | $145,524,570 |
| Oil & Gas | $125,947,199 |

In comparison Gun-rights organizations spent $12,453,572 in 2018 and Gun-control organizations spent just $2,039,212 [ccxii].

So, in the sense that contributions made by gun-rights advocacy groups are significantly less than those made by many other industries they are not big players. Gun-rights groups do however spend more relative to their size i.e. as a proportion of their revenue or net capital, than other major industries. What is more important for gun-related issues is the comparison between contributions made by gun-control and gun-rights groups. As can be seen from the above figures the gun-rights groups provided 6 times more contributions than the gun-control groups. It thus follows that gun-rights groups are more likely to influence politicians than gun-control groups.

A more detailed analysis of spending by Gun-rights and Gun-control groups, published by the Guardian in 2012, provides a starker variance between the money raised and hence political influence of the Gun-rights and Gun-control groups. This breaks down expenditure into 3 categories – Contributions – Lobbying – Outside Spending, which are defined as follows:

- Contributions – Money from an organization's employees, their family, or the organization's own PAC to a political candidate. These donations have a cap.
- Lobbying - Spending on firms to lobby for the organization's issues.
- Outside Spending - Money contributed by an organization, its employees, or employee's families to an outside spending group such as a super PAC.

Below is a comparison of the 2011/2012 expenditure[ccxiii]:

| Type of spending | Gun-rights Groups | Gun-control Groups |
| --- | --- | --- |
| Contributions | $1,713,984 | $3,018 |
| Lobbying | $9,309,869 | $420,000 |
| Outside spending | $19,634,906 | $0 |
| -Total | $30,658,759 | $423,018 |

In simple terms, the Gun-rights Groups outspent the Gun-control Groups over 72 times. The NRA provided over $25m of the Gun-rights Groups total, of which nearly $19m fell into the Outside Spending category. Much of this money was raised and spent by the NRA Political Action Committee (PAC) – National Rifle Association of America Political Victory Fund.

A PAC is a political committee organized for the specific purpose of raising and spending money to elect preferred candidates and to defeat candidates with opposing viewpoints, which in this case would be to help defeat those who are in favor of more gun control. This is something in which the Gun-rights Groups and in particular the NRA are very efficient. They are able to raise huge sums of money to promote their causes, help elect gun-friendly politicians, and influence elected politicians.

There are several ways in which the NRA influence politicians which include the following[ccxiv]:

Scorecards - The NRA sends a questionnaire to each candidate, which asks how they will vote on gun issues. The questionnaire, combined with any past votes and public statements on these issues, forms a "scorecard." The NRA publishes the ratings in its magazines and online, for its members to see, as well as sending them in e-mails and mailings. An "A" rating will generally earn a candidate the endorsement unless another candidate also scores an "A." Neither the questions nor the answers are made public.

The NRA grading system is defined as follows[ccxv]:

A+: A legislator with not only an excellent voting record on all critical NRA issues but who has also made a vigorous effort to promote and defend the Second Amendment.

A: Solidly pro-gun candidate. A candidate who has supported NRA positions on key votes in elective office or a candidate with a demonstrated record of support on Second Amendment issues.

AQ: A pro-gun candidate whose rating is based solely on the candidate's responses to the NRA Candidate Questionnaire and who does not have a voting record on Second Amendment issues.

B: A generally pro-gun candidate. However, a "B" candidate may have opposed some pro-gun reform or supported some restrictive legislation in the past.

D: An anti-gun candidate who usually supports restrictive gun-control legislation and opposes pro-gun reforms. Regardless of public statements, he can usually be counted on to vote wrong on key issues.

One Issue Agenda – Although the NRA typically support Republican candidates over Democratic candidates, they do not consider party affiliation when making endorsements. This is because of their one issue agenda and hence a politician's viewpoint on issues such as healthcare or the environment is irrelevant to the NRA. This means they will sometimes support Democrats, provided they are in favor of gun-rights. This increases the odds that multiple candidates in an election will support gun-rights.

Loyalty - Once a candidate is endorsed, as long as he or she maintains an "A" scorecard, the association maintains its endorsement. The NRA has a policy that it does not switch horses in midstream. That means incumbents always know they can count on the organization's support, provided they continue to align themselves with the NRA on gun issues.

Carrot and Stick – NRA endorsed candidates receive direct campaign contributions, grassroots support, advocacy on their behalf, and often independent expenditures, including advertisements. On the reverse side, when the NRA does not like a candidate's action, that candidate knows it.

NRA endorsement is particularly important for Republican candidates in Republican primary elections. With the majority of Republican primary voters supporting gun-rights any candidate who does not receive an A rating from the NRA is likely to be portrayed as weak on gun-rights and exposed as such by the NRA. Consequently, virtually all elected Republican politicians oppose even modest gun-control policies.

The wide-ranging impact of gun-rights groups on elected politicians is demonstrated by the number of Congress members and Senators who receive donations from them. This information is available on the Open Secrets website which details the money that Gun-rights Groups provide to Congress. For the 2016 election contributions by Gun-rights Groups to candidates were $5,727,094 of which $5,613,538 went to Republican candidates. These sums do not include money spent on lobbying, which totaled $11.24m in 2016.

More significant than the total sum of money spent is the number of candidates the money was spent on. Gun-rights Groups provided money to 230 Members of the House of Representatives (222 Republican and 8 Democrats) and 45 Senators (41 Republican and 4 Democrats). This means over 50% of House Representatives and just under 50% of Senators have been bought by Gun-rights organizations. It is very difficult for these Congressmen/Congresswomen and Senators to vote for anything their contributors oppose, which in this case means they are likely to vote down any proposal, no matter how much public support it may have, to enact sensible restrictions on gun ownership or gun purchases. In comparison in 2016 Gun-control Groups provided money to just 10 Congressmen/Congresswomen and 2 Senators.[ccxvi] [ccxvii]

No wonder Congress has failed to implement any recent gun-control proposals, they have in effect been bought out by Gun-rights Groups. This is a huge obstacle in preventing sensible new laws, which would reduce the annual firearm-related death toll, from being implemented. It is however clearly not just the gun industry that has a hold on Congress and as noted earlier in the chapter, industries such as the Pharmaceutical sector spend much more money. It is well recognized that individuals in Congress tend to vote in favor of those who contribute and lobby on their behalf, rather than to vote for what they feel is morally right, or what is best for the country. Consequently, public support for Congress is extremely low. As of May 2019, only 20 percent of the U.S. population approved of the way Congress was handling its job[ccxviii]. There should, therefore, be some scope in attacking Congress for their voting record on gun-related issues.

# 23. Register and Research Ban

If you own a motor vehicle in the United States, the law requires you to have a Certificate of Ownership or Title to prove you are the legal owner. The Certificate of Ownership details the owner's name and address, the registration plate number, and other details about the vehicle. Vehicle registration is managed by each state's department of motor vehicles (DMV). From these details, a Vehicle Registry can be maintained. The motor vehicle registry is helpful in many ways, such as identifying vehicles that have not passed necessary state inspection tests, or in identifying the owners of vehicles involved in accidents or crimes.

One would expect a similar registry to be available for firearms, however, this is not the case. Indeed, the laws surrounding the registration of firearms act in the opposite direction to those surrounding the registration of motor vehicles. Whilst the laws surrounding motor vehicles are that they must be registered, the law surrounding firearms makes it illegal to create a firearm registry in most instances.

The law in question is The Firearm Owners Protection Act of 1986 (FOPA) which makes it illegal for the national government or any state in the country to keep any sort of database or registry that ties firearms directly to their owner. The exact wording of the provision is as follows:

*No such rule or regulation prescribed [by the Attorney General] after the date of the enactment of the Firearms Owners Protection Act may require that records required to be maintained under this chapter or any portion of the contents of such records, be recorded at or transferred to a facility owned, managed, or controlled by the United States or any State or any political subdivision thereof, nor that any system of registration of firearms, firearms owners, or firearms transactions or disposition be established. Nothing in this section expands or restricts the Secretary's authority to inquire into the disposition of any firearm in the course of a criminal investigation.[ccxix]*

To determine the merits of this law it is necessary to understand the advantages and disadvantages of creating a firearm registry. The case in favor of a firearm registry is well made by Giffords Law Center to Prevent Gun Violence who have published a web page detailing the advantages of maintaining a register of firearms, which include the following[ccxx]:

Crime Gun Tracing – Firearm registration helps law enforcement to identify the source of firearms recovered from crime scenes. This is because Firearm registration laws create comprehensive records of firearm ownership, which include a full description of each firearm and identify the owner. Comprehensive registration laws also require a firearm to be re-registered whenever title to the firearm is transferred, and law enforcement to be notified whenever the weapon is lost or stolen. As a result, registration laws help law enforcement quickly and reliably identify the owner of any firearm used in a crime.

Disarming Dangerous People - Comprehensive registration laws require gun owners to renew their registration annually or explain why they should no longer be legally responsible for the weapon. During the renewal process, owners undergo additional background checks to ensure that they have not fallen into a class prohibited from possessing firearms. The renewal process, therefore, creates an opportunity for law enforcement to remove illegally possessed firearms.

Gun Owner Accountability - Registration laws help reduce illegal firearm sales and transfers by creating accountability for gun owners. A firearm owner who knows that law enforcement can trace the firearm back to him or her may be deterred from transferring the firearm to a potentially dangerous individual and maybe encouraged to store his or her firearm safely to prevent unauthorized access or theft. Registration laws also help deter "straw purchases," in which an eligible person purchases a firearm on behalf of an ineligible person or someone who wants to avoid having the gun traced back to them.

For a different perspective on the merits of gun registration and to argue the case against a firearm registry we turn to the NRA and in particular their Executive Vice President, Wayne LaPierre who quoted the following at a Conservative Political Action Conference (CPAC) with regards to a federal firearm registry:

*"That's what [the feds] are after, the names of good, decent people all over this country, who happen to own firearms to go into a federal database or universal registration, every lawful gun owner in America," LaPierre said in a speech at the Conservative Political Action Conference. "That's their answer to criminal violence... are they insane?"*[ccxxi]

So, the argument against a federal database would appear to be that it is an invasion of privacy i.e. why should law-abiding gun owners be on a database. This seems to miss the point that being on a register would only have a negative impact on the gun owner if the gun were used in a crime. Car owners don't complain about having their details on a database, so why should gun owners complain. A gun registry may even help lawful gun owners retrieve their guns if they are stolen and later recovered since they would easily be able to show they are the legal gun owner.

There is a certain irony in the NRA viewpoint in that they have built up their own database of gun owners. With a national gun database containing names and addresses, the NRA has the power to target certain markets and influence Americans to support them[ccxxii].

A third website published by Bustle provides a more balanced review of the advantages and disadvantages of a gun registry[ccxxiii]. This lists 3 advantages and 2 disadvantages. The advantages noted below mirror those of the Giffords Law Center, namely:

- Cops could identify guns recovered at crime scenes

- It could disarm criminals and domestic abusers

- Illegal gun sales would drop

With regards to the 1st disadvantage, it notes that whilst law enforcement could identify legally held guns recovered at crime scenes, guns held illegally would not be in the database and that the majority of firearms used in crimes would still not be traceable. The issue of illegal guns is a valid point (which will be reviewed in the final section of the book) as most guns used in crimes are held illegally, but it just limits the effectiveness of a gun database rather than providing a reason not to have a gun database. Additionally, a firearm register would reduce the number of illegal guns in circulation as it would deter legal gun owners from selling their firearms illegally and put more pressure on them to report stolen firearms.

The second disadvantage of a gun registry noted by Bustle is that this may lead to the government disarming everyone. This type of argument is a typical example of the fear-mongering used by gun-rights advocates, as this clearly would not happen. Public support for the right to bear arms and the 2nd Amendment ensures that the government would never even attempt to disarm everyone. What a gun registry may do is disarm certain individuals who pose a greater risk to themselves or others such as mentally disabled individuals or domestic abusers. Surely this is a good thing that would help reduce the number of firearm suicides and murders.

It is important to note that the creation of a firearm registry has much popular support. In February 2018 a Politico/Morning Consult poll found that 78% of voters were in favor of creating a national database providing information about each gun sale.[ccxxiv]

Finally, the best way to evaluate the merits of having a firearm register is to examine the gun death rates of states that currently do hold a gun register. Hawaii and the District of Columbia have state laws requiring registration of all firearms and New York has a law requiring the registration of all handguns. Giffords Law Center to Prevent Gun Violence does not provide a ranking for the District of Colombia but it is probably no coincidence that in their 2018 annual gun law scorecard Hawaii had the lowest statewide gun death rate and New York state the 3rd lowest gun death rates in the country[ccxxv].

In addition to the firearm register ban, there has until recently been an effective ban on firearm research by the Centers for Disease Control and Prevention (CDC). This was a consequence of the Dickey Amendment, a provision enacted in the 1996 spending bill mandating that no funds made available to the CDC for injury prevention and control may be used to advocate or promote gun control. In the same spending bill, Congress removed $2.6m from the CDC's budget, the exact amount that had previously been allocated to the agency for firearms research the previous year. The Dickey Amendment was lobbied by the NRA in response to a 1993 CDC funded study showing that guns in the home were associated with an increased risk of homicide in the home and it is frequently described as a ban on gun violence research by the CDC[ccxxvi].

In March 2018 an Omnibus spending bill clarified that the CDC is allowed to research gun violence[ccxxvii], however, the Dickey Amendment is still active in that there is still a ban on the CDC promoting gun-control. Consequently, the CDC is reluctant to conduct any research which may have the appearance of promoting gun-control. An additional problem relates to the funding of the CDC, as Congress has continued to block dedicated funding to gun violence research.

Following the Dickey Amendment, CDC funding for firearm injury prevention fell 96%, down to $100,000, from 1996 to 2013. The CDC was not alone in avoiding firearm studies, the National Institute of Justice, an arm of the U.S. Department of Justice, funded 32 gun-related studies from 1993 to 1999, but none from 2009-2013, according to Mayors Against Illegal Guns. Sponsors were spooked to fund stuff that had to do with guns. Apparently studying firearms was not a way to attract vital grant funding[ccxxviii].

It is very telling that the CDC is reluctant to research gun violence since on the surface this would not necessarily be promoting gun-control. If research showed for example that having a gun at home reduced the chances of residents being injured or killed then the research would help promote gun-rights. In reality, the CDC knows that research will highlight the negative impacts on gun ownership and that inevitably the research will be seen as promoting gun-control, which is still forbidden under the Dickey Amendment. It stands to reason that the only ones to benefit from a ban on researching gun violence are those who are fearful of the result. No wonder the NRA has been so supportive of the Dickey Amendment.

Finally, it should be noted that in 2015 Jay Dickey the author of the Dickey Amendment stated that he regretted the fact that his amendment had in effect restricted funding for research into gun violence and its effect on public health[ccxxix].

# 24. The Words "Freedom" and "Control"

Advocates for Gun-rights have one big advantage over advocates for Gun Restrictions and that is simply the main word they are associated with. The word associated with Gun-rights is "Freedom", whilst the word associated with Gun Restriction is "Control".

Examining the meanings of these words outside the context of guns is quite revealing. The English Oxford dictionary gives the 2 following definitions of "Freedom"[ccxxx]

*The power or right to act, speak, or think as one wants.*
The state of not being imprisoned or enslaved.

Freedom is clearly highly desirable since everyone would like to be able to act, speak, and think as they want without interference. Additionally, no-one wants to be imprisoned or enslaved and freedom is the exact opposite of imprisonment or enslavement.

The importance of freedom to Americans must not be underestimated and it is enshrined in the Bill of Rights, which could easily have been named the Bill of Freedoms. The Bill of Rights includes the following Rights, or Freedoms[ccxxxi].

Freedom of religion
Freedom of speech
Freedom of the press
Freedom of assembly
Freedom of petition
The right to bear arms
No quartering right
The right to equal justice
The right to own private property
The right to enjoy many other freedoms

America quite rightly prides itself on being the "Land of the Free" and there is no denying that freedom is a good thing, although as we shall see later in this chapter unfettered freedom can be dangerous.

With regards to the word "Control" the definitions are as follows:[ccxxxii]

The power to influence or direct people's behavior or the course of events.
*The ability to manage a machine, vehicle, or other moving object.*

The second definition can be ignored as this is using the word control in a different context to how it is used in connection with gun-control. With regard to the 1st definition, this is likely to be seen negatively. In general, people should be able to determine their own behavior without undue influence from others trying to control them. Similarly, most people do not have a desire or believe it is correct, to exert control over others. In particular control by the government as a way of subduing its citizens is seen in a very negative light.

Within the context of firearms, any form of restriction proposed by the government is likely to be seen as the government infringing on the right to bear arms i.e. an attempt to prevent law-abiding American citizens from having the freedom to decide themselves if they wish to purchase and own firearms. As an example, a proposal to ban semi-automatic weapons would be seen as the government using "Control" to prevent law-abiding citizens from having the "Freedom" to purchase a weapon of their choice.

To counter the "Freedom" good, "Control" bad obstacle it is first necessary to demonstrate that unrestrained freedom is a bad thing. If individuals were free to do as they wish there would be no laws and crime would be rampant. In an extreme form, this would lead to Anarchy which can be defined as an absence of government and absolute freedom of the individual. Now clearly even the most fervent supporters of freedom realize there have to be some constraints on freedoms and that all civilized countries must have a set of laws that have to be obeyed.

Everyone would agree that murder should be illegal i.e. an individual should not have the freedom to kill someone, except under extreme circumstances e.g. self-defense, but there are some less clear freedoms. Individuals should have the freedom to drink at home and the freedom to drive, but they should not have the freedom to drink and drive. The reason for this is that drinking and driving is a dangerous combination that impacts the safety of the driver, their passengers, and other road users. Even the freedom of driving sober has to be controlled in that individuals who have not passed their driving test must require supervision. At the time of writing 48 states have passed laws against texting and driving[ccxxxiii], for the very good reason that texting whilst driving is dangerous and impacts the safety of both the individual texting and other road users. All these driving-related examples are areas in which safety issues outweigh freedom issues.

Another reason why there has to be some control on freedom is that one person's freedom can have a negative impact on other people's freedom. Someone who feels they have the right or freedom to shout repeatedly in a library is denying others the freedom to read or study without distraction. A good example of where freedoms can clash is with smoking. Should people be allowed to smoke in public areas? Generally, this is allowed outside but prohibited inside. The reason for this is that outside the freedom to smoke may outweigh the inconvenience to a passerby, whilst inside the negative impacts of smoke, such as smells and the detrimental health impact on others, outweighs the freedom to smoke.

Even when related to firearm freedom, most gun-rights advocates would except there has to be some limits to their right to bear arms. They would probably agree that those who have previously been convicted of a violent crime should not be allowed access to firearms. Must gun-rights enthusiasts would also agree that there must be some limits as to the weapons which can be purchased e.g. being in favor of banning the right to buy a bomb or a grenade.

So, having accepted there must be some limits to "Freedom" we now need to determine if "Control" is the most appropriate word to use when promoting policies that aim to place restrictions on gun purchases and gun ownership. Although these policies do involve control, the actual objective is to reduce the number of firearm injuries and fatalities. This is similar to policies aimed at reducing driving fatalities such as the mandatory wearing of seat belts. A seat belt is considered to be necessary for "Safety" purposes and not for "Control" purposes, although technically it involves control in that you are told you must wear a seat belt. The end game is safety and innovations aimed at reducing motor vehicle fatalities are referred to as safety innovations, not control innovations. For this very reason policies and innovations aimed at reducing firearm fatalities should be referred to as gun-safety policies instead of gun-control policies. "Gun-control" suggests the main aim is to restrict freedom on gun ownership, whilst "Gun-safety" suggests the main aim is to reduce the number of firearm fatalities and injuries.

In addition to being more accurate, rebranding "Gun-control policies" as "Gun-safety policies" removes the obstacle of policies being associated with the word "Control" and the negative connotations this may have, particularly when associated with control by the government.

Turning the focus to safety as opposed to control we can define safety as follows:[ccxxxiv]

*The condition of being protected from or unlikely to cause danger, risk, or injury.*

Safety is seen as a very positive thing, the importance of which is well illustrated in Maslow's Hierarchy of Needs. This is a theory proposed by the American psychologist Abraham Maslow in a 1943 paper "A Theory of Human Motivation". These needs are summarized as follows:[ccxxxv]

| Hierarchy | Need |
| --- | --- |
| Level 1 | Physiological |
| Level 2 | Safety |
| Level 3 | Love and belonging |
| Level 4 | Esteem |
| Level 5 | Self-actualization |

This hierarchy remains a popular framework in sociology research and the basic theory is that the lower-level needs must be met before striving to satisfy the higher-level needs. Physiological needs are considered the main physical requirements for human survival and include ensuring you have water, food, shelter, and sleep. Having established the basic survival requirements the next most important need is that of Safety, which is all about keeping us safe from harm. Safety needs must be met before attempting to meet higher levels of survival and include personal security, financial security, health, and reducing the risk of accidents. Safety is such a fundamental requirement and one we teach our children from an early age. For example, we tell children to look carefully for traffic before crossing the road or to stay away from a cliff edge.

Frequently the compromise between freedom and safety can be a matter of personal choice e.g. someone who decides they want to go parachuting is exercising their freedom to do something they enjoy although it involves an element of danger i.e. it compromises safety. Sometimes however the tradeoff between freedom and safety is set by higher levels of authority, ranging from parents, teachers, organizations, employers, courts, states, and the federal government. As an example, a gas station will have a rule that smoking is not allowed whilst pumping gas. This rule removing the freedom to smoke is essential to prevent a potential explosion i.e. the rule is there for the safety of the gas station's employees and customers.

Gun-rights advocates will frequently argue that there is no conflict between freedom and safety when it comes to their freedom to bear arms. After all, they believe that owning and carrying guns makes them safer, so this is a win-win situation in their eyes as they are enjoying the freedom and making themselves safer. In reality, as we have previously discovered owning and possessing a gun reduces safety both for the gun owner and their family. Fortunately, the majority of Americans do understand that in relation to firearms there is a trade-off between freedom to unlimited gun ownership and safety and generally support many policies aimed at reducing gun fatalities. The American public is however more likely to support a policy aimed at increasing safety than a policy marketed as a control on gun ownership.

In summary, both freedom and safety are essential things, although sometimes one has to be sacrificed at the expense of the other. Control and especially control by the government is seen as a bad thing and consequently promoting gun-control policies is difficult. Those seeking more restrictions on gun ownership need to emphasize the reason for wanting to limit firearm freedom i.e. to reduce firearm injuries and fatalities and to reduce overall homicide and suicide rates, or in simple terms to make us safer. The word control is an obstacle that can be overcome by stressing the objective is gun-safety as opposed to gun-control.

# 25. Fearmongering

Another obstacle that those wanting to reduce firearm violence have to face is the use of "Fearmongering" by gun-rights activists. Fearmongering is defined as follows:[ccxxxvi]

*The action of deliberately arousing public fear or alarm about a particular issue.*

Fearmongering is frequently carried out by politicians and indeed the example of the use of the word provided by the Lexico Oxford English Dictionaries website is as follows:

*his campaign for re-election was based on fearmongering and deception.*[ccxxxvii]

The use of the word deception in the above example is interesting in that it correctly implies that frequently the arousing of public fear is not warranted based on facts. Fearmongering tends to either greatly exaggerate existing risks or predicts unwelcome outcomes which are never likely to occur.

Firearm-related fearmongering usually takes one of the following forms:

- The fear of being left defenseless if someone attacks you and you have no way of protecting yourself
- Stoking fears by accusing anyone who wishes to introduce gun safety measures, especially politicians, as instigating the start of a slippery slope which will eventually lead to the abolition of the 2nd Amendment and the confiscation of all civilian held firearms.

The 2016 NRA commercial referred to in Chapter 16 titled "Don't let Hillary Clinton leave you defenseless" uses both of these forms of fearmongering. It highlights the fear of waking up to the sound of breaking glass and not having a firearm to protect yourself and it also highlights the fear that Hillary would somehow be able to remove the 2<sup>nd</sup> Amendment and enforce the removal of all civilian held firearms.

Focusing first on the defenseless fear, the NRA and gun manufacturers have been very successful in drumming up this fear. They argue that you are in constant danger and defenseless without quick access to a firearm, despite all the evidence indicating that those who own guns are more likely to be shot than those who do not have access to guns. Consequently, many people believe they need to have continual access to firearms to be safe and the NRA has built on this fear to promote the custom of allowing concealed carry. At the time of writing all 50 states issue concealed carry permits.

An article published by the American Prospect titled Concealed Carry and the Triumph of Fear provides a good analysis on how gun advocates have marketed fear as a motive to carry guns and enabled this to be a focus in changing laws so that as many people as possible can carry as many guns as possible into as many places as possible. The article explains the profound psychological difference between someone who has a gun in his home and someone who decides to carry a gun wherever he goes i.e. a concealed gun carrier. The concealed gun carrier has in effect transformed his view of the world into one in which every person he encounters is a potential assailant and every space he walks into is a potential scene of carnage. For the concealed gun carrier, the battlefield could be anywhere such as supermarkets, parks, sidewalks, or schools. His life is gripped with fear and to the concealed gun carrier things would be even better if everybody was carrying so that everyone was gripped by the same fear as him, the fear that anyone might try to kill us at any moment, the fear that can only be handled by being able and willing to kill first.[ccxxxviii]

Why are so many Americans gripped with a fear and paranoia that makes them feel the need to carry at all times and to be on a continual lookout for danger? The answer is Fearmongering which was so typically demonstrated by the NRA in their 2014 annual convention which had the slogan "Stand and Fight". At this convention, the CEO, Wayne LaPierre, evoked a nation in peril and demise and gave the following speech "There are terrorists and home invaders and drug cartels and carjackers and knockout gamers and rapers, haters, campus killers, airport killers. I ask you: do you trust the government to protect you? We are on our own, the things we care about most are changing. It's why more and more Americans are buying firearms and ammunition."[ccxxxix]

This demonstrates how the NRA uses fear as a way of marketing the value of firearms. It is also worth noting that in the speech no reference was made to domestic abusers or oneself who represent the main danger to most people, particularly when a firearm is present.

In addition to stoking the fear of being attacked and helpless without a firearm to protect yourself, the NRA are also champions in promoting the fear that very soon your right to purchase or own a firearm will be removed. Shortly after President Obama's re-election in 2012, Wayne LaPierre explained, "No wonder Americans are buying guns in record numbers right now, while they still can and before their choice about which firearm is right for their family is taken away forever." In the same piece, he described the NRA as "the indispensable shield against the destruction of our nation's Second Amendment rights" and "the only chance gun owners have to withstand the coming siege."[ccxl] The use of the word siege is a blatant example of Fearmongering.

The NRA and gun manufacturers have learned that nothing sells guns like fear. In the aftermath of mass shootings, worries that this may lead to gun restrictions often lead to sharp increases in handgun purchases. Sure enough, gun stocks rose on Wall Street in the days immediately following America's deadliest mass shooting at Las Vegas in October 2017.[ccxli] Sad to say that no improved gun safety measures were introduced following this deadly and tragic incident and that the only impact appears to have been an increase in gun sales. Clearly fearmongering is a significant obstacle.

An extreme example of firearm-related fearmongering is when a parallel is drawn with Nazi Germany. A claim frequently made by Gun-rights advocates is that Gun-control laws enabled the rise of the Nazis and led to the extermination of 6 million Jews in the Holocaust. The claim being that German citizens were disarmed by their government in the late 1930s, which allowed the Nazis to "carry out their evil intentions with relatively little resistance." This is misleading as although Jews were subject to having their weapons seized, the Nazi period was one in which gun regulations were loosened, not tightened. The reason the Nazis were able to carry out their atrocities was due to significant popular support and not lack of guns in the hands of citizens. This claim was rated as False by PolitiFact.[ccxlii] Regardless of the accuracy of this claim, it puts fear into the minds of people who may believe a nasty chain of events starting with a modest gun safety regulation leading eventually to the government committing genocide on some of its citizens. This is clearly fearmongering in the extreme.

Fearmongering can be effective in 2 ways. Firstly, and in the way intended it motivates those who support gun-rights. It scares them into buying firearms for both protection and to buy them whilst they can, since those nasty gun-control people may take away your right to bear arms. There is also an indirect way in which fearmongering can be effective and that is on how it can influence those who support gun safety to keep quiet. This can best be illustrated by using a hypothetical example as outlined below:

Scenario 1 - Following a high-profile mass shooting where the perpetrator was able to kill and injure many victims using a semi-automatic rifle, gun-control advocates campaigned hard to enforce a ban on all semi-automatic weapons. This led to gun-rights advocates using fearmongering to suggest that soon all weapon sales will be banned. The result being a significant increase in gun sales, particularly semi-automatic weapons and no new gun safety regulations being passed.

Scenario 2 – Following this mass shooting gun-control advocates realize nothing ever gets done and keep quiet. The result is no new gun safety regulations being passed but no significant increase in gun sales.

It is important for gun safety advocates not to fall into the trap of believing the best thing to do, is to do nothing. The United States has a massive gun problem that will not be resolved by doing nothing. Gun safety advocates must have the resolve to keep a high profile and not give up in their quest to reduce the number of firearm victims. There are many ways in which this can be done as will be reviewed in Step 5 of the book.

# 26. Money

The biggest obstacle facing those who would like to see the introduction of sensible gun reform aimed at reducing firearm fatalities can be summed up by one word and that is "Money". Money talks and money has an enormous influence on American policy decisions. As discussed in Chapter 11 The National Shooting Sports Foundation (NSSF) has published figures showing that the total economic impact of the firearms and ammunition industry in the United States was a staggering $51.4 billion in 2017.[ccxliii]

With such huge amounts of money supporting the firearm industry, it is not surprising that the industry and its advocates have been so successful in encouraging relatively unrestricted gun ownership. Money flows from the gun manufacturers to their advocacy groups such as the NRA and from there it flows to politicians who then under the influence of the firearm industries money and lobbying vote down any regulation the firearm industry does not like. Additionally, the firearm industry uses its money on effective marketing to portray the image that guns are cool and save lives. This marketing combined with a strong gun culture in the United States encourages Americans to purchase ever-increasing numbers of firearms. Add to the mix the fearmongering that one day you will not be able to purchase guns and it is unsurprising that nearly half of all worldwide civilian firearms are held by Americans.

The gun industry understands the importance of the NRA in promoting the supposed benefits of gun ownership and funds the NRA in several ways as detailed below based on an article published in January 2013 by Business Insider[ccxliv].

Firstly, between 2005 and 2012, the gun industry and its corporate allies gave between $20 million and $52.6 million to the NRA through the NRA Ring of Freedom sponsor program. Donors included firearm companies like Midway USA, Springfield Armory

Inc, Pierce Bullet Seal Target Systems, and Beretta USA Corporation. Other supporters from the gun industry included Cabala's, Sturm Rugar & Co, and Smith & Wesson.

Secondly, The NRA made $20.9 million in 2010 from selling advertising to industry companies marketing products in its many publications, according to the IRS Form 990.

Thirdly, some companies donate portions of sales directly to the NRA. Crimson Trace, which makes laser sights, donates 10 percent of each sale to the NRA. Taurus buys an NRA membership for everyone who buys one of their guns. Sturm Rugar gives $1 to the NRA for each gun sold, which amounts to millions. The NRA's revenues are intrinsically linked to the success of the gun business.

Finally, the NRA Foundation also collects hundreds of thousands of dollars from the industry, which it then gives to local-level organizations for training and equipment purchases. "Today's NRA is a virtual subsidiary of the gun industry," said Josh Sugarmann, executive director of the Violence Policy Center. "While the NRA portrays itself as protecting the 'freedom' of individual gun owners, it's actually working to protect the freedom of the gun industry to manufacture and sell virtually any weapon or accessory."

Clearly with the amount of funds flowing into the NRA and other Gun-rights advocacy groups it is difficult for Gun-control advocacy groups to compete. That said there are several Gun-control Groups who are valiantly trying to do something about curtailing the horrendous death toll and injuries attributed to gun violence in the United States. This includes the following groups:

Brady United Against Gun Violence [ccxlv] – Founded in 1974, Brady United Against Gun Violence is named after James "Jim" Brady who was permanently disabled as a result of the Ronald Reagan assassination attempt in 1981 and Jim's wife Sarah Brady, a leading advocate for gun control. The organization incorporates Brady's Comprehensive Plan to prevent gun violence which includes initiatives such as expanding background checks, restricting the categories of persons prohibited from purchasing guns, and restricting access to assault weapons and high-capacity magazines.

Giffords Law Center to Prevent Gun Violence [ccxlvi] – The Giffords Law Center (originally named Americans for Responsible Solutions) was formed in 2012 by Gabby Giffords and her husband Mark Kelly. Gabby having recovered from being seriously injured in a 2011 mass shooting which had killed 6 people in Arizona. The organization provides legal assistance to elected officials, government attorneys, and activists in the United States to promote gun-control and to oppose gun violence. Each year the Giffords Law Center publishes an Annual Gun Law Scorecard which grades states based on the strength of their gun laws and this provides clear evidence demonstrating that gun laws save lives in the states with the courage to enact them.

Coalition to Stop Gun Violence (CSGV)[ccxlvii] – Formed in 1974 the CSGV and its sister organization the Educational Fund to Stop Gun Violence (EFSGV), are two parts of a national, non-profit gun-control advocacy organization whose mission is to advocate for evidence-based solutions to reduce gun injury and death in all its forms from suicide to intimate partner homicide. CSGV is dedicated to taking on the NRA and what they describe as their toxic agenda.

Violence Policy Center (VPC) [ccxlviii] – The VPC is an American nonprofit organization that advocates for gun control. Using data from federal agencies such as the Federal Bureau of Investigation and the Centers for Disease Control and Prevention, the VPC publishes annual state-by-state reports on the effects of gun violence.

Everytown For Gun Safety [ccxlix] – Everytown for Gun Safety is an American nonprofit organization that was founded by Michael Bloomberg in 2013, combining 'Mayors Against Illegal Guns' and 'Moms Demand Action for Gun Sense in America'. Their aim is to end gun violence and build safer communities in every town in America. Nearly 6 million mayors, moms, cops, teachers, survivors, gun owners, students, and everyday Americans have come together to make their communities safer by fighting for the changes to gun policies they know will save lives.

These Gun-control advocacy groups are doing an excellent job of informing people of the dangers of guns and the need for promoting policies that will reduce the number of firearm fatalities and injuries. Unfortunately, the money available to these groups is dwarfed by the money available to the Firearm industry and its associates. In 2016 NRA revenue was $433.9m and expenditure was $475.9m.[ccl] In comparison, Everytown for Gun Safety had revenue of $35.7m and expenditure of $32.6m in 2017[ccli].

There is no way in which Gun-control groups can compete with Gun-rights groups in terms of money for the simple reason that if you support a major industry you will get financed by that industry, but if you oppose a major industry financing must come from individual members or philanthropists. The sale of a firearm leads to revenue which is then used to produce more firearms, market firearms, and influence politicians to be friendly to the firearm industry. On the flip side, there is no money generated from preventing the sale of a firearm.

Money is used to influence the public by for example the NRA airing commercials to help promote gun ownership and elect gun-friendly politicians, or gun manufacturers marketing impressive looking firearms. The effectiveness of the money spent by the firearm industry and its advocates is however limited by the underlying message i.e. the adverse impact caused by the abundance of firearms and lack of restrictions on sales and ownership.

So, if the firearm industry has the advantage of money, gun safety advocates have the advantage of having a poignant message to portray that is backed up by empirical evidence. This message is that firearms are dangerous and that more guns lead to more fatalities and injuries.

Whilst on the subject of money researchers from Johns Hopkins University have published an article quantifying the financial burden of gun violence in the United States and concluded that the annual cost of gun violence is approximately $2.8 billion in emergency-room and inpatient charges alone. If lost wages are factored in, the financial burden rises to $45 billion each year.[cclii]

In this section of the book, we have seen that many obstacles are standing in the way of changing the gun culture and restricting easy access to firearms in the United States. These are however not insurmountable and in Step 5 of the book, we will examine the many ways in which the gun problem in the United States can be resolved, enabling many thousands of lives to be saved in the process.

# STEP 5

# The Way Forward

# 27. Preventing Illegal Possession

Evidence suggests that the vast majority of firearm crimes are committed by those who illegally possess the gun involved. Consequently, gun-rights advocacy supporters frequently claim there is no point in putting further restrictions on gun ownership since criminals will not follow the law and all you are doing is penalizing law-abiding gun owners. This is a very defeatist attitude implying that since it is difficult stopping criminals from obtaining firearms why even bother to try and stop them. As we shall see later in this chapter there are several ways in which it can be made more difficult for criminals to obtain firearms. Additionally, we will review the broader concept of illegal possession which is not just confined to criminals.

So just how many firearm crimes involve illegal possession? The only federal data available was tracked in 2004 when the U.S. Bureau of Justice Statistics surveyed inmates in federal and state prisons, asking those who had a gun during their crime where they originally obtained it. About 48 percent of state prison inmates surveyed said they got their gun from a family member, friend, gun store, pawnshop, flea market, or gun show. Some of these 48% would be legal and some would be illegal depending precisely on how the gun was obtained and their criminal status at the time of possession. Forty percent of state prison inmates admitted they obtained the gun illegally on the black market, from a drug dealer, or by stealing it. This would leave just 12% purchased through licensed gun stores which would require some form of background check.[ccliii]

Regional studies also tend to find a high share of criminals who did not legally possess a gun when they committed their crimes. For example, researchers at the University of Pittsburgh teamed up with the Pittsburgh Police Department in 2016 to look at almost 900 firearms recovered from crime scenes in 2008. They found the criminals did not legally possess their guns in 80 percent of the cases [ccliv].
The Pittsburgh study also found that more than 30 percent of the

guns that ended up at crime scenes had been stolen and that more than 40 percent of those stolen guns weren't reported by the owners as stolen until after police contacted them when the gun was used in a crime. One of the more concerning findings in the study was that with 62% of guns recovered, the place where the owner lost possession of the firearm was unknown.[cclv]

Based on inmate surveys it would appear that gang members, violent criminals, underage youths, and other dangerous people usually get their guns from an acquaintance or family member. They get these guns in many ways including purchasing, swapping, borrowing, sharing, or stealing them. Social networks also play an important role in facilitating firearm transactions and gang members who hang out with people who have guns will find it relatively easy to obtain a gun. Effective policing of the underground gun market would help to separate guns from everyday violent crime, but currently, it is rare for those who provide guns to offenders to face any legal consequences.[cclvi]

Although determined criminals will always be able to get their hands on a gun, it would make sense to make gun owners more responsible for not allowing guns to get into the wrong hands. The Giffords Law Center has published a helpful website summarizing the laws surrounding the reporting of lost or stolen firearms[cclvii]. Surprisingly, federal law does not require individual gun owners to report the loss or theft of a firearm to law enforcement, even though the public overwhelmingly supports laws requiring the reporting of lost or stolen firearms. A nationwide poll in 2011 found that 94% of registered voters supported laws to require the reporting of lost or stolen firearms[cclviii]. At the time of writing, just nine states and the District of Columbia require firearm owners to report the loss or theft of any firearms to law enforcement.

Researchers have estimated that more than half a million firearms are lost or stolen from private residences in a single year, but according to the Bureau of Alcohol, Tobacco, Firearms and Explosives (ATF) data, private individuals only reported the loss or theft of 173,000 guns nationwide in 2012. This discrepancy suggests that the majority of lost or stolen firearms are never reported to law enforcement. Laws requiring the reporting of lost or stolen firearms are useful to law enforcement for several reasons.

Firstly, when a crime gun is traced by law enforcement to the last purchaser of record, the person who purchased the gun may often claim that the weapon was lost or stolen to hide his or her involvement in the crime or in intentionally trafficking the gun to a prohibited person. Reporting laws provide an important tool for law enforcement to detect this behavior and charge criminals who engage in it. Additionally, individuals who repeatedly report their guns lost or stolen also put law enforcement on notice that they may be trafficking firearms on the black market.

Secondly, reporting laws help to disarm prohibited persons. When a person who legally owned a gun falls into a prohibited category, such as after a serious criminal conviction or domestic violence restraining order, it is crucial that law enforcement remove the firearm from his or her possession. However, when required to relinquish firearms, a prohibited offender or abuser may falsely claim that his or her gun was previously lost or stolen. Mandatory reporting laws provide a check against this behavior.

Thirdly, the reporting requirement helps law enforcement track down missing guns and return them to lawful owners before they fall into dangerous hands.

Finally, reporting laws make gun owners more accountable for their weapons and help protect rightful gun owners from unwarranted criminal accusations when a gun that was lost or stolen from them is later recovered at a crime scene.

Where enacted, these laws have been shown to correlate with significant reductions in illegal gun trafficking. One study found that, per capita, states without lost or stolen reporting laws are the source of more than 2.5 times as many crime gun recoveries compared to states with a lost or stolen reporting requirement.[cclix]

Giffords Law Center has identified "Gun Trafficking" as the main way in which guns end up being held illegally, with "Gun

Trafficking" being defined as the diversion of guns from lawful commerce into the illegal market. Studies of gun trafficking have identified the following major channels of trafficked guns:

Corrupt gun dealers - ATF data confirms that corrupt or irresponsible gun dealers are the leading source of guns on the black market, responsible for nearly half of the total number of trafficked firearms, uncovered in ATF investigations. Gun dealers' access to large numbers of firearms makes them a particular threat to public safety when they fail to comply with the law. On average, ATF trafficking investigations implicating a gun dealer involve over 350 black market guns per investigation. Strong dealer regulations, such as laws requiring licensing, inspections, employee background checks, and videotaping of gun purchases, can prevent this conduct.

Unlicensed Sellers - Federal law allows people who are not licensed gun dealers to sell guns at gun shows, online, and in person. These unlicensed private sellers are not required to conduct background checks or maintain records of purchasers. As a result, they play a significant role in gun trafficking.

Lost or Stolen Guns - Gun traffickers often falsely claim that guns they purchased were lost or stolen to hide their involvement in crime. Laws that require the reporting of lost or stolen firearms to law enforcement can provide a check against this behavior.

Bulk Firearm Sales - Gun traffickers often buy large quantities of guns at once in order to supply them to convicted felons and other prohibited persons. A 2007 University of Pennsylvania report to the National Institute of Justice found that guns purchased in bulk were up to 64% more likely to be used for illegal purposes than guns purchased individually. Laws limiting the number of guns that may be purchased in a single transaction help deter this conduct.

Straw Purchases - A "straw purchase" occurs when the actual buyer of a firearm uses another person, a "straw purchaser," to execute the paperwork necessary to purchase a firearm from a firearms dealer. People who are prohibited from purchasing firearms and people who do not want to be identified through crime gun tracing often obtain firearms through straw purchases. By intentionally buying firearms for someone else, straw purchasers undermine background checks and gun safety laws and allow firearms to be funneled to violent criminals, domestic abusers, and other prohibited people. In 2000, an ATF study of 1,530-gun trafficking cases determined that straw purchasers were involved in almost one-half (46%) of the investigations, and were associated with nearly 26,000 illegally trafficked firearms. Subsequent ATF investigations at gun shows also uncovered "widespread" straw purchasing from gun dealers, where guns were diverted to "convicted felons and local and international gangs. In 2009, New York City officials investigated gun shows across the US to test whether, among other things, gun dealers would be willing to sell guns to someone who appeared to be a straw purchaser. New York's investigation found that 16 out of 17 (or 94% of) dealers approached by investigators willingly sold to an apparent straw purchaser.[cclx]

The fact that over 90% of gun dealers are happy to sell to probable straw purchasers illustrates how profit takes precedence over safety. The dealer knows he will not be held liable for any crime committed by the eventual user of the gun and the dealer's livelihood is selling guns, not worrying about whether the gun will ever be used in a crime, or if the gun will be used to injure or kill someone.

Although the focus of this chapter has been on criminal activity, it must be noted that illegal possession also covers underage possession of firearms and those who have mental disabilities which makes it unsafe for them to possess firearms. Underage possession covers both firearms illegally transferred or sold to underage teenagers, who may want to commit crimes and younger children who get hold of guns in their family environment. With regards to younger children, parents need to be made more aware of the dangers of not storing firearms securely, since as we saw in Chapter 3 firearm accidents involving children can frequently have tragic consequences.

Concerning mental illness, current federal laws on preventing those with mental disabilities from accessing firearms are relatively weak. Under federal law, a person can be tallied in a database and barred from purchasing or possessing a firearm due to a mental illness under two conditions only; Firstly if he is involuntarily committed to a mental hospital, or if a court or government body declares him mentally incompetent.[cclxi] This however excludes the majority of mentally ill people, such as those voluntarily requesting to attend a mental hospital, those being looked after by family members, or those who have not been reviewed by a court or government body.

Attempts have been made to broaden the categories of mentally disabled people who would be prevented from possessing firearms under federal law. These were however overturned in 2017 when President Trump signed a measure that removed a regulation aimed at keeping guns out of the hands of people who were either receiving full disability benefits because of mental illness and couldn't work, or people who were unable to manage their own Social Security benefits and needed the help of third parties. The failure to introduce these additional regulations is a typical example of freedom under 2nd Amendment rights being considered to be more important than safety to both the general population and in particular the safety of those mentally disabled people wanting guns. Suicide is a huge risk for those with mental illness and recent studies have found that individuals with learning disabilities were significantly more likely to attempt suicide than those without.[cclxii] Giving these mentally disabled people easy access to firearms dramatically increases the chances that they will successfully commit suicide and is truly not in the best interest of the individuals concerned.

Finally, it should be noted that although the majority of firearm crimes are committed by those who illegally possess the gun involved, the majority of shooting victims are shot by legally held weapons. This will certainly be the case for most suicides and accidents but it also applies to homicide victims. Additionally, a study of mass shootings in the United States between 1982 and February 2020 found that legally obtained weapons were used in 82 out of 117 mass shootings.[cclxiii]. These findings highlight that in addition to preventing illegal ownership, gun safety policies need also to focus on tightening restrictions on legal ownership.

# 28. Lessons to Learn from Cars and Tobacco

There has been much success over the last several decades in reducing both motor vehicle fatalities and smoking-related deaths. Motor vehicle fatalities have been significantly reduced due to improved safety features such as seat belts and laws such as speed limits, and smoking-related deaths have been reduced due to changing public opinion on the sociability and dangers of smoking, which in turn has led to a significant reduction in the number of people who smoke. Both gun-rights and gun-safety advocates have a lot to learn from how safety features have reduced motor vehicle fatalities and how fewer people smoking is reducing tobacco-related deaths. We will commence by comparing firearm-related deaths with motor vehicle-related deaths.

In 1981 there were 49,301 motor vehicle fatalities and 34,050 firearm fatalities in the United States, which compares to 36,560 motor vehicle fatalities and 39,740 firearm fatalities in 2018. This represents a 27% reduction in motor vehicle fatalities and an 18% increase in firearm fatalities over this 37-year timespan.[cclxiv][cclxv] The success in reducing the number of motor vehicle fatalities is all the more remarkable when considering the dramatic increase in both the number of cars on the road and vehicle miles travelled. Indeed, the fatalities per 100 million vehicle miles travelled (VMT) fell from 3.17 in 1981 to 1.13 in 2018. Going back further in time it should be noted that the motor vehicle fatalities per 100 million VMT was over 10 until 1945[cclxvi]. There are many factors behind the declining rate in motor vehicle fatalities per mile driven, which include the following:

- Mandatory driving tests
- Installation of seat belts
- Laws requiring the compulsory wearing of front seat belts
- Laws requiring the compulsory wearing of rear seat belts

- Speed limits
- Driving under influence laws
- Public attitude to drinking and driving
- Distracted driving laws
- Child safety and booster seats
- Airbags
- Other car safety features e.g. Anti-lock braking system (ABS)
- Marketing the safety features of cars

Many of the above factors involve a tradeoff between freedom and safety, and in general public opinion and regulations have sided on the side of safety. This is without a doubt a good thing which has saved countless lives over the years, many of them being children. Using a base figure of 10 fatalities per 100 million VMT which was prevalent during the 1940's we can estimate the number of fatalities there would have been in 2018, if the fatalities per 100 million VMT rate had remained at 10, as opposed to falling to 1.13. In 2018 total VMT was 3,240 billion[cclxvii], which would have resulted in a staggering 324,000 motor vehicle fatalities in 2018 alone if fatalities per VMT had remained constant. As noted above actual motor vehicle fatalities were 36,560 in 2018, i.e. 287,440 less than they would have been if sensible safety features and laws had not been introduced with the specific aim of reducing motor vehicle fatalities and injuries.

It is also good to see that the emphasis on safety continues and in May 2018 a new law came into force requiring all new cars to be fitted with a "backup camera". This is a camera that shows what is behind you when reversing and according to the federal government's National Highway Traffic Safety Administration (NHTSA), backup cameras will go a long way toward preventing injury and death, especially among children. Roughly 200 people are killed each year and another 14,000 are injured in so-called backover accidents when drivers reverse over another person without noticing him or her. The vast majority of the victims are children, largely because their small size makes them harder to see from the driver's seat.[cclxviii]

In addition to the numerous safety features and laws designed to reduce motor vehicle fatalities, there is also much more regulation in the motor vehicle industry than in the firearm industry. All vehicle purchases and sales have to be registered and every vehicle must have a certificate of ownership showing the name and address of the registered owner. All drivers must pass a driving test and all owners must ensure they have adequate insurance. To ensure motor vehicles are roadworthy many States require cars to pass a Vehicle Inspection test.

The message which gun safety advocates need to stress is how motor vehicle safety features and sensible laws prioritizing safety over freedom have been successful in saving countless lives over the years. There is also much to be learnt about terminology, in that the seat belt designed to reduce the chance of injury or death in the event of an accident is frequently referred to as a safety belt and not a control, or restraining belt. The emphasis must always be on safety and not control. Additionally, it must be stressed that the introduction of car safety features and laws such as speed limits have not led to the collapse of the motor vehicle industry or any suggestion that your car is going to be taken away.

It should be pointed out that the argument gun-rights advocates frequently state that "cars kill more people than guns, but nobody's suggesting banning cars" is no longer just irrelevant, it is now statistically incorrect. The argument is irrelevant firstly because no one is suggesting banning guns and secondly, cars are vital to a country's economy and guns are not, so it is a ridiculous comparison. The argument is now also statistically incorrect as since 2013 there have been more firearm fatalities than motor vehicle fatalities.[cclxix cclxx]

The final point to make with regards to comparing the decline in motor vehicle fatalities to the increase in firearm fatalities since 1981 is that in the motor vehicle industry there has been both an acceptance of new regulations and also a desire to actively promote and market safety features. In contrast, within the firearm industry, there is a continuing reluctance to make any changes that would improve safety and even a ban on research that would assist in this matter. The challenge for gun safety advocates is to demonstrate the success the motor vehicle industry has had in reducing fatalities and injuries and to explain to gun-rights advocates that they too should be promoting policies that reduce firearm fatalities. After all, it is in everyone's interest to reduce firearm homicides, suicides & accidents i.e. there is a common goal.

Turning now to the tobacco industry it should be noted that unlike the car industry, little progress has been made in reducing the dangers of smoking, with the only attempt to make cigarettes somewhat less harmful being the cigarette filter which was introduced in the 1960s. The reasons for the lack of action in the tobacco industry are similar to those in the firearm industry. Money. as the saying goes is the root of all evil and since the tobacco industry makes huge amounts of money from selling cigarettes and other tobacco-related products, they can spend large amounts of money on political lobbying promoting their industry, to ensure there are not too many restrictions on the sale of tobacco products.

Despite the political lobbying on behalf of the tobacco industry, smoking-related deaths although still extremely high are declining, due largely to a significant decrease in the number of American citizens who actively smoke. A Gallup poll conducted in July 2018 found that 16% of U.S. adults smoked a cigarette in the past week. This was the lowest level on record since Gallup first asked this question in 1944. In 1944, 41% of U.S. adults said they smoked and this figure held steady for the several decades, even after the federal government warned the public in the early 1960s that smoking was a health threat. At the start of the 1970s, four in 10 Americans still reported smoking, but by 1977, the rate had fallen to 36%. Twelve years later, in 1989, the smoking rate fell below the 30% mark for the first time. In the late 2000s, smoking levels began to slowly drop again, when many cities and states started passing public smoking bans.[cclxxi]

Estimating the number of deaths related to tobacco use is difficult but the Centers for Disease Control and Prevention (CDC) estimate that there are more than 480,000 smoking-related deaths annually (this includes deaths from secondhand smoking). The CDC also noted that life expectancy for smokers is at least 10 years shorter than for nonsmokers.[cclxxii] Tracking the reduction in death rates arising from a fall in the number of smokers is difficult because of the large time lag but a good estimate can be found by examining the rate of cancer mortality. Figures from the American Cancer Society show that the death rate from cancer in the US has declined steadily over the past 2 decades. As of 2015, the cancer death rate for men and women combined had fallen 26% from its peak in 1991. This decline translates to nearly 2.4 million deaths averted during this period and a decline in consumption of cigarettes is credited with being the most important factor in the drop of cancer death rates. Lung cancer death rates declined 45% from 1990 to 2015 among men and 19% from 2002 to 2015 among women. From 2005 to 2014, the rates of new lung cancer cases dropped by 2.5% per year in men and 1.2% per year in women. The differences reflect historical patterns in tobacco use, where women began smoking in large numbers many years later than men and were slower to quit.[cclxxiii]

The above analysis demonstrates that the fall in the number of smokers is the major factor behind the fall in cancer death rates, but why has the number of smokers fallen from 41% of the adult population to 16%? The answer is that there has been a change in the public attitude with regards to smoking over recent years. In the 1960's thanks to effective marketing from the tobacco industry, smoking was considered to be sophisticated and desirable. Even following all the scientific evidence on the dangers of smoking, cigarettes remained popular. It was probably the discovery regarding the dangers of secondary smoking that accelerated the reduction in smoking. This encouraged parents to stop smoking to protect the health of their children. Additionally, it encouraged the banning of smoking in public places. Eventually, a tipping point was reached in which smoking was generally considered to be both unsocial and undesirable.

Whilst the success in reducing motor vehicle fatalities is based on improved safety features and laws designed to protect drivers, passengers, and pedestrians; the success of reducing smoking tobacco-related deaths is due to changing public attitudes towards smoking. The next challenge is to transfer the lessons learnt from the car and tobacco industries i.e. increased emphasis on safety and a change in public opinion and incorporate them into a gun safety strategy.

The reluctance of the firearm industry and their lobbyists to introduce laws and safety features to reduce firearm fatalities makes the requirement to change public opinion on guns all the more important. This leads us neatly into the next chapter, in which we will examine public attitudes towards gun-rights and gun-control (safety) and investigate ways in which the pendulum can be moved towards greater support for gun safety.

# 29. Building on Public Opinion

According to a September 2018 Pew Research poll, 52% of respondents stated that they believe it is more important to control gun ownership than to protect the right of Americans to own guns. This compares to 44% of respondents stating that the right to own guns is more important than to control ownership. From around 2010 similar Pew polls have indicated that there is a relatively even split between those supporting control and those supporting the right to bear arms.[cclxxiv] These polls may however underestimate those who would wish to see safety issues take priority over relatively unrestricted rights to own guns because the words "controlling gun ownership" are used in the polling question and as we have previously reviewed, the very word "Control" has negative connotations. Indeed, both Gallup and Politico morning Consult polls show more support for stricter laws surrounding firearms.

Gallup polls use the following more neutral terminology in their polling question "In general, do you feel that the laws covering the sale of firearms should be made more strict, less strict or kept as they are now?" This seems a very fair way to frame the question and should give a good indication of the general public attitude towards gun policy in America. The good news for those promoting gun safety is that in the Gallup poll conducted in October 2018, 61% of respondents favored stricter laws, with 30% wanting laws left unchanged and 8% favoring less strict laws.[cclxxv] Support for stricter laws fell steadily from 2000 to October 2011 when just 43% of respondents favored stricter laws. In December 2012 those supporting stricter laws rose to 58%. This rise from 2011 was almost certainly in response to the December 2012 Sandy Hook school mass shooting. In the aftermath of a significant mass shooting public support for stricter gun laws spikes and then falls again until the next major mass shooting. Following the Parkland mass shooting in February 2018, the March 2018 Gallup poll found that support for stricter laws rose to 67%, the highest level since 1993.[cclxxvi]

The bad news for those promoting gun safety is that public support for stricter gun laws has been higher in the past particularly in the 1990s and little was done then to resolve America's gun problem. Also, the October 2018 Gallup poll represents a 6% fall in those wanting stricter laws from March 2018. This demonstrates that the impact of mass shootings on public opinion is short-lived. Nevertheless, these polls do suggest there is a public appetite for stricter laws surrounding guns.

A Politico/Morning Consult poll conducted in February 2018 found that support for stricter gun laws among registered voters was 68 percent, compared with just 25 percent who opposed stricter gun laws. This poll was conducted after the Parkland Florida shooting and as noted support for gun-control does tick up in the aftermath of mass shootings, but the percentage of Americans who want more restrictive gun laws is greater now than after any other recent shooting. Morning Consult polling goes back only two years, but support for stricter gun laws was at 58 percent following the 2016 Pulse nightclub shooting that killed 49 people, 64 percent following the 2017 mass shooting that resulted in 58 deaths at a country-music festival in Las Vegas and 60 percent in November 2017, after a shooter killed 26 people inside a church in Sutherland Springs, Texas.[cclxxvii]

When it comes to specific questions relating to gun policies, public support for policies designed to help reduce firearm fatalities and injuries are overwhelmingly popular, as can be seen from the following responses to the question do you support or oppose:[cclxxviii]

- Preventing sales of all firearms to people who have been reported as dangerous to law enforcement by a mental-health provider – Support 89%   Oppose 5%
- Requiring background checks on all gun sales – Support 88% Oppose 6%
- Preventing sales of all firearms to people who have been convicted of violent misdemeanors – Support 84%   Oppose 9%

- Making private gun sales and sales at gun shows subject to background checks – Support 82%   Oppose 10%
- Barring gun purchases by people on the federal no-fly or watch lists – Support 81%   Oppose 10%
- Requiring a person to be 21 in order to purchase a gun – Support 81%   Oppose 13%
- Creating a national database with information about each gun sale – Support 78% Oppose 16%
- Requiring a mandatory waiting period of three days after a gun is purchased before it can be taken home – Support 78% Oppose 14%
- Banning the use of bump stocks, which are gun accessories that allow a shooter to fire hundreds of rounds per minute – Support 77%   Oppose 14%
- Requiring that all gun owners store their guns in a safe storage unit - Support 76% Oppose 16%
- Banning high-capacity magazines – Support 70%   Oppose 20%
- Banning assault-style weapons – Support 68%   Oppose 25%

The public support for all these sensible suggestions is very encouraging but appears to be having little effect on influencing politicians to enact any of these proposals (except for a law banning bump stocks which was passed in March 2019)[cclxxix]. Part of the problem lies in the fact that there is extreme partisanship in American politics which leads to Republicans and Democrats having widely diverging views on gun policy. For example, the response to the Gallup question "In general, do you feel that the laws covering the sale of firearms should be made more strict, less strict or kept as they are now? By political affiliation was as follows:[cclxxx]

| Gun Laws | Republicans | Independents | Democrats | Total |
|---|---|---|---|---|
| More strict | 31% | 61% | 87% | 61% |
| Kept as they are | 55% | 28% | 10% | 30% |
| Less strict | 13% | 7% | 3% | 8% |

It is not surprising therefore that Republican politicians are reluctant to introduce stricter gun laws. In addition to getting financial support from gun lobbyists such as the NRA to protect gun-rights, the Republican base itself is reluctant to make laws stricter. Partisanship is clearly an obstacle to enable sensible new gun laws to be enacted. Additionally, gun enthusiasts feel passionately about protecting gun-rights, whilst those in favor of stricter gun laws, unless they have been directly impacted by gun violence, are less likely to feel so strongly on this matter.

Gun safety advocates should, however, take heart from both the general and specific polls on gun policy, and then determine the best way forward, to both make use of the existing high levels of public support and also to build on these levels of public support, to enact sensible new laws which will help to reduce the number of firearm-related injuries and fatalities? This can be done in three ways, the first two taking advantage of current levels of public support and the third way demonstrating how public opinion can be influenced to provide even greater support

Firstly, politicians who are in favor of stricter gun laws should feel empowered by the strong support there is for a wide range of specific gun safety policies and should not be shy in making gun safety an important and well-publicized policy objective.

Secondly, gun safety policies that have universal support amongst Democrats, Independents & Republican voters should be prioritized. The February 2018 Politico/Morning Consult poll on gun-control breaks down the results by political affiliation and therefore provides a good indication as to which policies have universal support across Democratic, Republican, and Independent voters. The following proposed policies, ordered by Republican support, are all approved by over 50% of Democratic, Republican, and Independent voters.

Do you support or oppose each of the following?

- Preventing sales of all firearms to people who have been reported as dangerous to law enforcement by a mental health provider?
    o Democrat        92%
    o Independent    84%
    o Republican     90%

- Requiring background checks on all gun sales?
    o Democrat        92%
    o Independent    83%
    o Republican     88%

- Preventing sales of all firearms to people who have been convicted of violent misdemeanors?
    o Democrat        87%
    o Independent    77%
    o Republican     87%

- Barring gun purchases by people on the federal no-fly or watchlists?
    o Democrat        85%
    o Independent    76%
    o Republican     82%

- Making private gun sales and sales at gun shows subject to background checks?
    o Democrat        87%
    o Independent    78%
    o Republican     81%

- Requiring a person to be 21 in order to purchase a gun?
    o Democrat        88%
    o Independent    76%
    o Republican     79%

- Banning the use of bump fire stocks, which is a gun accessory that allows a shooter to fire hundreds of rounds per minute?

- o Democrat 86%
  - o Independent 69%
  - o Republican 76%

- Requiring a mandatory waiting period of three days after a gun is purchased before it can be taken home?
  - o Democrat 87%
  - o Independent 72%
  - o Republican 75%

- Requiring that all gun owners store their guns in a safe storage unit?
  - o Democrat 84%
  - o Independent 71%
  - o Republican 73%

- Creating a national database with information about each gun sale?
  - o Democrat 88%
  - o Independent 74%
  - o Republican 71%

- Banning high-capacity ammunition magazines?
  - o Democrat 87%
  - o Independent 65%
  - o Republican 60%

- Limiting the number of guns that can be purchased to one per month?
  - o Democrat 78%
  - o Independent 58%
  - o Republican 60%

- Banning assault-style weapons?
  - o Democrat 87%
  - o Independent 61%
  - o Republican 53%

- Limiting the amount of ammunition, you can purchase within a given period?
    - o Democrat      85%
    - o Independent   61%
    - o Republican    52%

A good starting point for reducing gun fatalities in the United States would be to focus on the 1st 5 proposals listed above which are namely:

- Preventing sales of all firearms to people who have been reported as dangerous to law enforcement by a mental health provider
- Requiring background checks on all gun sales
- Preventing sales of all firearms to people who have been convicted of violent misdemeanors
- Barring gun purchases by people on the federal no-fly or watchlists
- Making private gun sales and sales at gun shows subject to background checks

The above policies are all supported by over 80% of Republicans and fall into 2 categories which work together hand in hand, namely preventing sales to those deemed to be most likely to be dangerous and ensuring all sales have background checks which would identify those who should not be allowed to possess a firearm. There can be no excuse for not enforcing the above policies which have near-universal support amongst voters of all political persuasion.

There does appear to be a dichotomy between public opinion on specific sensible gun safety policies and public opinion on gun policy as a whole, which is encapsulated by the following February 2018 Politico/Morning Consult polling question:

Generally, if Congress passes legislation placing additional regulations on gun ownership, which of the following is more likely to happen?[cclxxxi]

Gun violence will decrease by making it more difficult for criminals and persons with mental health issues to access guns, or Gun violence will increase by making it more difficult for people to defend themselves against criminals and persons with mental health issues?

| Party affiliation | Gun violence will decrease | Gun violence will increase |
| --- | --- | --- |
| Democrat | 66% | 14% |
| Independent | 38% | 34% |
| Republican | 29% | 45% |
| Overall | 44% | 31% |

As long as Independent voters are roughly evenly split and Republican voters believe restricting gun ownership is more likely to increase gun violence than reduce it, there will be a continual block to enacting sensible gun safety regulations, even though most individual gun safety proposals are universally supported by Democrats, Independents, and Republicans.

Public opinion is on the side of gun safety advocates, but it just needs to reach a critical mass which will force politicians to support gun safety policies or face the consequences. This leads us to the third and perhaps the most important way in which gun safety advocates can use public support to enable the introduction of sensible new laws which will help to reduce the number of firearm-related injuries and fatalities and that is namely educating the public on the dangers of firearms.

Gun safety advocates and politicians who support gun safety need to repeatedly publicize the dangers of firearms and the dreadful impact they have on so many lives. There are a lot of simple messages on the danger of firearms which need to be portrayed to the public, of which the following are just a few examples:

- The United States' intentional homicide rate of 5.3 per 100,000 residents is over 6 times greater than the average of the other 19 countries, which make up the 20 most highly developed countries in the world. This, as the next bullet point indicates, is entirely due to firearm homicides.[cclxxxii]

- The United States' intentional firearm homicide rate of 4.46 per 100,000 residents[cclxxxiii] is over 25 times greater than the average of the other 19 countries, which make up the 20 most highly developed countries in the world. The reason for this is simple and that is the sheer volume and ease of access to firearms in the United States.

- In 2017 there were 39,773 firearm-related deaths in the United States, which equates to 109 firearm deaths per day, or around 3 million firearm deaths in the average lifespan of an American citizen.

- Guns make it easy to kill others and to kill oneself

- There is more than 1 accidental gun-related death every day in the United States. These often involve children.

The most important message to publicize however, is that guns are not only ineffective in providing protection, they increase the risk of death or injury to those residing in households where a firearm is present. It is worth repeating the findings of the March 2018 NBC/Wall Street Journal poll [cclxxxiv] and the UC San Francisco research published in the Annals of Internal Medicine in January 2014[cclxxxv]. The former shows a clear majority of US citizens believe that gun ownership increases safety by allowing law-abiding citizens to protect themselves, whilst the latter concludes that someone with access to firearms is three times more likely to commit suicide and nearly twice as likely to be the victim of a homicide as someone who does not have access.

The challenge for gun safety advocates is to resolve the mismatch between the perception that guns protect and the reality that guns increase the risk of homicide, suicide, and accidents. The dangers of owning firearms need to be repeatedly publicized and new research conducted on this matter. If US citizens understood that the dangers of owning firearms outweigh the advantages, public support for greater gun safety laws and initiatives would be overwhelming and would pave the way to enable changes in gun laws and attitudes which would save many thousands if not millions of lives.

# 30. Setting Goals and Targets

Gun safety and gun-rights advocates may not have a lot in common, but one would hope something they do agree on is that it is desirable to see both a reduction in the level of firearm-related deaths and the level of intentional homicides in the United States. A good strategy therefore for gun safety advocates would be to set well-publicized targets for the reduction of firearm-related deaths and intentional homicides. For example, a target could be set to reduce annual firearm fatalities by 25% in 5 years, or to reduce annual intentional homicides by 5,000 in 10 years, or to reduce annual firearm fatalities to below 20,000 in 15 years. There may be disagreement surrounding the achievability of targets but no one can argue that it would not be desirable to reduce firearm fatalities and intentional homicides. Ideally, targets should be set at both state and federal levels.

Whilst realistic firearm-related targets may be both desirable and achievable, in isolation they are not actionable e.g. setting a target to reduce the level of annual intentional homicides by 5,000 will do nothing to stop people committing murder. To achieve the target, it is necessary to set actionable goals that will assist in reaching the desired target. As an example, a goal could be set to make it harder for individuals who have committed an act of violence to possess firearms. Several goals will probably need to be achieved to meet the set target. Whilst targets are achievable, goals are actionable and ones in which the setter has some influence on the outcome.[cclxxxvi]

With regards to targets, the objective is to set easy to understand, challenging, but achievable targets. If the targets are too complex, they will be difficult to publicize. If they are too ambitious, they will be seen as unrealistic with no hope of achievement and the targets would soon be forgotten. If the targets are too modest, they may fail to encourage the significant action required to dramatically reduce the number of firearm fatalities and intentional homicides.

So, what would be an effective target for a reduction in firearm-related fatalities, which should include suicides, accidents, homicides, justified and undetermined deaths? In 2017 there were 39,773 firearm-related deaths[cclxxxvii] which was 1,115 more than the 38,658 deaths recorded in 2016. Reflecting a continual increase since 2014 a good proxy figure therefore for firearm-related deaths is 40,000 per annum. This is the equivalent of 110 deaths per day or around 4 million deaths per century. A bold easy to publicize target would be to reduce firearm fatalities by 50% reducing the annual carnage from 40,000 to 20,000; but is this realistic? Given a sufficient timescale and a general change in attitude concerning firearms this target is not as farfetched as may initially seem. Again, an easy to publicize message which is ambitious yet achievable would be a target to reduce firearm fatalities by 1,000 annually, Thus, a good example of a firearm fatality target would be to aim to reduce annual fatalities from 40,000 to 20,000 over twenty years. Given that fatalities increased by over 1,000 from 2016 to 2017 an annual reduction of 1,000 is not unrealistic, but it will require sustained and significant action and most importantly a change in attitude towards firearms.

Next, we need to consider what a suitable target would be for a reduction in intentional homicides. The target should be set not just for firearm-related homicides, but for all intentional homicides. This is partly to stop doubters from saying that a drop in firearm homicides would be matched by a corresponding increase in non-firearm homicides (there would be an increase but the increase in non-firearm homicides would be less than the reduction in firearm homicides), but more importantly to demonstrate that policies aimed at reducing firearm fatalities will also succeed in reducing overall homicide rates. There is a strong positive correlation between total firearm fatalities and total intentional homicides as demonstrated by the following figures:[cclxxxviii cclxxxix]

| Year | Total firearm fatalities | Total intentional homicides |
|---|---|---|
| 2010 | 31,672 | 14.722 |
| 2011 | 32,351 | 14,661 |
| 2012 | 33,563 | 14,856 |
| 2013 | 33,636 | 14,319 |
| 2014 | 33,594 | 14,164 |
| 2015 | 36,252 | 15,883 |
| 2016 | 38,658 | 17,413 |
| 2017 | 39,773 | 17,284 |

Thus, policies aimed at reducing the number of firearm fatalities, if successful, are extremely likely to also reduce the number of intentional homicides. That said the impact of policies aimed specifically at reducing firearm fatalities will probably have a smaller proportional impact on total intentional homicides than on total firearm fatalities and an ambitious realistic target in line with the 50% target for firearm fatalities would be to reduce intentional homicides to 10,000 a year. This would represent around a 42% reduction of intentional homicides from the 2017 figure of 17,284. Although this seems to be an ambitious target it should be noted that even if the United States was successful in reducing intentional homicides to 10,000 a year this would still represent an intentional homicide rate of around 3 per 100,000 residents (based on their 2019 population of around 329 million) which would still be a significantly higher rate than any other of the 20 most highly developed countries in the world.

In reality, the targets would be set through consultation between gun safety advocates and politicians and would need to be carefully scrutinized for achievability before being made public and hence the following proposed targets are just potential examples:

Target 1        Reduce annual firearm fatalities from 40,000 to 20,000 over 20 years.

Target 2        Reduce annual intentional homicides from 17,284 to
                10,000 over 20 years.

The perfect way to introduce these targets to ensure maximum
publicity would be for them to be announced by a pro-gun safety
president at the annual State of the Union address.

Now we need to determine some appropriate goals which will help
to achieve these ambitious targets? These goals will fall into the
following broad categories:

- Non-firearm-related goals
- Goals aimed at restricting who can have access to firearms
- Goals aimed at restricting the most dangerous firearms
- Goals aimed to encourage the safe storage of firearms
- Goals to make the public more aware of the dangers of
  firearms
- Goals to reward states which take the most positive action

Examples of non-firearm-related goals may include the following:

- Improving counselling for those deemed most likely to
  commit suicide e.g. setting up help-lines for the most
  vulnerable
- Improving mental health services
- Targeting gangs
- Targeting drug traffickers
- Providing greater resources to police officers

Examples of goals aimed at restricting who can have access to
firearms may include the following:

- Enforcing existing laws
- Requiring background checks for all gun sales
- Improving the effectiveness of background checks
- Preventing those with history of violence possessing firearms
- Raising the minimum age to purchase a gun to 21

- Creating a firearm registry
- Harsher penalties i.e. longer prison sentences for those illegally possessing weapons
- Harsher penalties for those supplying firearms to criminals
- Setting up a confidential helpline to report potential illegal possession of firearms

Examples of goals aimed at restricting the most dangerous firearms may include the following:

- A ban on semi-automatic weapons
- Banning the use of bump stocks
- Limits on the amount of ammunition which can be purchased

Examples of goals aimed to encourage the safe storage of firearms may include the following:

- Encouraging the use of gun safes
- Laws enforcing safe storage when children are present
- Encouraging gun clubs to store firearms
- Encouraging hunting lodges to store firearms

Examples of goals aimed to make the public more aware of the dangers of firearms may include the following:

- Publicizing the statistics covered in Chapter 1 of this book
- Publicizing the fact that possession of a firearm endangers individuals far more than protecting them
- Publicizing the fact that possession of a firearm in the home increases the risk of accidents, suicides, and homicides
- Publicizing the fact that most homicides are committed by people known to the victim
- Publicizing the popularity of most sensible gun safety proposals
- Publicizing the fact that most politicians blocking sensible gun safety laws have received money from the NRA

Examples of goals rewarding states which take the most positive action may include the following:

- Financial reward from the federal government for states which actively target reductions in firearm deaths and homicides
- Financial reward from the federal government for states which succeed in reducing firearm deaths and homicides
- Financial reward from the federal government for states with the best ratings on Giffords Law Center
- Financial reward from the federal government for states which improve their ratings on Giffords Law Center

This last set of goals emphasizes the importance of setting well-publicized targets and goals at a state-level as well as a federal level since many firearm-related laws and procedures are set at the state level. Any state which refuses to set targets for a reduction in firearm fatalities and intentional homicides should be named and shamed. Additionally, annual rankings of the states, based both on actual firearm fatalities and intentional homicide rates and also on the reduction in firearm fatalities and intentional homicide rates should be published, which will hopefully encourage states to take actions which will help save lives.

In reality, even if many of the proposed goals were acted upon it will be extremely difficult to reduce annual firearm fatalities to 20,000 and intentional homicides to 10,000, without there being a wholesale change in the attitude towards guns in the United States. There is hope however and as we saw in the previous chapter public support is generally on the side of gun safety. It may only take a few states to lead the way in successfully using targets and goals to reduce firearm fatalities before other more reticent states follow suit. This in turn will lead to more publicity resulting in even greater public support for gun safety and increase the chances that more federal action will be taken to reduce firearm fatalities.

# 31. Technological Advances

With the development of technology, firearms have become deadlier as evidenced by the fact that the technologically advanced AR-15 semi-automatic (or other similar) weapon has been used in six of the ten deadliest mass shooting events in the United States. These weapons are so much more lethal than earlier more primitive weapons such as muskets that were used in the American Revolutionary war. With technological advances, weapons become more dangerous and it is no coincidence that the 2 most deadly mass shootings in the United States have occurred in recent years (Las Vegas 2017) & (Orlando 2016).[ccxc]

Whilst it makes sense to continue to make technological advances to make weapons deadlier for military purposes, the exact opposite is the case for civilian purposes. There is no need for civilians to possess weapons and ammunition which can kill scores of people in a short time. Indeed, modern technology should be used to ensure weapons held by civilians are less deadly. If this could be done successfully there would a dramatic drop in the number of firearm suicides, accidents, and homicides.

One way in which guns could be made safer is through the development of smart guns[ccxci] which is a weapon that only specific users can fire and there are several gun technologies aimed at preventing unauthorized or accidental discharge. Dome smart guns use Radio Frequency Identification (RFID) systems equipped with a locking mechanism that releases only when a gun draws close to a device broadcasting a particular radio band. An RFID gun was introduced to the U.S. in 2013 that activates when a person enters a PIN on a nearby paired watch. Gun-rights advocates may argue that it is not practical to quickly find your watch and enter a pin if the gun is required for immediate self-defense. So, a better option which has also been produced in the United States is a gun that automatically unlocks when the owner's ring, which contains an authorization tag, comes within two inches of a reader in the weapon's handle. These, or other similar types of guns would significantly reduce the number of teen suicides and accidental shootings.

An alternative form of smart gun uses biometrics to require proof of identity. The biometrics can be based on voice or a retinal scan, but most versions available analyze hand-related features, such as fingerprints. Fingerprint-access gun technology allows user-authentication to be quick and effortless. This technology is already widely used in smartphones and security devices and offers a simple solution to prevent others from using your firearm. When an authorized user presses their finger to a fingerprint scanner on the gun, the scanner compares the print to its internal database, finds a match, and allows the user full access to the firearm. Unauthorized users cannot fire the weapon. This technology can be programmed for an unlimited number of users, allowing gun owners to give other family members access to their firearm or enabling police departments to authorize an entire police force access to the same firearm. Biofire Technologies is a startup company aiming to build the next generation of smart firearms and they have developed a gun with a fingerprint scanner that can be programmed for a virtually unlimited number of users and boasts a 99.99% accurate recognition rate.[ccxcii]

Technology can also assist with the use of microstamping. This technique imprints tiny identifying marks from a gun onto a cartridge as it fires. This would help law enforcement quickly link an individual weapon, and therefore a suspect, to a shooting.[ccxciii] This technology may deter criminals from using stolen firearms but would not be as effective as RFID or biometric technology which would make it impossible to use stolen firearms. Additionally, microstamping will not assist in reducing suicides and accidental shootings.

Despite the obvious lifesaving potential in the development of smart guns at the time of writing they are generally not available for sale in the United States. There are many obstacles to their development including cost however, the main obstacle, as usual, is that traditional firearm manufacturers and their advocacy groups such as the NRA are opposed to the development of smart firearm technology. In November 2018 a journalist from Forbes asked 2 contacts from the National Shooting Sports Foundation (NSSF) why they were so opposed to the development of smart firearms and produced an article providing the following 5 reasons for their opposition.[ccxciv]

1. Guns may be less reliable with a chip or other technology - The NSSF view is that the technological developments introduce points of failure that could put the lives of lawful and authorized users at risk when they need those firearms to preserve lives. This viewpoint is contradicted by testing on the iGun smart gun which was found to be more reliable than most commercial firearms available. In reality, the new technology will need to be rigorously tested for reliability and it would be hoped that only the most reliable firearms would successfully make it into commercial production.

2. Product liability issues - "If a manufacturer were to overcome the significant technological challenges inherent in developing a safe and equally reliable firearm incorporating "authorized user recognition" technology, would they be exposing themselves to product liability lawsuits alleging that all their other products that do not incorporate this technology are somehow "defectively designed," or that their previously manufactured products are also "defectively designed" because they did not incorporate this feature soon enough?" wrote the NSSF in a fact sheet about the technology. This is an extraordinary statement which is in effect stating that we don't want to make things safer because we may be sued for continuing to sell less safe products.

3. They fear mandates - In 2002, New Jersey passed a law saying that once "personalized handguns are available" anywhere in the country, all handguns sold in New Jersey must be smart guns within 30 months. This well-intentioned law has had the unfortunate effect of actually preventing the development and sale of smart guns. Anyone selling a smart gun in any state would in effect be imposing a handgun ban in New Jersey. The negative impact of this law is evidenced by a couple of retailers that announced they would stock the Armatix iP1, a German-made gun that only fires if the owner is wearing a special watch. The response was quick and intense with

both stores being flooded with angry calls and messages from people who consider the New Jersey law an infringement of the Second Amendment's right to bear arms. One of the store owners reported he received multiple death threats and both stores quickly backed down on their plans to sell the Armatix gun.[ccxcv]

4. The market may be small - The NSSF surveyed its members and found that 14% would be likely to buy a smart gun. In 2015, Penn Shoen Berland found 40% of Americans would consider swapping their current gun for a smart gun. The underlying data in the latter study suggests older gun owners are less likely to be interested in smart guns. Although the NSSF may think this is a small market even if only 14% of gun sales were smart guns this would represent around 3.5 million sales based on estimated gun sales of around 25m for 2017[ccxcvi]. Additionally, the market for smart guns would grow as the technology advances and more smart guns are available and the price becomes more competitive.

5. The technology may be hard – As an example, an NSSF spokesman said what do you do about batteries: "If a homeowner keeps a gun locked with the use of "smart gun" technology and stores the gun, perhaps in an accessible place to enable quick access in the event of an emergency, but then the gun is not used for months, maybe years, what is the failure mode when the battery or power source dies?" Sure, the technology may be hard but that applies to all new technology and if there is a will and sufficient resources there is no doubt that technologically advanced firearms could be as, if not more, reliable than traditional firearms.

At the time of writing in 2019, a new generation of Entrepreneurs thinks it can revive the smart gun[ccxcvii]. This next generation of products promises to chamber more popular types of ammunition, be better shielded against hacking, and perhaps most important: be reliable when it matters. The optimism among entrepreneurs was on full display on January 16 2019 when an array of gun safety device startups converged on a technical college just outside of Milwaukee to show off their inventions. The exhibition was the second such event sponsored by a national coalition of religious groups and community organizations intent on harnessing the purchasing power of public entities to popularize technologies that have long been relegated to the margins of American gun culture. It is a well-tested strategy, drawn from the likes of Glock, Smith & Wesson, and Colt, whose weapons gained prestige among civilians after being adopted by law enforcement.

"If it's accepted by the military and police, then it will be accepted by the general public," said Milwaukee County District Attorney John Chisholm, one of dozens of law enforcement officials and elected leaders who attended the Firearm Safety Expo at the Milwaukee Area Technical College. "There's optimism about this now, and I think some of that resistance you've seen is going to dissipate once we show that this technology is reliable."

Some models are tantalizingly close to launch: Kloepfer, whose company built a fingerprint-activated, .40-caliber handgun, said the weapon could be sold as early as 2020. A Swiss company, SAAR, is aiming to roll out an assault-style rifle with user-recognition technology for law enforcement within months, first in Europe, but with an eye toward the American market. And Pennsylvania's LodeStar Firearms could be offering a 9mm pistol activated by radio-frequency identification (or RFID) or a pin code in 18 months. Gareth Glaser, LodeStar's CEO, said that he had received a verbal commitment from a major retailer to sell the company's debut model.

"Getting national distribution is a huge issue," Glaser said. "When we are ready to get this out there, it will probably start in a handful of stores, and then expand from there." The push for smart guns has been fueled by a smattering of benefactors, including big-name Silicon Valley investors and a former gun industry heavyweight.

Despite these advances, the NRA has continued to urge caution on smart guns and repeatedly denounced mandates like New Jersey's as unwarranted government intrusion in the marketplace. On that latter point, smart-gun makers agree, saying the New Jersey mandate needs to be scrapped before their inventions can succeed.

There is one potential technological advance that could have an even bigger impact on gun violence than the development of smart guns and that is a technology that would enable firearms to immobilize a target without the risk of serious injury or death. The ideal solution would be a firearm that sends the target to sleep rather than injuring or killing them i.e. some form of tranquilizer gun. These exist for animals and so it should be possible to develop something similar for humans. This technology does not currently exist and would require a tremendous amount of research and testing to ensure the weapons and ammunition developed fulfilled the following minimum requirements:

- Simple to use and aim at the target
- Immediately render the target unable to retaliate
- Ensure target is immobilized for sufficient time to allow law enforcement officers to arrive and take the necessary action
- Be equally effective wherever on the body the target is hit e.g. hand, leg or chest
- Not be fatal to children
- Not to be fatal when shot at point-blank range (necessary to prevent suicides)
- Leave no lasting damage to the target

Ideally, this weapon should incorporate the smart technology previously discussed to prevent unauthorized users from shooting for fun e.g. children messing around with their parent's firearm.

The cost involved in developing such a firearm would probably be prohibitive for private companies and would need the backing for government-funded research. The ultimate prize however would be huge, if non-lethal weapons could replace traditional firearms on a large scale. The number of accidental firearm deaths would dramatically drop and there would be a significant reduction in suicides. There would also be a fall in the number of intentional homicides although this reduction would be less significant, whilst traditional firearms are still readily available. Someone intent on murder will want to kill their victim rather than send them to sleep, however, there would be a fall in unpremeditated murders where someone fires a gun on impulse without thinking of the consequences.

The number of justifiable homicides would also fall significantly with the introduction of non-lethal firearms, as many homeowners would choose to protect themselves with a weapon that sends their target to sleep rather than kill them. Indeed, a non-lethal weapon which immediately renders the target incapable of retaliation offers the following advantages when used for protection or self-defense purposes:

- If a burglar is apprehended a homeowner will be less hesitant to use a weapon knowing the consequences will not be fatal
- Most criminals do not deserve to be killed and it should be left to the courts to determine the appropriate punishment for burglars or robbers.
- It will remove the risk that someone else in a household will take the gun to kill themselves or another household member e.g. remove the risk of someone killing a spouse or partner
- It removes the risk that a child can get hold of the weapon and kill themselves or another family member
- The negative psychological impact on the shooter of knowing they have killed or seriously injured their target will be removed.
- Specifically, for law enforcers the negative publicity surrounding dubiously justified or unjustified killings would be removed if non-lethal weapons were used

So, what can be done to encourage the technological development of weapons which will neutralize as opposed to kill their target? This probably requires the 2 following steps:

1. A commitment from the government to provide the necessary funding to carry out the required technological research and development to produce a safe and effective non-lethal weapon. To achieve the maximum publicity, ideally, this commitment should be announced by the President in a State of Union address at the same time that targets to reduce

firearm fatalities and intentional homicides are announced.

2. Following the announcement of the funding, appropriate companies should be approached and requested to provide tenders on how they could develop the required technology. The successful company or research department would then be provided with the necessary funding to develop the new technologically advanced weapons.

The development of smart guns and non-lethal weapons will go a long way to help reduce the number of firearm fatalities however, it must be recognized that even if they were to become readily available at competitive prices, current traditional firearms estimated to be between 270 and 310 million[ccxcviii] will still exist and will not suddenly disappear. It will take time for public attitudes towards firearms to change but it is hoped that eventually traditional firearms will be seen as dangerous and unnecessary and no longer be considered beneficial for protection.

Compulsory gun buy-backs are clearly not constitutional in the United States however, if non-lethal weapons were to become publicly available there would be an excellent opportunity to introduce voluntary buy-backs in which traditional firearms were exchanged for safer modern non-lethal weapons.

Technology if harnessed correctly could have a huge impact on reducing the number of firearm fatalities in the United States.

# 32. Post Parkland

On February 14, 2018, a gunman opened fire at Marjory Stoneman Douglas High School in Parkland, Florida, killing seventeen students and staff members and injuring seventeen others.[ccxcix]

The Federal response to this tragedy was lamentable. Apart from the usual thoughts and prayers the only suggestion President Trump came up with following a White House meeting with students was to arm up to 20% of teachers. This is a crazy idea since teachers should be fully focused on teaching and not on how to safely use firearms. Armed guards would make more sense than armed teachers due to their training and experience, but even their ability to stop a mass shooting is limited as evidenced by the fact that there was an armed deputy sheriff present at the Marjory Stoneman Douglas High School when the shooting occurred who failed to engage the shooter. The following comment comes from a teacher whose husband was killed in the shooting and sums up the problems of arming teachers: "Classroom teachers cannot and should not be distracted with the responsibility of being armed inside a classroom, even if they think they want to. The probability of something going wrong clearly outweighs that one time that there may be a shooting in the classroom."[ccc]. It is difficult to determine what the outcome would be if an aggressive student tried to forcefully obtain a firearm from an armed teacher, but the presence of a firearm significantly increase the chances of serious injury or death, to either a teacher or student.

The State response to this tragedy was somewhat better than the Federal response as summarized by the Giffords Law Center – "Florida significantly raised its grade in 2018, from an F to a C-. After the mass shooting in Parkland in February, the state legislature passed a package of gun safety bills that included an extreme risk protection law, a higher minimum age for buying firearms, and stronger waiting periods. To save more lives and further raise its grade, Florida should adopt universal background checks and regulate military-style weapons and magazines" [ccci]. All efforts to introduce new gun safety bills must be encouraged, however, it is unfortunate that the tragedy had to occur before any action was taken. To save lives, states should introduce sensible gun safety regulations as a matter of priority and not wait until a mass shooting occurs before taking any action. Indeed, as detailed in the next paragraph these actions taken by Florida were in response to pressure from the students of Marjory Stoneman Douglas High School.

By far the most impressive response to the Marjory Stoneman Douglas High School mass shooting came directly from some of the school's students. Shortly after the shooting, a group of twenty students formed the "Never Again (MSD)" movement [cccii] with MSD representing the initials of the Marjory Stoneman Douglas High School. This is a student-led political action committee for gun-control advocating tighter regulations to prevent gun violence. The organization staged protests demanding legislative action to be taken to prevent similar shootings in the future and has vocally condemned U.S. lawmakers who have received political contributions from the National Rifle Association (NRA). It was credited in the Washington Post as winning a "stunning victory" against the NRA in the Florida legislature in March 2018 when both houses voted for various gun-control measures. The law increased funding for school security and raised the required age to buy a gun from 18 to 21. Within days the group announced a nationwide protest, for March 24, 2018. The March 24 protest involved millions of people in over 800 sites across the US and other countries and was named "March for Our Lives". This march was described by several media outlets as a possible tipping point for gun-control legislation.[ccciii] Protesters urged for universal background checks on all gun sales, raising the federal age of gun ownership and possession to 21, closing of the gun show loophole, a restoration of the 1994 Federal Assault Weapons Ban, and a ban on the sale of high-capacity magazines and bump stocks in the United States. Turnout was estimated to be between 1.2 and 2 million people in the US, making it one of the largest protests in American history. March for Our Lives was among the biggest youth-led protests since the Vietnam War era with estimates of participation at the main event in Washington, D.C. ranging from 200,000 to 800,000. The speakers, all of whom were high schoolers or younger included many Marjory Stoneman Douglas students.

Other participants included those who had lost close relatives to gun violence. One of the students. Emma González after speaking and naming the seventeen victims, stood silent for over four minutes, after which a cellphone alarm went off and she announced that it was the 6 minutes and 20 seconds point in her speech, equal to the length of the Parkland shooting. González ended her speech saying since the time that I came out here, it has been 6 minutes and 20 seconds. The shooter has ceased shooting, and will soon abandon his rifle, blend in with the students as they escape, and walk free for an hour before arrest. Fight for your lives before it's someone else's job, then walked off stage as the entire crowd along Pennsylvania Avenue applauded loudly. To add publicity for the March for Our Lives many high-profile celebrities provided donations and support. [ccciv]

Whilst the March for Our Lives gave momentary publicity to the gun problem in the United States, of much greater importance is whether the Never Again movement will have any lasting impact on the gun issue in the United States. On the 1st anniversary of the Marjory Stoneman Douglas, The Washington Post published an article titled "One year after the Parkland shooting, is the #NeverAgain movement on track to succeed?"[cccv]

Although one year later, the Parkland young people haven't stopped mass shootings and the policies they've promoted and the less dangerous world they imagined are still distant, it cannot yet be argued that the #NeverAgain movement has failed. This is largely because, as the Washington Post article explains, success rarely comes overnight. The Never Again movement has built broad coalitions, sharing their spotlight with young people from very different backgrounds, defining the problem of gun violence to include crime, suicide, and police violence. Their organization, March for Our Lives, joined a coalition of other gun-control organizations that formed in the wake of other shootings, including Moms Demand Action, Everytown for Gun Safety, and Courage to Fight Gun Violence.

Importantly the Never Again movement is strategizing for the long term, not only looking at immediate gains. They've offered an agenda and identified an opponent: the NRA. They've put unusual pressure on companies that do business with it by threatening boycotts. By keeping gun violence in the news and staging repeated events, the Parkland kids helped recruit thousands of new young activists and voters, helping to put new voices in Congress. It is still too early to determine how successful the Never Again movement will be in the long term, but what is important is that it continues with a sense of urgency, claim partial victories and navigate a long road forward since as we saw in Step 4 of the book there are many obstacles in the way.

What is encouraging for the future is that the younger generation does seem to be more focused on gun safety than previous generations. If the Never Again movement can help achieve the following 3 goals, they will have gone a long way to resolving America's gun issue:

1. Successfully get across the message that America does have a gun problem
2. Promotion of sensible gun safety policies
3. Making politicians aware that supporting gun-rights advocates such as the NRA is a vote loser and that promoting gun safety policies is a vote winner

The final point above will only occur after public opinion has moved sufficiently in the direction towards gun safety and away from gun-rights. This is a big challenge for gun safety advocates but it is not unsurmountable.

# 33. Gun Safety Strategy

There is so much potential to make positive changes which will reduce the number of firearm fatalities and injuries in the United States. In this chapter, we will consider a 20-point strategy which if followed would dramatically reduce the overall number of firearm-related fatalities and injuries. The strategy consists of a mixture of publicity, education, realism, enforcing existing laws, and introducing new laws, all of which have the sole purpose of saving lives.

1. Keep publicizing the fact that America does have a gun problem. Despite overwhelming evidence that there is a gun problem, there is a reluctance to accept this obvious fact. The extent of America's gun problem is detailed in Step 1 of this book but can be summarized by the following fact reported in the American Journal of Medicine "US homicide rates were 7.0 times higher than in other high-income countries, driven by a gun homicide rate that was 25.2 times higher"[cccvi]. This is a vital first step as until it is accepted that there is a gun problem nothing will be done to resolve the problem. The message to get across is very simple i.e. more guns = more suicides = more homicides = more gun accidents = more deaths and injuries.

2. Ensure the annual number of firearm fatalities and injuries are well-publicized. Provide a split between suicides, intentional homicides, justified homicides, accidents, and undetermined. The significant increase in both firearm fatalities and total homicides since 2014 needs to be highlighted to demonstrate that the gun problem is getting worse. A trend that is likely to continue unless significant action is taken.

3. Be realistic – e.g. A ban on handguns which has been effective in other countries is not a realistic possibility in the United States. Public opinion would be opposed to a handgun

ban and additionally, such a ban would fall foul of the Constitution as set by the 2nd amendment. The 2nd amendment is extremely popular and gun safety proponents must stress that they are not looking to overturn this amendment.

4. Counter fearmongering – for example by publicizing the fact that a proposal to enforce background checks is not the 1st step towards a ban on guns. The District of Columbia v Heller Supreme Court ruling should be quoted as a reminder that even if some gun safety proponents would like to see a firearm ban this is not constitutionally possible and should not be feared.

5. Emphasize the fact that the presence of a gun in the household endangers rather than protects the residents. The UC San Francisco research [cccvii] which concluded that someone with access to firearms is three times more likely to commit suicide and nearly twice as likely to be a homicide victim as someone who does not have access needs to be well-publicized. This is critical as the majority of people believe guns help protect when in reality the exact opposite is true. Further research into the impact of having firearms in the home should be encouraged.

6. Emphasize the most obvious reason why guns are so dangerous, which is that they were designed to kill people efficiently and effectively. Counter the stupid argument that "guns don't kill people, people kill people" with the more relevant statement that "guns make it easy for people to kill people".

7. Show respect to gun owners who possess their firearms for either hunting or target shooting purposes, but introduce policies which will encourage safe weapon storage at hunting lodges or target ranges, as opposed to storing guns in the home and having to transport them to and from the lodge or range.

8. Encourage more respect between gun-rights and gun safety advocates. Gun safety advocates should accept that most gun owners are responsible individuals who do not wish to harm others. Gun-rights advocates should accept that guns in the wrong hands are a danger to everyone and accept minor inconveniences such as not being able to purchase a gun without a thorough background check.

9. Publicize the Giffords Law Center to prevent gun violence website and analysis.[cccviii] This website has so much useful information including the Annual Gun Law Scorecard which shows clear evidence that states with stronger gun laws have lower gun death rates, year after year. The website also provides helpful and detailed reports on several gun-related policy areas including the following:

   a. Background checks
   b. Who can have a gun?
   c. Gun sales
   d. Owner responsibilities
   e. Guns in public
   f. Hardware and ammunition
   g. Crime guns

The Giffords Law Center provides advice for each state giving praise and criticism where merited. For example, the summary provided for Pennsylvania which has a C rating is as follows: "Pennsylvania strengthened its gun laws in 2018 by prohibiting firearm possession by individuals who have been convicted of domestic abuse or are subject to domestic violence protective orders and requiring those individuals to relinquish their firearms. Pennsylvania could further raise its grade and save lives by allowing local governments to regulate firearms and enacting extreme risk protection order legislation".

10. Enforce and expand existing policies to deter criminals from obtaining and using firearms. Gun-rights advocates frequently state that there is no point in introducing new laws when criminals do not obey existing laws. Whilst criminals are indeed unlikely to follow laws, there are many ways in which criminals can be deterred and prevented from possessing firearms, including the following:

   - Enforcing more severe punishment for those caught possessing firearms not legally obtained. Ideally through the setting up of federal minimum sentencing requirements
   - Enforce more severe penalties for gun traffickers
   - Encouraging individuals to report suspected illegal possession by setting up anonymous whistleblowing helplines
   - Using commercials to encourage the reporting of stolen or lost firearms and to discourage the sale of firearms to third parties e.g. a commercial that shows someone buying a gun legally and then selling it to someone who would not pass a background check. The commercial would then cut to the aftermath of a homicide committed with this firearm.
   - Through the development of smart guns such as fingerprint technology which would prevent criminals from using stolen or gifted guns.

11. Introduce new safety proposals designed specifically to prevent criminals from obtaining or possessing firearms. Whilst enforcing existing policies is essential there is also a dire need to introduce new policies that will help to prevent criminals from obtaining firearms. This would include the following proposals all of which have overwhelming public support:

   - Requiring background checks for all firearm sales

- Preventing sales of all firearms to people who have been reported as dangerous to law enforcement by a mental-health provider
- Preventing sales of all firearms to people who have been convicted of violent misdemeanors
- Barring gun purchases by people on the federal no-fly or watch lists

12. Introduce new safety proposals designed at making firearms less dangerous. It makes no sense to allow civilians access to weapons that can injure or kill multiple people in rapid succession. Appropriate policies would include the following:

- A ban on assault-style weapons such as the AR-15
- A ban on bump stocks. It is pleasing to see that this law was created in March 2019[cccix].
- Banning high capacity magazines
- Encourage technological research to develop non-lethal alternatives to firearms
- Ensure that all firearms are sold with child safety locks. This would help reduce accidental firearm injuries and deaths

13. Enforce mandatory registration for all firearms in all states. Currently, only the District of Columbia and Hawaii require registration of all firearms. By contrast, every motor vehicle in all states must have a certificate of ownership generally referred to as the "Title" showing the name of the registered owner, the registration plate number, and other vehicle details. If this can be done for cars it makes no sense not to enforce similar documentation and databases for firearms. The benefits of a universal gun register in assisting the tracing of guns used in crimes, the disarming of dangerous people, and encouraging gun owner accountability were detailed in Chapter 23.

14. Provide federal funding to the Centers for Disease Control and Prevention (CDC) for immediate firearm research and ensure the findings, which are likely to highlight the dangers that easy access to firearms pose are well-publicized. This is essential to educate the public and influence public opinion on this matter.

15. Emphasize the word safety and avoid using the word control. A gun safety policy suggests that the principal aim of the policy is to remove a danger and consequently reduce firearm-related deaths and injuries. A gun-control policy suggests that the principal aim is to restrict the rights of citizens to buy or possess guns.

16. Publicize the overwhelming public support for virtually all sensible gun safety proposals. As an example, 88% of respondents support mandatory background checks for all gun sales, with just 6% opposing[cccx].

17. Publicize the reason why politicians fail to act on sensible gun safety proposals? This is namely money and corruption. Politicians who fail to support sensible gun safety issues should be named and shamed e.g. publicize the fact that a politician who voted against a proposal to introduce mandatory background checks for all gun sales received large sums of money from the NRA.

18. Emphasize the importance of setting gun safety policies at the federal level. Whilst city and state laws designed to promote gun safety are to be encouraged, their impact is limited due to the ease of mobility of firearms from neighboring districts or states.

19. Develop and publicize federal targets for annual reductions in firearm fatalities and intentional homicide levels and provide financial rewards to the states which take the most positive actions in achieving these targets.

20. Persevere – Some gun safety advocates have given up the fight to resolve America's gun problem. They argue that proposing gun policies that may restrict purchases or ownership only results in increased firearm sales. Whilst this may have been true in recent years, it is a defeatist attitude. With determination and perseverance, gun safety advocates can introduce policies that will dramatically reduce the number of firearm fatalities and save thousands of livers every year. Public opinion is on the side of gun safety advocates and with perseverance, positive changes can be made which will go a long way to resolve America's gun problem.

# Conclusion

On reading Step 1 of this book it is difficult for anyone with an open mind on the subject to come to any conclusion other than the fact that America does have a significant gun problem which results in the needless loss of life of thousands of Americans every year. This is a problem which is unique amongst highly developed countries and is summed up by the American Journal of Medicine study published in February 2016 which concluded the following[cccxi]:

- Americans are 10 times more likely to be killed by guns than people in other developed countries
- Compared to 22 other high-income nations, the United States' gun-related murder rate is 25 times higher
- Compared to those in the same age groups in other wealthy countries, Americans aged 15-24 are 49 times more likely to be the victim of a gun-related murder

So why, despite the overwhelming evidence showing that the presence of guns results in far more lives being lost than being saved, do so many Americans believe that owning and having easy access to guns is a good thing? The answer to this question is complex but reasons include a general lack of awareness of the dangers of guns, which is best demonstrated by the fact that most Americans believe a gun in the home makes you safer, when indeed as we have seen the exact opposite is true. Another reason Americans believe having a gun is a good thing is that they believe it may one day be necessary for armed citizens to overthrow a tyrannical government. As reviewed in Chapter 8 the concept of armed militia, even if by some miracle they were all on the same side, overpowering a government backed by the world's strongest military is ludicrous. A third reason for the popularity of guns is a strong gun culture in which children are frequently taught how to handle a gun at a relatively young age. In summary, Americans think guns are a good thing for the following reasons:

- Protection
- The 2<sup>nd</sup> amendment
- Culture

As a consequence of the popularity of guns, it is estimated that one or more guns are to be found in around 37% of households in the United States[cccxii]. The combination of the popularity of guns and the fact that they are so dangerous is a difficult conundrum to resolve as gun supporters tend to turn a blind eye on all the negative statistics and insist that there is no gun problem and oppose all sensible suggestions to resolve what they believe to be a non-existent problem. This viewpoint is then reinforced by gun-rights advocates such as the NRA who use their resources to fund gun supporting politicians. As we have seen in Step 4 of this book, the obstacles preventing sensible action to reduce firearm fatalities and injuries are huge. The District of Columbia v Heller Supreme Court ruling, NRA leadership, political lobbying, a ban on firearm research, fearmongering, and money provided by gun-rights advocates all make any significant changes to gun laws difficult to enact.

To compound the difficulty in overcoming obstacles preventing sensible gun safety legislation from being implemented is a belief held by many that promoting gun safety is not only ineffective, it can also be counter-productive. This is best demonstrated by the fact that following President Obama's election in 2008 there was a sharp increase in gun sales as people were concerned that President Obama who had a strong reputation for promoting gun-control, would crack down on gun ownership. Consequently, some gun safety advocates say that the best policy is to shut up and do nothing, since proposing gun-control measures such as mandatory background checks on all gun sales will fail in Congress or Senate and only have the impact of increasing gun sales by those who fear a background check.

The above viewpoint is a defeatist attitude, however, and as we saw in the final chapters of this book many positive actions can be taken to resolve America's gun problem. These actions include deterring illegal possession by increasing penalties for illegal possession and making illegal possession easier to identify by creating a gun registry. Other positive actions include more effective publicity on the danger of firearms and by drawing a comparison with the motor vehicle and tobacco industries. Motor vehicle fatalities per mile driven have fallen because the motor industry, unlike the firearm industry, has embraced new and improved safety features. Tobacco-related deaths have fallen because the dangers of smoking are well-publicized and this has led to a significant fall in the number of smokers.

Whilst public opinion on guns is less negative than it is on tobacco, there is significant public support for most sensible gun safety strategies and the challenge for gun safety advocates is to initially focus on initiatives that currently have majority support amongst Democrats, Republicans, and Independents. At the same time, the strategy needs to continue to sway public opinion on the side of gun safety. This includes avoiding the term "Gun-control" and using the term "Gun-safety". This reinforces the message that the underlying objective for placing restrictions on gun ownership is not to take away guns, but rather to make everyone safer by reducing both gun fatalities and overall homicide and suicide rates. The concept that safety is paramount can then be reinforced by the setting of realistic targets to reduce both the number of firearm fatalities and the overall homicide rate. As we saw in Chapter 30 there is a strong correlation between firearm fatalities and intentional homicides, so that when the number of firearm fatalities falls the level of intentional homicides is also likely to fall. Targets are helpful because they provide publicity to the alarming levels of firearm fatalities and the close link between firearm fatalities and overall homicide rates. Moreover, effective targets are difficult for gun-rights advocates to oppose. For example, if a President were to announce the setting of a target to reduce firearm fatalities by 25% over a specific period, how could anyone or any organization object?

The next essential step for those wishing to reduce firearm fatalities and overall homicide and suicide levels is to embrace technology. Smart technology for firearms already exists and needs to be marketed more effectively so that gun owners swap their traditional firearms for smart firearms. Can you imagine the relief of parents who discover that when their toddler found a loaded gun and attempted to fire it at their brother or sister, nothing happened, thanks to fingerprint recognition? Additionally, research needs to continue in finding a safe alternative to existing firearms. If a weapon could be invented which neutralizes the target without causing any long-term injury then it would remove the requirement for the possession of traditional firearms and there would be a huge reduction in firearm fatalities and a significant reduction in homicide and suicide levels.

It is encouraging that it is mainly the younger generation who wish to promote gun safety and the post Parkland – "Never Again" and "March for Our Lives" movements need to be encouraged. Hopefully, this will lead to future generations being more inclined to take effective action on reducing gun violence.

In the final chapter of this book, a 20-point gun safety strategy was proposed that, even if only some of the proposals were acted upon, would significantly reduce the overall number of firearm-related fatalities and injuries and also the overall level of homicides and suicides. Just how many lives that can be saved is impossible to predict but the numbers would be significant.

There is, of course, one way in finding out many lives could be saved and that is to enact a comprehensive gun safety strategy incorporating as many of the goals detailed in Chapter 30 and strategies proposed in the final Chapter as practical and then measure the inevitable reduction in firearm fatalities, firearm accidents, overall homicides, and overall suicides.

Wake up America! You have a serious gun problem which has been getting steadily worse in recent years. Now is the time to take positive action to reduce gun violence as opposed to doing nothing and blaming everything but the gun.

# Endnotes

---

[i] NBC News (2014, November 23). Cops Kill Boy, 12, Carrying 'Airsoft' Toy Gun in Cleveland. Retrieved from https://www.nbcnews.com/news/us-news/cops-kill-boy-12-carrying-airsoft-toy-gun-cleveland-n254251

[ii] Ellis, R, Fantz A, Karimi F, McLaughlin E. (2016, June 13), Orlando shooting – 49 killed, shooter pledged ISIS allegiance. Retrieved from https://edition.cnn.com/2016/06/12/us/orlando-nightclub-shooting/index.html

[iii] Quinnipiac University poll (2016, June 30), Overwhelming Support For No-Fly, No-Buy Gun Law, Quinnipiac University National Poll Finds; Support For Background Checks Tops 90 Percent Again. Retrieved from https://poll.qu.edu/national/release-detail?ReleaseID=2364

[iv] USA Facts, Firearm Deaths, Retrieved from https://usafacts.org/data/topics/security-safety/crime-and-justice/firearms/firearm-deaths/

[v] USA Facts, Firearm Deaths, Retrieved from https://usafacts.org/data/topics/security-safety/crime-and-justice/firearms/firearm-deaths/

[vi] USA Facts, Firearm Deaths, Retrieved from https://usafacts.org/data/topics/security-safety/crime-and-justice/firearms/firearm-deaths/

[vii] USA Facts, Firearm Deaths, Retrieved from https://usafacts.org/data/topics/security-safety/crime-and-justice/firearms/firearm-deaths/

[viii] NSSF The Firearm Industry Trade, (2018, April 10). Firearms and Ammunition Industry Economic Impact Report 2018. Retrieved from https://www.nssf.org/firearms-industry-economic-impact-rises-169-since-2008/Association,

[ix] Knoema, (2019, August 5), UNODC International Homicide Statistics. Retrieved from https://knoema.com/UNODCHIS2017/unodc-international-homicide-statistics

[x] The World Bank Group, UN Office on Drugs and Crime's International Homicide Statistics database, Intentional homicides (per 100,000 people). Retrieved from https://data.worldbank.org/indicator/VC.IHR.PSRC.P5

[xi] Knoema World Data Atlas – Rankings crime statistics Homicide rate 2017. Retrieved from https://knoema.com/atlas/ranks/Homicide-rate

[xii] United Nations Development Programme (UNDP), Latest Human Development Index (HDI) Ranking. Retrieved 2020, June 14 from http://hdr.undp.org/

[xiii] Knoema World Data Atlas – Rankings crime statistics Homicide rate 2017. Retrieved from https://knoema.com/atlas/ranks/Homicide-rate

[xiv] Gun Policy.Org – Gun Homicides, Liechtenstein 2016, Hong Kong 2017, Singapore 2015, Japan 2015, United Kingdom 2015, Norway 2015, Germany 2015, Austria 2016, Australia 2018, Switzerland 2018, Netherlands 2016, Finland

2016, Denmark 2015, New Zealand 2016, Belgium 2015, Iceland 2016, Ireland 2014, Sweden 2017, Canada 2018, United States 2017. Retrieved from https://www.gunpolicy.org/

xv GunPolicy.org, United States. Gun Facts, Figures and the Law, Gun Homicides 2017. Retrieved from https://www.gunpolicy.org/firearms/region/united-states

xvi Lopez G, (2015, October 2), The ridiculous number of guns owned by Americans, in one chart. Retrieved from https://www.vox.com/policy-and-politics/2015/10/2/9439909/the-ridiculous-number-of-guns-owned-by-americans-in-one-chart

xvii Gun Policy.Org – Total number of gun deaths -  Hong Kong 2015, Singapore 2015, Japan 2015, United Kingdom 2015, Norway 2015, Germany 2015, Austria 2016, Australia 2018, Switzerland 2015, Netherlands 2016, Finland 2015, Denmark 2015, New Zealand 2015, Belgium 2015, Iceland 2016, Ireland 2014, Sweden 2016, Canada 2018, United States 2017. Retrieved from https://www.gunpolicy.org/

xviii USA Facts, Firearm Deaths by Type 2017. Retrieved from https://usafacts.org/data/topics/security-safety/crime-and-justice/firearms/firearm-deaths/

xix Pane, N. (2018, February 22).  Data Point: Gun violence is the most common cause of death for young men. Retrieved from https://www.childtrends.org/gun-violence-common-cause-death-young-men

xx Parker, K. Horowitz, J. Igielnik, R. Oliphant, J. Brown, A (2017, June 22) Pew Research Center Social & Demographic Trends Americas Complex Relationship with Guns. Retrieved from https://www.pewsocialtrends.org/2017/06/22/views-on-gun-policy/

xxi BBC News US & Canada (2017, June 19). Guns kill 1,300 US children every year, study finds. Retrieved from https://www.bbc.co.uk/news/world-us-canada-40336048

xxii Gun Policy.Org – Suicide any method -  Hong Kong 2015, Singapore 2015, Japan 2015, United Kingdom 2015, Norway 2015, Germany 2015, Austria 2016, Australia 2018, Switzerland 2015, Netherlands 2016, Finland 2015, Denmark 2015, New Zealand 2015, Belgium 2015, Iceland 2016, Ireland 2014, Sweden 2016, Canada 2018, United States 2017. Retrieved from https://www.gunpolicy.org/

xxiii Peterson, M. Stoppler, M. (2019, September 24). Suicidal Thoughts. Retrieved from https://www.emedicinehealth.com/suicidal_thoughts/article_em.htm https://www.thetrace.org/2016/09/10-essential-facts-guns-suicide/

xxiv Shaw, K. (2016, September 6). The Trace, 10 Essential Facts About Guns and Suicide. Retrieved from https://www.thetrace.org/2016/09/10-essential-facts-guns-suicide/

xxv Harvard T.H. Chan. Lethality of Suicide Methods Case Fatality Rates by Suicide Method, 8 U.S. States, 1989-1997. Retrieved from https://www.hsph.harvard.edu/means-matter/means-matter/case-fatality/

[xxvi] Signer, M. (2016, April 28). States with "the highest gun ownership rates also have the highest suicide rates.". Retrieved from https://www.politifact.com/factchecks/2016/apr/11/myra-signer/myra-signer-says-state-highest-gun-ownership-rates/

[xxvii] Siegel, M. Rothman, E. (2016, June 10). Firearm Ownership and Suicide Rates Among US Men and Women, 1981–2013. Retrieved from https://ajph.aphapublications.org/doi/full/10.2105/AJPH.2016.303182

[xxviii] Shaw, K. (2016, September 6). 10 Essential Facts About Guns and Suicide More than two-thirds of all gun deaths are self-inflicted. Retrieved from https://www.thetrace.org/2016/09/10-essential-facts-guns-suicide/

[xxix] Shaw, K. (2016, September 6). 10 Essential Facts About Guns and Suicide More than two-thirds of all gun deaths are self-inflicted. Retrieved from https://www.thetrace.org/2016/09/10-essential-facts-guns-suicide/

[xxx] Brady Guns Suicide Report 2016 – The Truth About Suicide and Guns. Retrieved from http://www.bradycampaign.org/sites/default/files/Brady-Guns-Suicide-Report-2016.pdf

[xxxi] Anglemyer, A., Horvath, T., & Rutherford, G. (2014, January 21). The accessibility of firearms and risk for suicide and homicide victimization among household members: A systematic review and meta-analysis. Retrieved from https://pubmed.ncbi.nlm.nih.gov/24592495/

[xxxii] CDC Centers for Disease Control and Prevention Injury Prevention & Control. Report generated from the CDC Web-Based Injury Statistics Query & Reporting System (WISQARS). Retrieved from https://www.cdc.gov/injury/wisqars/index.html

[xxxiii] CDC Centers for Disease Control and Prevention Injury Prevention & Control. Report generated from the CDC Web-Based Injury Statistics Query & Reporting System (WISQARS). Retrieved from https://www.cdc.gov/injury/wisqars/index.html

[xxxiv] Miller, M. Azrael, D. Hemenway, D. (2001, July 4). Firearm availability and unintentional firearm deaths. Retrieved from https://www.sciencedirect.com/science/article/abs/pii/S0001457500000610

xxxv United States General Accounting Office. (1991, March). *Accidental Shootings: Many Deaths and Injuries Caused by Firearms Could Be Prevented.* Retrieved from https://www.gao.gov/assets/160/150353.pdf

[xxxvi] Azrael, D. Cohen, J. Salhi, C. Miller, M (2018). Firearm Storage in Gun-owning Households with Children: Results of a 2015 National Survey. Retrieved from https://www.thetrace.org/wp-content/uploads/2018/05/Firearm-Storage-in-Households-with-Children_JUH.pdf

[xxxvii] Schuster M, MD PhD. Franke, TM PhD. Bastian A M MPH. Sor S, MD. Halfon N. MD MPH (2000, April). *Firearm Storage Patterns in U.S. Homes with Children,* 90 Am. J. Pub. Health 588, 590 Retrieved from http://www.rand.org/content/dam/rand/pubs/reprints/2005/RAND_RP890.pdf.

xxxviii Baxley, F. Miller, M. (2006, May 1). Parental Misperceptions About

Children and Firearms. Retrieved from
https://europepmc.org/article/med/16651499
xxxix Giffords Law Center To Prevent Gun Violence. Safe Storage. Retrieved from
https://lawcenter.giffords.org/gun-laws/policy-areas/child-consumer-safety/safe-
storage/
xl Giffords Law Center To Prevent Gun Violence. Annual Gun Law Scorecard 2019.
Retrieved from https://lawcenter.giffords.org/scorecard/
xli Everytown for Gun Safety. "NotAnAccident Index. Retrieved from
https://everytownresearch.org/notanaccident/#16294
xlii Harbarger, M. The Oregonian (2017, November 13). 7-year-old shoots sibling,
2, in head, Hermiston police say. Retrieved from
https://www.oregonlive.com/pacific-northwest-news/2017/11/2-year-
old_shot_in_head_by_sib.html
xliii Andrews, T. (2017, November 13). 1-year-old dies after being shot with
father's gun by 3-year-old, police say. Retrieved from
https://www.washingtonpost.com/
xliv Walsh, L. (2017, October 24). Teen dies in accidental shooting; Cullman
community mourns loss. Retrieved from
https://abc3340.com/news/local/cullman-teen-dies-in-accidental-shooting
xlv Pettit, E. (2017, June 22). 2-year-old Arkansas boy dies of gunshot wound,
officials say. Retrieved from
https://www.arkansasonline.com/news/2017/jun/22/arkansas-boy-2-dies-
gunshot-wound-apparent-acciden/
xlvi WFTS Webteam. (2017, May 29). Police: 10-year-old boy expected to be OK
after accidental shooting in St. Pete. Retrieved from
https://www.abcactionnews.com/news/crime/police-juvenile-boy-seriously-
injured-after-shooting-in-south-st-pete
xlvii Osborne, R. (2017, March 17). 2 young boys accidentally shot outside Fort
Worth Chuck E. Cheese's. Retrieved from
https://www.abcactionnews.com/news/crime/police-juvenile-boy-seriously-
injured-after-shooting-in-south-st-pete
xlviii Howard, M. (2017, February 1). Baby recovering after shot by 4-year-old
brother. Retrieved from https://www.wlbt.com/story/34397119/baby-
recovering-after-shot-by-4-year-old-brother/
xlix AP News. (2017, January 17). Girl, 10, identified as victim of deadly Missouri
shooting. Retrieved from
https://apnews.com/088ed73913fd4553a5b40660543701fa
l USA Facts, Firearm Deaths by Type 2017. Retrieved from
https://usafacts.org/data/topics/security-safety/crime-and-
justice/firearms/firearm-deaths/
li FBI:UCR. 2014 Crime in the United States. Expanded Homicide Data Table 15,
Justifiable Homicide
by Weapon, Private Citizen,1 2010–2014. Retrieved from

https://ucr.fbi.gov/crime-in-the-u.s/2014/crime-in-the-u.s.-2014/tables/expanded-homicide-data/expanded_homicide_data_table_15_justifiable_homicide_by_weapon_private_citizen_2010-2014.xls

[lii] McDowall, D. Wiersema, B. (1994, December). The incidence of defensive firearm use by US crime victims, 1987 through 1990. Retrieved from https://www.ncbi.nlm.nih.gov/pmc/articles/PMC1615397/

[liii] Democratic Underground.com. (2016, April 25). As we suspected: NRA's Myth of Defensive Gun Use is largely just a myth. Retrieved from https://www.democraticunderground.com/126210508

[liv] Japan Today. (2012, October 20). Louisiana 'Freeze' shooting tragedy remembered 20 years on. Retrieved from https://japantoday.com/category/features/kuchikomi/louisiana-freeze-shooting-tragedy-remembered-20-years-on

[lv] USA Today. (2013, December 7). Suffering from Alzheimer's, Ga. man fatally shot. Retrieved from https://eu.usatoday.com/story/news/nation/2013/12/07/suffering-from-alzheimers-ga-man-fatally-shot/3904791/

[lvi] US Department of Justice. (2013, May). Firearm Violence, 1993-2011. Table11 Self-protective behaviors, by type of crime, 2007–2011. Retrieved from https://www.bjs.gov/content/pub/pdf/fv9311.pdf

[lvii] BBC News. (2016, July 18). US police shootings: How many die each year? Retrieved from https://www.bbc.co.uk/news/magazine-36826297

[lviii] The Washington Post. Police Shootings 2016 database. Retrieved from https://www.washingtonpost.com/graphics/national/police-shootings-2016/

[lix] The Washington Post. Police Shootings 2017 database. Retrieved from https://www.washingtonpost.com/graphics/national/police-shootings-2017/

[lx] Lartey, J. (2015, June 9). By the numbers: US police kill more in days than other countries do in years. Retrieved from https://www.theguardian.com/us-news/2015/jun/09/the-counted-police-killings-us-vs-other-countries?

lxi Statista. Number of fatal shootings by police in England and Wales from 2004/05 to 2018/19. Retrieved from https://www.statista.com/statistics/319246/police-fatal-shootings-england-wales/

lxii The Conversation. (2014, November 25). Shoot to kill: the use of lethal force by police in Australia. Retrieved from https://theconversation.com/shoot-to-kill-the-use-of-lethal-force-by-police-in-australia-34578

lxiii Gagnon, M. (2017, May 14). Police in Germany kill more than you think. Retrieved from https://www.dw.com/en/police-in-germany-kill-more-than-you-think/a-38822484

[lxiv] McCarthy, N. (2017, August 8). Where Are The World's Unarmed Police Officers? Retrieved from https://www.statista.com/chart/10601/where-are-the-worlds-unarmed-police-officers/

[lxv] Washington Post. Fatal force, Police shootings database 2015-2020. Retrieved from https://www.washingtonpost.com/graphics/investigations/police-shootings-database/

[lxvi] Siemaszko, C, McCausland, P. (2017 December 22), Texas boy, 6, killed in deputy-involved shooting days before Christmas Retrieved from. https://www.nbcnews.com/news/us-news/texas-boy-age-6-killed-deputy-involved-shooting-days-christmas-n832166

[lxvii] National Law Enforcement Officers Memorial Fund, (2019, March 29). Causes of Law Enforcement Deaths. Retrieved from https://nleomf.org/facts-figures/causes-of-law-enforcement-deaths

[lxviii] BBC News. (2017, April 7). Westminster attack: What happened. Retrieved from https://www.bbc.co.uk/news/uk-39355108

[lxix] BBC News. (2018, January 31). PC Gareth Browning death: Man jailed for manslaughter. Retrieved from https://www.bbc.co.uk/news/uk-england-berkshire-42889088

[lxx] Williams, R. (2012, September 18). Two unarmed female police officers 'lured to their deaths' in Greater Manchester. Retrieved from https://www.independent.co.uk/news/uk/crime/two-unarmed-female-police-officers-lured-to-their-deaths-in-greater-manchester-8152771.html

[lxxi] Office for National Statistics, (2018, February 8). Homicide in England and Wales: year ending March 2017. Retrieved from https://www.ons.gov.uk/peoplepopulationandcommunity/crimeandjustice/articles/homicideinenglandandwales/yearendingmarch2017

[lxxii] Harrell, E. (2012, December). U.S. Department of Justice, Violent Victimization Committed by Strangers, 1993-2010. Retrieved from https://bjs.gov/content/pub/pdf/vvcs9310.pdf

[lxxiii] Violence Policy Center. (2018, June), American Roulette Murder-Suicide in the United States. Retrieved from https://vpc.org/studies/amroul2018.pdf

[lxxiv] GVA Gun Violence Archive. Past Summary Ledgers. Gun Violence Archive 2016, Gun Violence Archive 2017. Retrieved from https://www.gunviolencearchive.org/past-tolls

[lxxv] FBI documents - Active Shooter Incidents in the United States in 2016 and 2017. Retrieved from https://www.fbi.gov/file-repository/active-shooter-incidents-us-2016-2017.pdf/view

[lxxvi] Lemeiux, F. (2015, December 3). Six things to know about mass shootings in America. Retrieved from https://theconversation.com/six-things-to-know-about-mass-shootings-in-america-48934

[lxxvii] Christensen, J. (2017, October 5). Why the US has the most mass shootings. Retrieved from https://edition.cnn.com/2015/08/27/health/u-s-most-mass-shootings/index.html

[lxxviii] CNN Editorial Research. (2020, May 3). Mass Shootings in the US Fast Facts. Retrieved from https://edition.cnn.com/2019/08/19/us/mass-shootings-fast-facts/index.html

[lxxix] National Museum Australia. Defining Moments. Port Arthur massacre. Retrieved from https://www.nma.gov.au/defining-moments/resources/port-arthur-massacre

[lxxx] Bright, D. Weatherburn, D. Goldsworthy, T. (2017, October 30). FactCheck Q&A: did government gun buybacks reduce the number of gun deaths in Australia? Retrieved from https://theconversation.com/factcheck-qanda-did-government-gun-buybacks-reduce-the-number-of-gun-deaths-in-australia-85836

[lxxxi] Bright, D. Weatherburn, D. Goldsworthy, T. (2017, October 30). FactCheck Q&A: did government gun buybacks reduce the number of gun deaths in Australia? Retrieved from https://theconversation.com/factcheck-qanda-did-government-gun-buybacks-reduce-the-number-of-gun-deaths-in-australia-85836

[lxxxii] Bauer, P. Dunblane school massacre school shooting, Dunblane, Scotland, United Kingdom [1996]. Retrieved from https://www.britannica.com/event/Dunblane-school-massacre

lxxxiii Hansard, (1996, October 16), The Cullen Report (Firearms). Retrieved from https://api.parliament.uk/historic-hansard/lords/1996/oct/16/the-cullen-report

[lxxxiv] Fredrik, (2016, May 6). Hungerford Massacre. Retrieved from http://crimescenedb.com/hungerford-massacre/

[lxxxv] BBC News (2011, March 25). Cumbria shootings: Timeline of Derrick Bird's rampage. Retrieved from https://www.bbc.co.uk/news/10259982

[lxxxvi] Barnett, D. (2017, December 16). Firearms Act: Twenty years on, has it made a difference? Retrieved from https://www.independent.co.uk/news/long_reads/firearms-act-twenty-years-on-has-it-made-a-difference-dunblane-port-arthur-a8110911.html

[lxxxvii] The New York Times. (2019, March 17). There Will Be Changes' to Gun Laws, New Zealand Prime Minister Says. Retrieved from https://www.nytimes.com/2019/03/17/world/asia/new-zealand-shooting.html

[lxxxviii] Channel News Asia. (2019, April 10). New Zealand votes to amend gun laws after Christchurch attack. Retrieved from https://www.channelnewsasia.com/news/world/new-zealand-votes-to-amend-gun-laws-after-christchurch-attack-11429852

[lxxxix] Delkic, M. (2017, December 14). Sandy Hook Anniversary: These Are the Gun Control Laws That Have Failed Since the Newtown Shooting. Retrieved from https://www.newsweek.com/sandy-hook-anniversary-gun-control-laws-failed-747415

[xc] BBC News. (2018, December 19) - US bans 'bump stock' gun device used in Las Vegas mass shooting. Retrieved from https://www.bbc.co.uk/news/world-us-canada-46614001

[xci] Cornell Law School. Second Amendment. Retrieved from https://www.law.cornell.edu/wex/second_amendment

[xcii] Cornell Law School. Second Amendment. Retrieved from https://www.law.cornell.edu/wex/second_amendment

[xciii] Military.com. Retrieved from https://www.military.com/national-guard

[xciv] Military Law. (2019, December 23). Naval militia. Retrieved from https://military.laws.com/naval-militia

[xcv] JUST IA US law. 2010 Georgia Code. Retrieved from https://law.justia.com/codes/georgia/2010/title-38/chapter-2/article-1/part-4/38-2-70/

[xcvi] The Editors of Encyclopaedia Britannica. U.S. Department of Defense. Retrieved from https://www.britannica.com/topic/US-Department-of-Defense

[xcvii] History Lists. 10 Deadliest American Wars. Retrieved from https://historylist.wordpress.com/2008/03/18/10-deadliest-american-wars/

[xcviii] Peterson, P. (2018, May 7), U.S. Defense Spending Compared to Other Countries. Retrieved from https://www.economicsvoodoo.com/wp-content/uploads/Peter-G.-Peterson-Foundation-U.S.-Defense-Spending-Compared-to-Other-Countries-2018-10-27.pdf

[xcix] Prof Frink, (2018, March 27). One in five Americans wants Second Amendment repeal: Poll. Retrieved from https://internationalfreepress.com/2018/03/27/one-in-five-americans-wants-second-amendment-repeal-poll/

[c] Lopez G, (2015, October 2), The ridiculous number of guns owned by Americans, in one chart. Retrieved from https://www.vox.com/policy-and-politics/2015/10/2/9439909/the-ridiculous-number-of-guns-owned-by-americans-in-one-chart

[ci] Parker, K. Horowitz, J. Igielnik, R. Oliphant, J. Brown, A. (2017, June 22). America's Complex Relationship With Guns. Retrieved from https://www.pewsocialtrends.org/2017/06/22/americas-complex-relationship-with-guns/

[cii] Murray, M. (2018, March 23). Poll: 58 percent say gun ownership increases safety. Retrieved from https://www.nbcnews.com/politics/first-read/poll-58-percent-say-gun-ownership-increases-safety-n859231

[ciii] Kurtzman, L. (2014, January 21). Access to Guns Increases Risk of Suicide, Homicide. Retrieved from https://www.ucsf.edu/news/2014/01/111286/access-guns-increases-risk-suicide-homicide

[civ] Yablon, A. (2017, July 18). 4 Out of 10 Self-Defense Handgun Owners Have Received No Formal Firearms Training. Retrieved from https://www.thetrace.org/2017/07/handgun-owners-self-defense-no-formal-training/

[cv] Crary, D. (2007, September 3). Number Of Hunters In U.S. Declining. Retrieved from https://www.cbsnews.com/news/number-of-hunters-in-us-declining/

[cvi] Lock, S. (2020, February 13). Number of participants in target shooting in the United States from 2006 to 2017 (in millions)*. Retrieved from https://www.statista.com/statistics/191962/participants-in-target-shooting-in-the-us-since-2006/

[cvii] Parker, K. Horowitz, J. Igielnik, R. Oliphant, J. Brown, A. (2017, June 22). America's Complex Relationship With Guns. Retrieved from https://www.pewsocialtrends.org/2017/06/22/americas-complex-relationship-

with-guns/
[cviii] Lopez G, (2015, October 2), The ridiculous number of guns owned by Americans, in one chart. Retrieved from https://www.vox.com/policy-and-politics/2015/10/2/9439909/the-ridiculous-number-of-guns-owned-by-americans-in-one-chart
[cix] Associated Press. (2018, June 19). Americans own nearly half the world's civilian firearms. Retrieved from https://nypost.com/2018/06/19/americans-own-nearly-half-the-worlds-civilian-firearms/
[cx] KDLYPEN. (2013, March 11). Hollywood's Unapologetic Portrayal of Gun Violence. Retrieved from http://yvpc.sph.umich.edu/hollywoods-unapologetic-portrayal-gun-violence/
[cxi] KDLYPEN. (2013, March 11). Hollywood's Unapologetic Portrayal of Gun Violence. Retrieved from http://yvpc.sph.umich.edu/hollywoods-unapologetic-portrayal-gun-violence/
[cxii] Businesswire. (2016, February 11). Activision Blizzard Announces Fourth Quarter and Full Year 2015 Financial Results. Retrieved from https://www.businesswire.com/news/home/20160211006451/en/Activision-Blizzard-Announces-Fourth-Quarter-Full-Year
[cxiii] The Violence Policy Center. Gun Shows in America. Retrieved from https://vpc.org/studies/tupthree.htm
[cxiv] Parker, K. Horowitz, J. Igielnik, R. Oliphant, J. Brown, A. (2017, June 22). America's Complex Relationship With Guns. Retrieved from https://www.pewsocialtrends.org/2017/06/22/americas-complex-relationship-with-guns/
[cxv] Spitzer, R (1995). *The Politics of Gun-control*. Chatham House Publishers.
[cxvi] ATF Bureau of Alcohol, Tobacco, Firearms and Explosives. Annual Firearms Manufacturing and export report Year 2016 Final. Retrieved from https://www.atf.gov/file/123801/download
[cxvii] Detrixhe, J. (2018, March 7). A third of guns in the US are imported, and foreign firearms makers want a say on gun control. Retrieved from https://qz.com/1222436/a-third-of-guns-in-the-us-are-imported-and-foreign-manufacturers-like-glock-and-beretta-want-a-say-on-gun-control-laws/
[cxviii] FBI. NICS Firearm Background Checks: Month/Year. Retrieved from https://www.fbi.gov/file-repository/nics_firearm_checks_-_month_year.pdf/view
[cxix] RUGER. LCP Model 3701 Caliber 380 Auto. Retrieved from https://ruger.com/products/lcp/specSheets/3701.html
[cxx] Wing, N. Reilly, M. (2018, February 15). Here's What You Need To Know About The Weapons Of War Used In Mass Shootings. Retrieved from https://www.huffingtonpost.co.uk/entry/ar-15-style-weapons_n_5a84cf09e4b0ab6daf45ab2d
[cxxi] Editorial Staff. (2010, March 3). Firearms Owner's Protection Act (1986). Retrieved from http://fbinicsystem.com/federal-and-us-gun-laws/firearms-

owners-protection-act-1986.html

[cxxii] Congress.Gov. (1989-1990). S.2070 - Gun-Free School Zones Act of 1990. Retrieved from https://www.congress.gov/bill/101st-congress/senate-bill/2070/text

[cxxiii] Govtrak. H.R. 1025 (103rd): Brady Handgun Violence Prevention Act. Retrieved from https://www.govtrack.us/congress/bills/103/hr1025

[cxxiv] Editorial Staff. (2010, March 3). Federal Assault Weapons Ban (1994 – 2004). Retrieved from http://fbinicsystem.com/federal-and-us-gun-laws/federal-assault-weapons-ban-1994-2004.html

[cxxv] Govtrak. S. 397 (109th): Protection of Lawful Commerce in Arms Act. Retrieved from https://www.govtrack.us/congress/bills/109/s397/summary

[cxxvi] Taylor, K. Hanbury, M. (2017, October 5). Here's how easy it is to legally buy a semiautomatic gun in the US. Retrieved from https://www.businessinsider.com.au/how-to-buy-a-gun-2017-10

[cxxvii] Taylor, K. Hanbury, M. (2017, October 5). Here's how easy it is to legally buy a semiautomatic gun in the US. Retrieved from https://www.businessinsider.com.au/how-to-buy-a-gun-2017-10

[cxxviii] Cratty, C. (2013, January 15). Criminal record top reason for U.S. gun-check rejection. Retrieved from https://edition.cnn.com/2013/01/14/justice/guns-background-check/index.html

[cxxix] NSSF The Firearm Industry Trade Association. (2018, April 10). Firearms Industry Economic Impact Rises 169% since 2008. Retrieved from https://www.nssf.org/firearms-industry-economic-impact-rises-169-since-2008/

[cxxx] Gun Owners of America. Retrieved from https://gunowners.org

[cxxxi] Second Amendment Foundation. Retrieved from https://www.saf.org/

[cxxxii] National Association for Gun Rights. Retrieved from https://nationalgunrights.org/

[cxxxiii] National Shooting Sports Foundation. Retrieved from https://www.nssf.org/

[cxxxiv] Valentine, M. (2013, September 12). The Gun Lobbying Group You Don't Hear About The NSSF is the NRA's smaller, highly effective cousin. Retrieved from https://www.theatlantic.com/national/archive/2013/09/the-gun-lobbying-group-you-dont-hear-about/279616/

[cxxxv] National Rifle Association. Retrieved from https://nra.org.uk/

[cxxxvi] NRA-ILA. (2017, July 7). Remarkable Finding from Pew Survey. Retrieved from https://www.nraila.org/articles/20170707/remarkable-finding-from-pew-survey

[cxxxvii] Parker, J. (2018 June). Live-Streaming the Apocalypse With NRATV. Retrieved from https://www.theatlantic.com/magazine/archive/2018/06/nratv-live-streaming-the-apocalypse/559139/

[cxxxviii] Spies, M. Balcerzak, A. (2016, November 9). The NRA Placed Big Bets on the 2016 Election, and Won Almost All of Them. Retrieved from https://www.opensecrets.org/news/2016/11/the-nra-placed-big-bets-on-the-2016-election-and-won-almost-all-of-them/

[cxxxix] Scher, B. (2018, February 19). Why the NRA Always Wins. Retrieved from

https://www.politico.com/magazine/story/2018/02/19/why-the-nra-always-wins-217028

[cxl] Bryan, B. (2018, March 21). Something historic is happening with how Americans see the NRA. Retrieved from https://www.businessinsider.com/nra-poll-popularity-favorability-more-americans-dislike-2018-3?r=US&IR=T

[cxli] Stone, P. (2019, March 1). NRA in crisis: how the gun group became ensnared in the Russia inquiry. Retrieved from https://www.theguardian.com/us-news/2019/mar/01/nra-russia-investigations-gun-lobby

[cxlii] Murray, S. Shortell, D. (2019, April 27). Alleged Russian agent Maria Butina sentenced to 18 months in prison on conspiracy charge. Retrieved from https://edition.cnn.com/2019/04/26/politics/maria-butina-sentencing/index.html

[cxliii] National Institute of Justice. (2019, February 26). Gun Violence in America. Retrieved from https://nij.ojp.gov/topics/articles/gun-violence-america

[cxliv] Office for National Statistics. (2020, February 13). Offences involving the use of weapons: data tables year ending March 2019. Retrieved from https://www.ons.gov.uk/peoplepopulationandcommunity/crimeandjustice/datasets/offencesinvolvingtheuseofweaponsdatatables

[cxlv] Associated Press. (2019, January 1). Homicides in Chicago decline in 2018, but still dwarf totals in Los Angeles and New York. Retrieved from https://www.latimes.com/nation/la-na-chicago-homicides-fall-20190101-story.html

[cxlvi] Mirabile, F. Nass, D. (2019, October 1). What's the Homicide Capital of America? Murder Rates in U.S. Cities, Ranked. Retrieved from https://www.thetrace.org/2018/04/highest-murder-rates-us-cities-list/

cxlvii Tarm, M. (2018, June 11). Social media altering Chicago street-gang culture, fueling violence. Retrieved from https://chicago.suntimes.com/2018/6/11/18405967/social-media-altering-chicago-street-gang-culture-fueling-violence

cxlviii Sun-Times Wire. (2019, January 1). Police release 2018 shooting numbers. Retrieved from https://chicago.suntimes.com/2019/1/1/18314536/police-release-2018-shooting-numbers

cxlix Aol. (2017, January 27). Debunked: Chicago has the strictest gun laws in the country. Retrieved from https://www.aol.com/article/news/2017/01/27/debunked-chicago-has-the-strictest-gun-laws-in-the/21701367/

[cl] Giffords Law Center. Annual Gun Law Scorecard. Retrieved from https://lawcenter.giffords.org/scorecard2017/

[cli] The Local. (2018, June 19). Switzerland ranks 16th for civilian firearms: survey. Retrieved from https://www.thelocal.ch/20180619/switzerland-ranks-16th-for-civilian-firearms-survey

[clii] Knoema. UNODC International Homicide Statistics. Retrieved from https://knoema.com/UNODCHIS2017/unodc-international-homicide-statistics

cliii Huppi.com. Myth: Switzerland proves that high gun-ownership doesn't increase murder. Retrieved from http://www.huppi.com/kangaroo/L-switzerland.htm?vm=r

cliv GunPolicy.org. Serbia- Gun Facts, Figures and the Law. Retrieved from https://www.gunpolicy.org/firearms/region/serbia

clv Lott J Jr. More Guns Less Crime originally published 1998

clvi Donohue, J. Aneja, A. Weber, K. (2017 June).  Right-to-Carry Laws and Violent Crime: A Comprehensive Assessment Using Panel Data and a State-Level Synthetic Control Analysis. Retrieved from https://www.nber.org/papers/w23510

clvii Hemenway, D. (206, August). Review of the book Firearms and violence: a critical review. Retrieved from https://www.ncbi.nlm.nih.gov/pmc/articles/PMC2586792/

clviii Lott J Jr. More Guns Less Crime. Third Edition, Chapter 5

clix Civitas Crime. (2006). Comparisons of Crime in OECD Countries. Retrieved from http://www.civitas.org.uk/content/files/crime_stats_oecdjan2012.pdf

clx Office for National Statistics. (2016, February 11). Overview of violent crime and sexual offences. Retrieved from https://www.ons.gov.uk/peoplepopulationandcommunity/crimeandjustice/compendium/focusonviolentcrimeandsexualoffences/yearendingmarch2015/chapter1overviewofviolentcrimeandsexualoffences

clxi FBI:UCR. 2017 Crime in the United States – Violent Crime. Retrieved from https://ucr.fbi.gov/crime-in-the-u.s/2017/crime-in-the-u.s.-2017/topic-pages/violent-crime#

clxii Kurtzman, L. (2014, January 21). Access to Guns Increases Risk of Suicide, Homicide. Retrieved from https://www.ucsf.edu/news/2014/01/111286/access-guns-increases-risk-suicide-homicide

clxiii Khazan, O. (2017, July 20). Nearly Half of All Murdered Women Are Killed by Romantic Partners. Retrieved from www.theatlantic.com/health/archive/2017/07/homicides-women/534306/

clxiv Dumenko, S. (2016, September 20). NEW NRA AD PLAYS LIKE A HORROR MOVIE: 'DON'T LET HILLARY CLINTON LEAVE YOU DEFENSELESS'. Retrieved from https://adage.com/article/campaign-trail/nra-ad-hillary-clinton-leave-defenseless/305929The Journal of Trauma: Injury, Infection, and Critical Care: July 1992 - p 1-5. R

clxv Kellermann, A. Mercy, J. (1992, July). The Journal of Trauma: Injury, Infection, and Critical Care: July 1992 - p 1-5. Retrieved from https://journals.lww.com/jtrauma/abstract/1992/07000/men,_women,_and_murder__gender_specific.1.aspx

clxvi Defilippis, E. (2014, February 23). Having a Gun in the House Doesn't Make a Woman Safer. Retrieved from https://www.theatlantic.com/national/archive/2014/02/having-a-gun-in-the-house-doesnt-make-a-woman-safer/284022/

clxvii Hemenway, D. Miller, M. Shinoda-Tagawa, T. (2002, February). Firearm availability and female homicide victimization rates among 25 populous high-income countries. Retrieved from https://www.researchgate.net/publication/11379728_Firearm_availability_and_female_homicide_victimization_rates_among_25_populous_high-income_countries

clxviii Violence Policy Center. (2017, May). Firearm Justifiable Homicides and Non-Fatal Self Defense Gun Use. Retrieved from https://www.vpc.org/studies/justifiable17.pdf

clxix Shaw, K. (2016, September 6). The Trace, 10 Essential Facts About Guns and Suicide. Retrieved from https://www.thetrace.org/2016/09/10-essential-facts-guns-suicide/

clxx Ingraham, C. (2018, April 3). Guns are now responsible for 75% of killings in America. Retrieved from https://www.independent.co.uk/news/world/americas/us-gun-deaths-killings-control-homicides-america-shootings-a8285916.html

clxxi Penn Medicine News. 2014, January 2). Survival Rates Similar for Gunshot, Stabbing Victims Whether Brought to the Hospital by Police or EMS, Penn Medicine Study Finds. Retrieved from https://www.pennmedicine.org/news/news-releases/2014/january/survival-rates-similar-for-gun84

clxxii Magrath, G. (2013, March 1). For 2013, Let's Ban Cars and Guns. Retrieved from https://www.huffpost.com/entry/gun-control-debate_b_2389047

clxxiii Pariona, A. (2020, January 9). Murder Rate By Country. Retrieved from https://www.worldatlas.com/articles/murder-rates-by-country.html

clxxiv Procon.org. (2017, August 8). International Firearm Homicide Rates 2010-2015. Retrieved from https://gun-control.procon.org/international-firearm-homicide-rates/

clxxv Mental Health America, The state of mental health in America 2018. Retrieved from https://www.mhanational.org/issues/state-mental-health-america-2018

clxxvi Walton, A. (2011, October 4). Why More Americans Suffer From Mental Disorders Than Anyone Else. Retrieved from https://www.theatlantic.com/health/archive/2011/10/why-more-americans-suffer-from-mental-disorders-than-anyone-else/246035/

clxxvii Nuwer, R. (2018 May 10). Is there a link between mass shootings and mental illness? Retrieved from https://www.bbc.com/future/article/20180509-is-there-a-link-between-mass-shooting-and-mental-illness

clxxviii Science Daily. (2010, December 6). People with severe mental illness 12 times more likely to commit suicide. Retrieved from https://www.sciencedaily.com/releases/2010/12/101206161740.htm

clxxix National Institute of Mental Health (NIH). Suicide in America Frequently Asked Questions. Retrieved from https://www.nimh.nih.gov/health/publications/suicide-faq/index.shtml

clxxx Baker, P. (2017, November 6). Trump Says Issue Is Mental Health, Not Gun Control. Retrieved from https://www.nytimes.com/2017/11/06/us/politics/trump-guns-mental-health.html

clxxxi Baker, P. (2017, November 6). Trump Says Issue Is Mental Health, Not Gun Control. Retrieved from https://www.nytimes.com/2017/11/06/us/politics/trump-guns-mental-health.html

clxxxii Giffords Law Center to prevent gun violence. Extreme Risk Protection Orders. Retrieved from https://lawcenter.giffords.org/gun-laws/policy-areas/who-can-have-a-gun/extreme-risk-protection-orders/

clxxxiii Slack, M. (2012, December 14). President Obama Speaks on the Shooting in Connecticut. Retrieved from https://obamawhitehouse.archives.gov/blog/2012/12/14/president-obama-speaks-shooting-connecticut

clxxxiv Conspiracies.net. (2017, April 7). SANDY HOOK – SCHOOL MASSACRE OR GOVERNMENT HOAX?. Retrieved from https://www.conspiracies.net/sandy-hook-school-massacre-government-hoax/

clxxxv Schwartz, S. (2012, December 23). Iranian TV Blames Sandy Hook Shootings on 'Israeli Death Squads,' Says Gunman Was Just the 'Fall Guy. Retrieved from https://www.theblaze.com/news/2012/12/23/iranian-tv-blames-sandy-hook-shootings-on-israeli-death-squads-says-gunman-was-just-the-fall-guy

clxxxvi Alvarez, L. (2016, January 6). Florida Professor Who Cast Doubt on Mass Shootings Is Fired. Retrieved from https://www.nytimes.com/2016/01/07/us/florida-professor-who-cast-doubt-on-mass-shootings-is-fired.html

clxxxvii Levine, D. (2018, July 10). Alex Jones & Sandy Hook: 5 Fast Facts You Need to Know. Retrieved from https://heavy.com/news/2017/06/alex-jones-sandy-hook-shooting-conspiracy-theory-megyn-kelly-apology/

clxxxviii Weston, P. (2018, September 11). Banned Infowars app launched by conspiracy theorist host Alex Jones is STILL online for Android's Google Play despite being kicked off Apple, Twitter, Facebook and Spotify. Retrieved from https://www.dailymail.co.uk/sciencetech/article-6154591/Banned-Infowars-app-launched-Alex-Jones-online-Androids-Google-Play.html

clxxxix Williamson, E. (2018, August 1). InfoWars host Alex Jones faces defamation case from Sandy Hook families over false conspiracy theory. Retrieved from https://www.independent.co.uk/news/world/americas/sandy-hook-alex-jones-info-wars-fake-conspiracy-theory-a8472301.html

cxc BBC News. (2019, December 31). Alex Jones ordered to pay $100,000 in Sandy Hook defamation case. Retrieved from https://www.bbc.co.uk/news/world-us-canada-50960730

cxci Zadrozny, B. (2018, May 23). Six more families sue Alex Jones over Sandy Hook conspiracy claims. Retrieved from https://www.nbcnews.com/business/business-news/six-more-families-sue-alex-jones-over-sandy-hook-conspiracy-n876881

[cxcii] IMDb. (2014, November). We Need to Talk About Sandy Hook. Retrieved from https://www.imdb.com/title/tt4245810/

[cxciii] Cassino, D. Jenkins, K. (2013, May 1). BELIEFS ABOUT SANDY HOOK COVER-UP, COMING REVOLUTION
UNDERLIE DIVIDE ON GUN CONTROL. Retrieved from https://portal.fdu.edu/newspubs/publicmind/2013/guncontrol/final.pdf

cxciv Hignett, K. (2017, December 8). Sandy Hook Mass Shooting Led to 3 Million Extra Gun Sales and Spike in Firearms Deaths, Researchers Say. Retrieved from https://www.newsweek.com/sandy-hook-mass-shooting-gun-sales-firearms-deaths-741965

[cxcv] Cornell Law School. Legal Information Institute. UNITED STATES v. MILLER et al. Retrieved from https://www.law.cornell.edu/supremecourt/text/307/174

[cxcvi] Cornell Law School. Legal Information Institute. DISTRICT OF COLUMBIA v. HELLER. Retrieved from https://www.law.cornell.edu/supremecourt/text/07-290

[cxcvii] Jones, J. (2008, June 26). Americans in Agreement with Supreme Court on Gun Rights. Retrieved from https://news.gallup.com/poll/108394/americans-agreement-supreme-court-gun-rights.aspx

cxcviii Rose, V. (2008, October 17). SUMMARY OF D.C. V. HELLER. Retrieved from https://www.cga.ct.gov/2008/rpt/2008-R-0578.htm

cxcix Flynn, M. Barbash, F. (2018, February 22). Does the Second Amendment really protect assault weapons? Four courts have said no. Retrieved from https://www.washingtonpost.com/news/morning-mix/wp/2018/02/22/does-the-second-amendment-really-protect-assault-weapons-four-courts-have-said-no/

[cc] The Week Staff, (2018, March 18). The surprising history of the NRA. Retrieved from https://theweek.com/articles/7610135/surprising-history-nra

[cci] Waxman, O. (2018, October 30). How the Gun Control Act of 1968 Changed America's Approach to Firearms—And What People Get Wrong About That History. Retrieved from https://time.com/5429002/gun-control-act-history-1968/

[ccii] Achenbach, J. Higham, S. Horwitz, S. (2013, January 12). How NRA's true believers converted a marksmanship group into a mighty gun lobby. Retrieved from https://www.washingtonpost.com/politics/how-nras-true-believers-converted-a-marksmanship-group-into-a-mighty-gun-lobby/2013/01/12/51c62288-59b9-11e2-88d0-c4cf65c3ad15_story.html

[cciii] The Week Staff, (2018, March 18). The surprising history of the NRA. Retrieved from https://theweek.com/articles/7610135/surprising-history-nra

[cciv] Shabad, R. (2016, June 20). Why more than 100 gun control proposals in Congress since 2011 have failed. Retrieved from https://www.cbsnews.com/news/how-many-gun-control-proposals-have-been-offered-since-2011/

[ccv] Shabad, R. (2016, June 20). Why more than 100 gun control proposals in Congress since 2011 have failed. Retrieved from

https://www.cbsnews.com/news/how-many-gun-control-proposals-have-been-offered-since-2011/

ccvi Mark, M. (2018, February, 21). The American public could be at a turning point on gun control. Retrieved from https://www.businessinsider.in/the-american-public-could-be-at-a-turning-point-on-gun-control/articleshow/63005813.cms

ccvii Mosendz, P, (2018, March 12). Most Gun Owners Support Stricter Laws—Even NRA Members. Retrieved from https://www.bloomberg.com/news/articles/2018-03-12/most-gun-owners-support-stricter-laws-even-nra-members

ccviii The Free Dictionary by Farlax. Lobbying. Retrieved from https://www.thefreedictionary.com/lobbying

ccix The Editors of Encyclopaedia Britannica. Lobbying. Retrieved from https://www.britannica.com/topic/lobbying

ccx Ingraham, C, (2017, April 14) Somebody just put a price tag on the 2016 election. It's a doozy. Retrieved from https://www.washingtonpost.com/news/wonk/wp/2017/04/14/somebody-just-put-a-price-tag-on-the-2016-election-its-a-doozy/

ccxi OpenSecrets.org. Industries. Retrieved from http://www.opensecrets.org/federal-lobbying/industries?cycle=2018

ccxii OpenSecrets.org. Gun Rights Vs Gun Control. Retrieved from http://www.opensecrets.org/news/issues/guns

ccxiii Guardian US Interactive Team. (2012, December, 27). Gun rights v gun control: how each group spends its money – interactive. Retrieved from https://www.theguardian.com/world/interactive/2012/dec/27/pro-gun-versus-gun-control-spending

ccxiv Bradford, B. (2012, September 13). Explainer: How Much Does the NRA Influence Elections? Retrieved from https://www.wnyc.org/story/237219-explainer-how-much-does-nra-influence-elections/

ccxv Daily KOS. (2014, May 27). This is How the NRA 'Grades' your Candidates. Retrieved from https://www.dailykos.com/stories/2014/5/27/1302266/-This-is-How-the-NRA-Grades-your-Candidates

ccxvi OpenSecrets.org. Gun Rights: Money to Congress 2016. Retrieved from https://www.opensecrets.org/industries/summary.php?cycle=2016&ind=q13

ccxvii OpenSecrets.org. Gun Control: Money to Congress 2016. Retrieved from https://www.opensecrets.org/industries/summary.php?ind=q12&recipdetail=A&sortorder=U&mem=Y&cycle=2016

ccxviii Brenan, M. (2019, May 24). Congressional Approval Steady at 20%. Retrieved from https://news.gallup.com/poll/257762/congressional-approval-steady.aspx

ccxix Paulsen, J. (2015, June 18). Are Guns Registered in a National Firearms Registry. Retrieved from https://www.concealedcarry.com/law/are-guns-registered/

ccxx Giffords Law Center to Prevent Gun Violence. Registration. Retrieved from https://lawcenter.giffords.org/gun-laws/policy-areas/gun-owner-responsibilities/registration/

ccxxi RT Question More. (2013, August 21). NRA built massive database of gun owners while opposing national gun registry. Retrieved from https://www.rt.com/usa/nra-database-guns-registry-811/

ccxxii RT Question More. (2013, August 21). NRA built massive database of gun owners while opposing national gun registry. Retrieved from https://www.rt.com/usa/nra-database-guns-registry-811/

ccxxiii Holter, L. (2018, June 1). These National Gun Registry Pros & Cons Show Why The Debate Is So Thorny. Retrieved from https://www.bustle.com/p/5-national-gun-registry-pros-cons-show-why-the-debate-is-so-thorny-9242571

ccxxiv Shepard, S. (2018, February 28). Gun control support surges in polls. Retrieved from https://www.politico.com/story/2018/02/28/gun-control-polling-parkland-430099

ccxxv Giffords Law Center to Prevent Gun Violence. Annual Gun Law Scorecard. Retrieved from https://lawcenter.giffords.org/scorecard2018/#rankings

ccxxvi The Dickey Amendment. Retrieved from https://appd.s3.amazonaws.com/docs/meetings/2017SpringPresentations/WS31HO4.pdf

ccxxvii Greenfieldboyce, N. (2018, March 23). Spending Bill Lets CDC Study Gun Violence; But Researchers Are Skeptical It Will Help. Retrieved from https://www.npr.org/sections/health-shots/2018/03/23/596413510/proposed-budget-allows-cdc-to-study-gun-violence-researchers-skeptical

ccxxviii Frankel, T. (2015, January 14). Why the CDC still isn't researching gun violence, despite the ban being lifted two years ago. Retrieved from https://www.washingtonpost.com/news/storyline/wp/2015/01/14/why-the-cdc-still-isnt-researching-gun-violence-despite-the-ban-being-lifted-two-years-ago/

ccxxix NPR Politics. (2015, October 9). Ex-Rep. Dickey Regrets Restrictive Law On Gun Violence Research. Retrieved from https://www.npr.org/2015/10/09/447098666/ex-rep-dickey-regrets-restrictive-law-on-gun-violence-research

ccxxx Lexico Oxford English Dictionary. Meaning of Freedom in English. Retrieved from https://www.lexico.com/definition/freedom

ccxxxi The Rights and Freedoms of Americans. (From: Hartley, William H., Vincent, William S. American Civics. N.Y., 1974, pp. 34ff). Retrieved from https://www.tep-online.info/laku/usa/rights.htm

ccxxxii Lexico Oxford English Dictionary. Meaning of Control in English. Retrieved from https://www.lexico.com/definition/control

ccxxxiii Governors Highway Safety Association. Distracted Driving. Retrieved from https://www.ghsa.org/state-laws/issues/distracted%20driving

ccxxxiv Lexico Oxford English Dictionary. Meaning of Safety in English. Retrieved

from https://www.lexico.com/definition/safety
[ccxxxv] Hopper, E. (2020, February 24). Maslow's Hierarchy of Needs Explained. Retrieved from https://www.thoughtco.com/maslows-hierarchy-of-needs-4582571
ccxxxvi Lexico Oxford English Dictionary. Meaning of Fearmongering in English. Retrieved from https://www.lexico.com/definition/fearmongering
[ccxxxvii] ccxxxvii Lexico Oxford English Dictionary. Meaning of Fearmongering in English. Retrieved from https://www.lexico.com/definition/fearmongering
[ccxxxviii] Waldman, P. (2012, December 19). Concealed Carry and the Triumph of Fear. Retrieved from https://prospect.org/power/concealed-carry-triumph-fear/
[ccxxxix] Younge, G. (2017, October 6). Why Americans won't give up their guns. Retrieved from https://www.theguardian.com/commentisfree/2017/oct/06/americans-guns-nra-las-vegas-shooting
ccxl Eidelson, R. (2017, October 5). Fear Is the NRA and Gun Industry's Deadliest Weapon. Retrieved from https://www.psychologytoday.com/us/blog/dangerous-ideas/201710/fear-is-the-nra-and-gun-industry-s-deadliest-weapon
[ccxli] Eidelson, R. (2017, October 5). Fear Is the NRA and Gun Industry's Deadliest Weapon. Retrieved from https://www.psychologytoday.com/us/blog/dangerous-ideas/201710/fear-is-the-nra-and-gun-industry-s-deadliest-weapon
ccxlii Greenberg, J. (2015, October 26). Fact-checking Ben Carson's claim that gun control laws allowed the Nazis to carry out Holocaust. Retrieved from https://www.politifact.com/factchecks/2015/oct/26/ben-carson/fact-checking-ben-carson-nazi-guns/
[ccxliii] NSSF The Firearm Industry Trade Association. (2018, April 10). Firearms Industry Economic Impact Rises 169% since 2008. Retrieved from https://www.nssf.org/firearms-industry-economic-impact-rises-169-since-2008/
ccxliv Hickey, W. (2013, January 16). How The Gun Industry Funnels Tens Of Millions Of Dollars To The NRA. Retrieved from https://www.businessinsider.com/gun-industry-funds-nra-2013-1?r=US&IR=T
[ccxlv] Brady United Against Gun Violence. Retrieved from https://www.bradyunited.org/
[ccxlvi] Giffords Law Center To Prevent Gun Violence. Retrieved from https://lawcenter.giffords.org/
[ccxlvii] CSGV The Coalition to Stop Gun Violence. Retrieved from https://www.csgv.org/
[ccxlviii] Violence Policy Center. Retrieved from vpc.org
[ccxlix] Everytown for Gun Safety. Retrieved from everytown.org
[ccl] Terrill, D. (2017, May 5). NRA RELEASES FINANCIAL STATEMENT SHOWING REVENUE, EXPENSES FOR 2016. Retrieved from https://www.guns.com/news/2017/05/05/nra-revenue-expenses-in-2016
[ccli] Nonprofit Explorer. Everytown For Gun Safety Action Fund Inc. Retrieved from https://projects.propublica.org/nonprofits/organizations/208802884

ccⁱⁱ Rubin, M. (2017, October 3). The cost of US gun violence has finally been calculated—at $2.8 billion a year. Retrieved from https://qz.com/1093144/us-gun-violence-costs-an-average-of-2-8-billion-a-year-a-johns-hopkins-study-reveals/

ccliii Clark, D. PolitiFact: Most guns in crimes obtained illegally. Retrieved from https://www.ajc.com/news/national-govt--politics/politifact-most-guns-crimes-obtained-illegally/FdPGcFG853OoZCqmknRl3K/

ccliv Clark, D. PolitiFact: Most guns in crimes obtained illegally. Retrieved from https://www.ajc.com/news/national-govt--politics/politifact-most-guns-crimes-obtained-illegally/FdPGcFG853OoZCqmknRl3K/

cclv Ingraham, C. (2016, July 27). New evidence confirms what gun rights advocates have said for a long time about crime. Retrieved from https://www.washingtonpost.com/news/wonk/wp/2016/07/27/new-evidence-confirms-what-gun-rights-advocates-have-been-saying-for-a-long-time-about-crime/

cclvi Cook, P. (2017, October 3). How dangerous people get their guns in America. Retrieved from https://www.cbsnews.com/news/gun-sales-how-dangerous-people-get-weapons/

cclvii Giffords Law Center to Prevent Gun Violence. Reporting Lost and Stolen Firearms. Retrieved from https://lawcenter.giffords.org/gun-laws/policy-areas/gun-owner-responsibilities/reporting-lost-stolen-guns/

cclviii Giffords Law Center to Prevent Gun Violence. Polling on Reporting of Lost or Stolen Firearms. Retrieved from https://lawcenter.giffords.org/polling-on-reporting-of-lost-or-stolen-firearms/

cclix Giffords Law Center to Prevent Gun Violence. Reporting Lost and Stolen Firearms. Retrieved from https://lawcenter.giffords.org/gun-laws/policy-areas/gun-owner-responsibilities/reporting-lost-stolen-guns/

cclx Giffords Law Center to Prevent Gun Violence. Trafficking & Straw Purchasing. Retrieved from https://lawcenter.giffords.org/gun-laws/policy-areas/crime-guns/trafficking-straw-purchasing/

cclxi Shortell, D. (2018, February 16). How do laws prevent mentally ill people from buying guns? Retrieved from https://edition.cnn.com/2018/02/15/politics/mental-health-gun-possession-explainer/index.html

cclxii Fuller-Thomson, E. (2017, July 5). Attempted suicide rates much higher in adults with learning disabilities. Retrieved from https://www.healio.com/news/psychiatry/20170629/attempted-suicide-rates-much-higher-in-adults-with-learning-disabilities

cclxiii Statista. (2020, February). Number of mass shootings in the United States between 1982 and February 2020, by legality of shooter's weapons. Retrieved from https://www.statista.com/statistics/476461/mass-shootings-in-the-us-by-legality-of-shooters-weapons/

cclxiv Motor Vehicle Traffic Fatalities and Fatality Rates, 1899-2018. Retrieved from

https://cdan.nhtsa.gov/tsftables/Fatalities%20and%20Fatality%20Rates.pdf
[cclxv] USA Facts Firearm deaths. Table. Retrieved from https://usafacts.org/data/topics/security-safety/crime-and-justice/firearms/firearm-deaths/
[cclxvi] Motor Vehicle Traffic Fatalities and Fatality Rates, 1899-2018. Retrieved from https://cdan.nhtsa.gov/tsftables/Fatalities%20and%20Fatality%20Rates.pdf
[cclxvii] Motor Vehicle Traffic Fatalities and Fatality Rates, 1899-2018. Retrieved from https://cdan.nhtsa.gov/tsftables/Fatalities%20and%20Fatality%20Rates.pdf
[cclxviii] Demuro, D. (2014, April 11). New Backup Camera Rule: Cameras Will Be Mandatory by 2018. Retrieved from https://www.autotrader.com/car-news/new-backup-camera-rule-cameras-will-be-mandatory-by-2018-223739
[cclxix] Motor Vehicle Traffic Fatalities and Fatality Rates, 1899-2018. Retrieved from https://cdan.nhtsa.gov/tsftables/Fatalities%20and%20Fatality%20Rates.pdf
[cclxx] USA Facts Firearm deaths. Table. Retrieved from https://usafacts.org/data/topics/security-safety/crime-and-justice/firearms/firearm-deaths/
[cclxxi] Dugan, A. (2018, July 24).  In U.S., Smoking Rate Hits New Low at 16%. Retrieved from https://news.gallup.com/poll/237908/smoking-rate-hits-new-low.aspx
[cclxxii] CDC Centers for Disease Control and Prevention. Tobacco-Related Mortality. Retrieved from https://www.cdc.gov/tobacco/data_statistics/fact_sheets/health_effects/tobacco_related_mortality/index.htm
[cclxxiii] Simon, S. (2018, January 4). Facts & Figures 2018: Rate of Deaths From Cancer Continues Decline. Retrieved from https://www.cancer.org/latest-news/facts-and-figures-2018-rate-of-deaths-from-cancer-continues-decline.html
[cclxxiv] Pew Research Center. (2018, October 18). Gun Policy Remains Divisive, But Several Proposals Still Draw Bipartisan Support. Retrieved from https://www.pewresearch.org/politics/2018/10/18/gun-policy-remains-divisive-but-several-proposals-still-draw-bipartisan-support/
[cclxxv] Reinhart, RJ. (2018, October 17). Six in 10 Americans Support Stricter Gun Laws. Retrieved from https://news.gallup.com/poll/243797/six-americans-support-stricter-gun-laws.aspx
[cclxxvi] Jones, JM. (2018, March 14). U.S. Preference for Stricter Gun Laws Highest Since 1993. Retrieved from https://news.gallup.com/poll/229562/preference-stricter-gun-laws-highest-1993.aspx
[cclxxvii] Shepard, S. (2018, February 28). Gun control support surges in polls. Retrieved from https://www.politico.com/story/2018/02/28/gun-control-polling-parkland-430099
[cclxxviii] Morning Consult National Tracking Poll #180217 February 22-26, 2018. Retrieved from https://morningconsult.com/wp-content/uploads/2018/02/180217_crosstabs_POLITICO_v1_DK-1.pdf
[cclxxix] BBC News. (2018, December 19).  US bans 'bump stock' gun device used in

Las Vegas mass shooting. Retrieved from https://www.bbc.co.uk/news/world-us-canada-46614001

[cclxxx] Reinhart, RJ. (2018, October 17). Six in 10 Americans Support Stricter Gun Laws. Retrieved from https://news.gallup.com/poll/243797/six-americans-support-stricter-gun-laws.aspx

[cclxxxi] Morning Consult National Tracking Poll #180217 February 22-26, 2018. Retrieved from https://morningconsult.com/wp-content/uploads/2018/02/180217_crosstabs_POLITICO_v1_DK-1.pdf

[cclxxxii] Knoema World Data Atlas – Rankings crime statistics Homicide rate 2017. Retrieved from https://knoema.com/atlas/ranks/Homicide-rate

[cclxxxiii] GunPolicy.org, United States. Gun Facts, Figures and the Law, Gun Homicides 2017. Retrieved from https://www.gunpolicy.org/firearms/region/united-states

[cclxxxiv] Murray, M. (2018, March 23). Poll: 58 percent say gun ownership increases safety. Retrieved from https://www.nbcnews.com/politics/first-read/poll-58-percent-say-gun-ownership-increases-safety-n859231

[cclxxxv] Kurtzman, L. (2014, January 21). Access to Guns Increases Risk of Suicide, Homicide. Retrieved from https://www.ucsf.edu/news/2014/01/111286/access-guns-increases-risk-suicide-homicide

[cclxxxvi] Haydon, J. (2010, December 15). The difference between goals and targets. Retrieved from https://www.johnhaydon.com/difference-goals-targets/

[cclxxxvii] Mervosh, S. (2018, December 18). Nearly 40,000 People Died From Guns in U.S. Last Year, Highest in 50 Years. Retrieved from https://www.nytimes.com/2018/12/18/us/gun-deaths.html

[cclxxxviii] USA Facts, Firearm Deaths by Type 2017. Retrieved from https://usafacts.org/data/topics/security-safety/crime-and-justice/firearms/firearm-deaths/

[cclxxxix] Countryeconomy.com. United States - Intentional homicides. Retrieved from https://countryeconomy.com/demography/homicides/usa

[ccxc] CNN Editorial Research. (2020, May 3). Mass Shootings in the US Fast Facts. Retrieved from https://edition.cnn.com/2019/08/19/us/mass-shootings-fast-facts/index.html

[ccxci] Schechter, E. (2015, October 1). How to Make Guns Safer - Biometrics, RFID and microstamping technologies aim to prevent deaths and crime. Retrieved from https://www.scientificamerican.com/article/how-to-make-guns-safer/

[ccxcii] SMART TECH Challenges Foundation. Fingerprint Guns. Retrieved from https://smarttechfoundation.org/smart-firearms-technology/fingerprint-guns/

[ccxciii] Schechter, E. (2015, October 1). How to Make Guns Safer - Biometrics, RFID and microstamping technologies aim to prevent deaths and crime. Retrieved from https://www.scientificamerican.com/article/how-to-make-guns-safer/

[ccxciv] Macbride, E. (2018, November 29). 5 Reasons Gun Companies Oppose Higher-Tech Guns. Retrieved from https://www.forbes.com/sites/elizabethmacbride/2018/11/29/from-the-

industry-perspective-5-reasons-to-oppose-higher-tech-guns/#39dc5134187f

ccxcv Rose, J. (2014, June 24). A New Jersey Law That's Kept Smart Guns Off Shelves Nationwide. Retrieved from https://www.npr.org/sections/alltechconsidered/2014/06/24/325178305/a-new-jersey-law-thats-kept-smart-guns-off-shelves-nationwide

ccxcvi Bedard, P. (2017, July 6). 2017 is second biggest year for gun sales ever, might top 2016. Retrieved from https://www.washingtonexaminer.com/2017-is-second-biggest-year-for-gun-sales-ever-might-top-2016

ccxcvii Freskos, B. (2019, January 21). A New Generation of Entrepreneurs Thinks It Can Revive the Smart Gun. Retrieved from https://www.thetrace.org/2019/01/a-new-generation-of-entrepreneurs-thinks-it-can-revive-the-smart-gun/

ccxcviii Zhou, Y. (2017, October 6). Three percent of the population own half of the civilian guns in the US. Retrieved from https://qz.com/1095899/gun-ownership-in-america-in-three-charts/

ccxcix This Day in History February 14. (2019, February 6). Teen gunman kills 17, injures 17 at Parkland, Florida high school. Retrieved from https://www.history.com/this-day-in-history/parkland-marjory-stoneman-douglas-school-shooting

ccc Mazzei, P. (2018, December 12). Slow Police Response and Chaos Contributed to Parkland Massacre, Report Finds. Retrieved from https://www.nytimes.com/2018/12/12/us/parkland-shooting-florida-commission-report.html

ccci Giffords Law Center to Prevent Gun Violence. Annual Gun Law Scorecard Florida C-. Retrieved from https://lawcenter.giffords.org/scorecard2018/#FL

cccii Sarfaraz, M. (2019, January 7). #NeverAgain MSD: from outrage to movement for gun control. Retrieved from https://www.diggitmagazine.com/articles/neveragain-msd-outrage-movement-gun-control

ccciii March For Our Lives. Retrieved from https://marchforourlives.com/

ccciv Walsh, J. (2018, March 24). 6 Minutes and 20 Seconds That Could Change the World. Retrieved from https://www.thenation.com/article/archive/6-minutes-and-20-seconds-that-could-change-the-world/

cccv Meyer, D S. (2019, February 14). One year after the Parkland shooting is the "NeverAgain movement on track to succeed? Retrieved from https://www.washingtonpost.com/news/monkey-cage/wp/2019/02/14/one-year-after-the-parkland-shooting-is-the-neveragain-movement-on-track-to-succeed/

cccvi Grinshteyn, E. Hemenway, D. (2015, November 6). Violent Death Rates: The US Compared with Other High-income OECD Countries, 2010. Retrieved from https://www.amjmed.com/article/S0002-9343(15)01030-X/abstract

cccvii Kurtzman, L. (2014, January 21). Access to Guns Increases Risk of Suicide, Homicide. Retrieved from https://www.ucsf.edu/news/2014/01/111286/access-guns-increases-risk-suicide-homicide

[cccviii] Giffords Law Center to Prevent Gun Violence. Retrieved from https://lawcenter.giffords.org/
[cccix] Chappell, B (2019, March 26). Bump Stock Ban Takes Effect As Gun Rights Groups Ask Supreme Court For Delay. Retrieved from https://www.npr.org/2019/03/26/706905757/bump-stock-ban-takes-effect-as-gun-rights-groups-ask-supreme-court-for-delay
[cccx] Morning Consult National Tracking Poll #180217 February 22-26, 2018. Retrieved from https://morningconsult.com/wp-content/uploads/2018/02/180217_crosstabs_POLITICO_v1_DK-1.pdf
[cccxi] Preidt, R. (2016, February 3). How U.S. gun deaths compare to other countries. Retrieved from https://www.cbsnews.com/news/how-u-s-gun-deaths-compare-to-other-countries/
[cccxii] Statista. (2019, October). Percentage of households in the United States owning one or more firearms from 1972 to 2019. Retrieved from https://www.statista.com/statistics/249740/percentage-of-households-in-the-united-states-owning-a-firearm/